THE SECRET SON OF WALLIS SIMPSON

"If you've had enough of tiresome tales of the Mitfords, reruns of starchy Downton Abbey or the gilded romanticism of Out of Africa, Selina Molteno's engrossing story of Joss de Wahl is a must-read piece of highly entertaining biographical detection. Who was he? Was his origin and identity as intriguing as he claimed it to have been? A superbly-orchestrated rummage through a rich and assorted set of circumstances and characters, including Britain's royal family, Winston Churchill and a nondescript South African dorp, the author's stylish prose and judicious eye brings this astonishing – and weird – story vividly and compellingly to life."

– Bill Nasson, Emeritus Professor in History,
Stellenbosch University.

"A deep dive into the British royal family and a careful psychological analysis of someone who claimed to have been disowned by his royal parents. This intriguing account, by someone who got to know him well, left me convinced that none of the logically possible explanations fit the meticulously checked facts – although one of them must be true!"

– Andrew Colman, Professor of Psychology,
University of Leicester.

"This is a page-turning story on a finely balanced set of believable circumstances. Is Joss truly the love-child of abdicated King Edward VIII and his lover Wallis Simpson? As he tells his tale, you find yourself believing that indeed he is – and then just wondering all over again. The story is told with fine skill and a light touch, which will make it a popular read for anyone fascinated by royal history and South Africa."

– Troth Wells, author of *The World in Your Kitchen*.

THE SECRET SON
OF WALLIS SIMPSON

My quest for the truth

Selina Molteno

Matador
Unit E2 Airfield Business Park,
Harrison Road, Market Harborough,
Leicestershire. LE16 7UL
Tel: 0116 2792299
Email: books@troubador.co.uk
Web: www.troubador.co.uk/matador
Twitter: @matadorbooks

ISBN 978 1803131 733

British Library Cataloguing in Publication Data.
A catalogue record for this book is available from the British Library.

Printed and bound in the UK by TJ Books Ltd, Padstow, Cornwall
Typeset in 11.5/15 Berkeley Oldstyle Pro by Oxford Publishing Services

Matador is an imprint of Troubador Publishing Ltd

Contents

Author Biography

SELINA MOLTENO IS the great granddaughter of Sir John Charles Molteno, the first prime minister of the Cape Colony. She continued the family tradition of politics, but in a rather unexpected direction. She was arrested during the apartheid era and worked subsequently for the Anti-Apartheid Movement in London.

Selina was a ballet dancer with the Grand Ballet de Marquis de Cuevas in Paris when Rudolf Nureyev defected to the company, her account of that period being published as *Letters from an Intrepid Ballet Dancer* (2015). She also lived in Nigeria during the civil war and in Trinidad. Her co-authored memoir of her Nigerian experience appeared as *An Expatriate Family in the Nigerian Civil War* (2020).

Selina has worked in academic publishing for over thirty years. She is married to a university professor, Robin Cohen, and lives in Oxford.

Note and Acknowledgements

THIS IS BOOK about a man who lived his life incognito. He was, pretended he was, or believed he was, the natural son of the Duke and Duchess of Windsor. At a very early age, while still in his infancy, he was sent to South Africa from Europe to be raised by foster parents who, he claimed, were known and selected by his natural father.

Listening to his rambling accounts of the wide range of people with whom he claimed to have been associated – many of whom certainly ranked among the celebrities of their time – was confusing to say the least. I have provided a context in the narrative, but for the convenience of those who may need a reminder and a longer explanation, I have included a list (titled Dramatis Personae) of the most important of these people at the back of the book, with a brief description of who they actually are or were. The more elevated people are, the more names and confusing titles they seem to acquire!

With respect to acknowledgements, I owe a debt to many people, the first and foremost of which must go to my cousin Georgina Stuttaford, who introduced me to Joss in the first place and has been an important person in my life ever since it began a very long time ago. For their help and constructive encouragement, I also wish to thank my husband Robin Cohen, our son Jason Cohen for his technical expertise and

NOTE AND ACKNOWLEDGEMENTS

general help, Sara Banerji for sharing her helpful authorial advice, Mimi Kester for her professional insights into complicated human minds, Joel David for his encouragement, Abebe Zegeye for being so good at making connections, and Rachel Browne for her incredibly helpful and useful suggestions.

I also owe a debt of gratitude to the team at Matador, notably Hannah Dakin, for finally getting the show on the road.

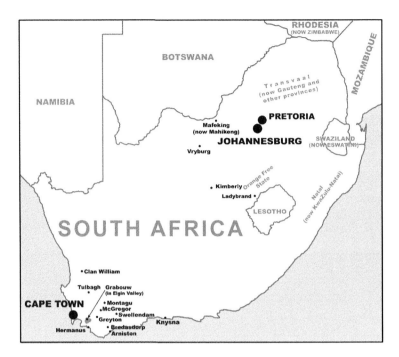

Southern Africa

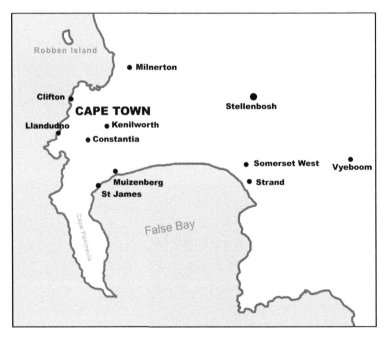

Cape Town and environs
(showing places mentioned in this book)

1

Introduction

THIS STORY STARTED on a bright winter's day in the Western Cape in June 1995 when my cousin Georgina Stuttaford, who was the South African agent for the London-based auctioneers, Phillips (which merged with Bonhams in 2001) received a telephone call. It was from her London employers who rang to tell her about a request from someone living in Bredasdorp regarding the sale of three ostensibly valuable pieces of furniture. Would she please look into it? Since she was living at the time on a farm at Vyeboom, a small farming village on the Garden Route about halfway between Cape Town and Bredasdorp, it would only take her about two hours to drive there. She was initially sceptical about the assignment because, as she explained, Bredasdorp is hardly the kind of place in which one would expect to find a Thomas Hope Regency bookcase, a commode made by the famous eighteenth-century Parisian cabinetmaker, Roger Vandercruse Lacroix, and a chiffonier that had belonged to Queen Mary.[1]

Bredasdorp is a rather quaint small town, or as South Africans would call it, a 'dorp,' on the slopes of a high hill in the Cape Agulhas municipality of the Western Cape. It has strong agricultural roots and serves the surrounding wheat, dairy, sheep, and protea farming area of the Overberg region. When Georgina reached her destination outside a pair of simple, white-washed, thatched-roofed cottages in Lourens

Street near the centre of Bredasdorp, a Mr Joss de Wahl was waiting to greet her. So began an association and then a friendship that was to last for 15 years until Joss de Wahl died on 26 June 2010.

If Georgina was going to be able to help her client realize the value of his furniture, she had to establish its provenance. Where had he acquired such unusual items? Mr de Wahl said he had them from his parents. When she asked him who his parents were, he replied that he was unable to tell her but that he was prepared to vouch for the authenticity of the furniture, though not in writing. Well, that was hardly helpful!

Joss de Wahl's cottage in Lourens Street, Bredasdorp.

Eventually, it transpired that Joss was the custodian of a considerable amount of European and Cape art, jewellery, and furniture, which he had either bought in South Africa or had received as gifts and bequests. As we shall see later in the chapter entitled 'Riches and Rogues', Joss had found himself in a difficult position and was being systematically dispossessed of his belongings and money. As the months passed by Joss became increasingly open with Georgina and, eventually, she agreed to try to help him trace and recover those of his possessions that had found their way out of South Africa. In a letter to Georgina dated 15 September 1995, he recognized that he was asking a lot of her but claimed to trust her because she was related to Miss Kathleen Murray (1891–1984), whom he associated with Princess Alice.

To explain this reference, I need to digress a little. Miss Kathleen Murray was an apple farmer at Grabouw in the Elgin Valley where two of her uncles, Ted and Harry Molteno, had started farming in the early 1900s and had eventually turned the district into the largest fruit-producing area in southern Africa, marketed in the UK as 'Cape Apples.' Kathleen Murray, whose mother had been a Molteno, befriended Princess Alice, the Countess of Athlone (1883–1981), during the period when her husband, the Earl of Athlone (1874–1957), was serving as the fourth governor-general of the Union of South Africa between 1923 and 1931. Princess Alice was the daughter of the Duke of Albany Prince Leopold, who was the youngest son of Queen Victoria and Prince Albert. She married Queen Mary's brother, Prince Alexander of Teck, in 1904.

Princess Alice had clearly liked the Cape, for she and the Earl of Athlone had built a beach house at Muizenberg and, after his death and right into her old age, each January she would sail with her lady-in-waiting, Miss Joan Lascelles, on the Union Castle mail ship from Southampton to Cape Town where she would remain, sometimes as Kathleen Murray's house guest, until April when she would return to her London home at Kensington Palace.

Joss claimed that these links with our family reassured him sufficiently to share with Georgina the astounding revelation that he was the son of Wallis Simpson and Edward VIII, the Duke and Duchess of Windsor.[2] When Georgina shared his extraordinary claim with me, my first response was one of incredulity. Aided by a couple of G&Ts, we burst out laughing. I would not say that either of us is an inveterate cynic, but we have both lived long, not over-protected lives, and have probably encountered more than our fair share of rascals, liars and chancers.

Was Joss insane? Even in a frontier society like South Africa, which harbours its fair share of eccentrics, imposters, fugitives, crooks, and swindlers, claiming to be the son of Wallis Simpson and Edward VIII was way off the wall. We all know that royal fakes have peppered the histories of the European royal houses since the beginning of time – with the story of Anastasia[3] being the first one to come to mind – so the likelihood of him also being one such fake was the first thought that occurred to me.

However, in a more sober mood, we began to kick around a ground-clearing discussion by asking ourselves a simple question. 'Could it even be possible for someone to live incognito in South Africa for sixty odd years?' Knowing something of white elites in South Africa and their capacity to persuade people in authority to bend the rules to achieve a desired outcome, the answer to that question is 'quite possibly.'

We thought it would be conceivable to live in the country anonymously for a range of reasons. For a start, white South African society is less rigidly stratified than Britain. Wealth plays more of a role in determining a person's social status than the subtle gradations of class and, in any case, white South Africans are unlikely to accord deference to anybody. It is alien to them, or at least was during the apartheid years, because they expected only to receive it. Their ears are less attuned to the nuances of accent that English people are so good at detecting and that enable them to distinguish a parvenu from the genuine object. In fact, South Africa would have been a good place in which to hide a member of the British royal family without arousing too much suspicion: he would simply blend into the morass of white privilege.

Using South Africa as a refuge is a tradition that continues today. The Cape attracts large numbers of wealthy Europeans, especially British people wishing to escape the winter months back home and many are clearly from the English upper classes. Some, the so-called 'Snowbirds,' own homes in two or even more jurisdictions and can, if they carefully time the length of their stay in each place, turn their lives into one long tax-free summer. Plenty of local professionals in the form of lawyers, accountants and financial advisers are available to help them spot the legal loopholes and maximize their advantages.

In addition, South Africa is where people with blemished careers in journalism, the professions or business can find a new start in life. It is also where people show up for cheap dental treatment, cosmetic surgery or even, as rumoured in the case of Princess Diana's brother, Charles Spencer, a cheap divorce. Mark Thatcher, the son of former British Prime Minister Margaret Thatcher, became a South African resident, presumably to get away from the bad publicity associated with his unethical business practices. Tolerant as they are of dodgy characters, there are limits to South African hospitality. The Royal Cape Golf Club 'blackballed' (a particularly inappropriate expression in the context) Mark Thatcher's application for membership on the grounds that they had their standards and did not accept 'Eurotrash.'4 Thatcher was subsequently tried and convicted in a South African court for his involvement in an incompetent attempt to supplant the president of Equatorial Guinea in a mercenary-led coup. While many European foreigners think themselves sophisticates living among hicks, the local sharks have sharp teeth and, as we shall see in this book, are perfectly capable of taking a few chunks out of the denizens' flesh.

I get recruited

Though we both remained highly sceptical, Georgina began to wonder if Joss's bizarre claim could possibly have any validity. I, Selina, had written a little and run a small business providing publishing services in the UK and since Joss had mentioned that he would like to have his story told after his death, she thought that I might be interested in the task. When my husband Robin and I next visited South Africa, we met Joss for the first time. He made an extraordinary impression on me, but that was mainly because he failed to fit into any category that I could identify. Tall, dark haired, square jawed, rather heavily built and, in voice and bearing, though definitely not in dress, Joss gave every appearance of being well-born. I was somewhat bewildered, but deeply intrigued by this strange man. White South African males are not known for their reticence in announcing what they 'do.' Joss apparently did not 'do' and had never 'done' *anything*, either to make a living or to pass the time.

It was one matter for Georgina to agree to try to help Joss track down his missing belongings, which involved consulting furniture houses, valuers, fine arts experts, lawyers and, ultimately, even the police. However, if I were to be involved in writing his story, I needed to convince myself that this was a pursuit that was not a total waste of my time. In short, I wanted to hear his own account in his own voice. Ultimately, this involved lengthy interviews transcribed to 599 single-spaced pages. While I have sometimes quoted Joss's words directly in this account, I have always sought where possible to authenticate his version of events against other sources.

Whereas Georgina was on the spot in South Africa, I lived in England. However, as luck would have it, my husband accepted an appointment at the University of Cape Town for three years between 2001 and 2004, which gave me ample opportunity to visit Joss in Bredasdorp, where he was by then living in a small flat with the Baroness Jean Tromp. Thereafter, Joss and I kept in touch by telephone, and I would always visit him whenever I happened to be in South Africa, sometimes alone, sometimes with Georgina, and occasionally with Robin as well.

Obviously, over a period of fifteen years, circumstances change, distractions intervene and there were times when I had far more pressing claims on my time. I never entirely gave up on the task of telling Joss's story, but decided, on advice, to wait for the deaths of several people mentioned in this book. The delay was also occasioned by Joss's request for a posthumous account. However, now that Joss and the people around him who would have objected to me telling his story have died, the time is right to tell this tale. Irrespective of who he really was, I have sought to bring him alive as a warm, amusing, self-reflective person who tried valiantly to cope with the cruel yet sometimes privileged hand that life had dealt him. I also remember him as hopelessly impractical, terribly lazy, and incurably disorganized.

Naturally, I address the question of his birth in this book. However, there are wider implications of his story. He provided compelling insights into the ins and outs of royal scandals and the entanglements of the British and white South African elites. He lived through the dog days of apartheid, when he was preoccupied not by the great moral and political questions of the day, but by how to protect his possessions. The depredations of those around him tell their own story. In the course of researching Joss's life I also turned up significant evidence of money laundering and smuggling among wealthy South Africans.

To be sure, much of this book revolves around Joss's take on his own life. He tells a story of staring forlornly through a shadowy veil at a world of glittering privilege. He claimed to have mingled with some of the twentieth century's most powerful and famous personalities and to have known some of their most intimate secrets. Yet, he said, he could never declare his identity or gain recognition and acceptance. He seemed convinced that to have exposed his origins would have guaranteed his immediate death and provided a threat to the monarchy. He never married or fathered a child. His is a story of secrecy, trust, friendship, greed, hope, betrayal, loss, and loneliness.

It is important to mention that Joss never sought public recognition, never harboured an ambition to claim any 'entitlement' to the British crown and never intended to rock any boats. Unlike his alleged father, he maintained he had little regard for money or wealth; he was not a greedy person. He did, however, place a high premium on friendship.

I feel relatively convinced that what Joss told me was the truth as he saw it. Joss was quite open about being vague and having a poor memory. He was the first to admit that his account was probably full of inaccuracies. On occasions, as I show later, he was trapped in the elaborate coils of his own narrative. He never kept diaries or any other substantial record of his life. Unlike most people, who can readily produce documentation of their early lives through family photographs, school reports, letters and so forth, Joss claimed that certain people took great care to ensure that his identity remained concealed. After all, to all intents and purposes, he was a prince who had never been born.

Joss claimed that Wallis Simpson sought him out and it was she who told him who he really was. The complex and presumably fictive relationship that Joss subsequently developed with his famous parents shows them in a new light, albeit in the distorted one of an unacknowledged son.

Historical background

In 1936, the newly crowned king of England, Edward VIII, gave up his office because of his love for Wallis Simpson.[5] At first sight, the match could hardly have been less suitable. She was a commoner, twice divorced and American. Her mother ran a boarding house in Baltimore. This unlikely romance captured, indeed transfixed, the public imagination. How did Wallis Simpson somehow persuade the most eligible bachelor of the time not only to marry her, but also to renounce the British crown to do so? With only a little exaggeration, the American columnist, H. L. Mencken, described the abdication as the 'greatest story since the Crucifixion.'[6]

However, according to the subject of this book, all was not what it seemed. What the public was not told, Joss claimed, was that Mrs Wallis Simpson, née Warfield, was the illegitimate daughter of American millionaire J. Pierpont Morgan and Roman aristocrat Princess Victoria Colonna.[7] Far from being a penniless *femme fatale* whose charms Edward VIII was incapable of resisting, Wallis Simpson herself had impeccable family credentials and was a beneficiary of one of the world's greatest fortunes. Julius Caesar had been a Colonna, as had the Empress Eugénie; no less a sculptor than Michelangelo had immortalized her beautiful ancestor. Wallis became heir to the legendary Colonna pearls from which, so the bizarre story goes, Caesar's blood sometimes oozes. Royal blood, albeit from the wrong side of the sheets, flowed through Wallis's veins. Pierpont Morgan made vast settlements on Victoria Colonna, which then went to Wallis. One could reasonably infer that the prospect of access to the fortune at her disposal sweetened the tip of the arrow from Cupid's bow that entrapped the Prince of Wales and occasioned unprecedented damage to the House of Windsor.

This revelation about Wallis's background will strain credulity, but I ask you, the reader, to hold your breath for an even more startling claim by the subject of this book. A few days after Edward VIII announced his intention to abdicate and a little over half a year before he and Wallis became free to marry in June 1937, Wallis purportedly bore Edward VIII a son. 'Robert Windsor' was born in France on 16 December 1936. The birth occurred at the Villa Lou Viei in Cannes, while Wallis was seeking refuge at the home of her close friends Katherine and Herman Rogers. Wallis had got to know Katherine (as Katherine Bigelow) in southern California in 1918 shortly after her first husband was killed in France during the First World War. Her second husband Herman Rogers, the son of a millionaire railroad tycoon, devoted his life to the pursuit of leisure and the acquisition of cultured and titled friends. This was a particularly difficult declaration to swallow as there is an extant photograph of Wallis purportedly taken just eight days earlier showing no signs of pregnancy. Joss knew about the photograph and vehemently contested its date, inferring also that the Rothermere press, where the photograph appeared, was engaged in a cover up. As I shall explain in Chapter 2, Cust's presence may also be significant as the Cust family was well practised in the art of concealing illegitimate children. We should also allow, of course, that some women do not show a prominent 'bump' when pregnant.

Herman Rogers; Katherine Rogers; Wallis and Peregrine Francis Adelbert Cust, 6th Baron Brownlow. Although we do not know when this photograph was taken, it appeared in the *Daily Express* on 8 December 1936.

While Britain was reeling from the shock of the abdication crisis and dark clouds were hovering over Europe during the build-up to the Second World War, the world was unaware of the supposed existence of a new-born 'prince,' for whom a new and covert identity was hurriedly being constructed. By the time young 'Robert Windsor' is old enough to remember anything at all, he is another child, on another continent, in another family. He is called Joss (short for Joseph) de Wahl and lives in South Africa. Joss asserts that he discovered his 'true' identity during the royal visit to South Africa in 1947, and thereafter began to live in both Europe and South Africa. Towards the end of his life porphyria inherited, he thought, from his father's side of the family, subjects him to frequent bouts of depression and internal bleeding.

Even if we were to accept Joss's extraordinary claim that Wallis was his birth mother, one cannot, of course, rule out the possibility that he may not have been the Duke of Windsor's son, for in the spring of 1936 there were rumours afoot that she was having a sexual relationship with Joachim von Ribbentrop. Ribbentrop, who was Hitler's special adviser on foreign affairs and ambassador without portfolio, served as German ambassador to the court of St James between 1936 and 1938. Charles Higham claimed that

> it was widely believed (among the alleged witnesses was Mary Raffray)[8] that Wallis was … having an affair with Ribbentrop and that he was paying her directly from German funds in Berlin to influence … the king. … Ribbentrop was constantly in the apartment at Bryanston Court,[9] and it is hard to believe that in this case the thick smoke of gossip had no fire at its source. … Frau von Ribbentrop had young children; she had a jealous possessive nature; and she must not be allowed to ruin Ribbentrop, but the people of Wallis's set were certain of it.[10]

Indeed, a breach of security was traced through Wallis to Ribbentrop.

Allowing for the moment his claimed provenance, Joss had some of Wallis's features and shared the distinctive hairline of the Duke of Windsor's father George V, but he bore no obvious

Joss (left) and the man he believed to be his paternal
grandfather (King George V) shared a distinctive hairline.

resemblance to the Duke of Windsor. Nonetheless, Joss was
convinced that he was the son of both Wallis and the Duke of
Windsor. Higham goes on to say that 'during the summer of
1936, severe censorship was applied to any mention of Wallis
in England. The newspaper magnates loyal to the king introduced a self-imposed edict that precluded either photographs
or articles which would disclose the relationship between her
and the monarch.'[11] These would have been the newspapers
that Max Aitken, 1st Baron Beaverbrook, known as the 'First
Baron of Fleet Street,' and the British newspaper proprietor
Harold Harmsworth, 1st Viscount Rothermere, owned, including the *Sunday Express*, *Daily Express*, *Daily Mail* and *Daily
Mirror*.

Questions, questions, questions

Even although Georgina and I had decided that it was, at least
theoretically, possible to conceal a royal baby in South Africa,
there remained an enormous gap between Joss's declaration
and what I was prepared to believe. Could I dismiss the
rumours of a pregnancy as unfounded and Joss's claim to being
the Duke and Duchess of Windsor's child as the delusions of a
madman? How could I objectively address his claims with an

open mind? I decided to rise to the challenge and posed five questions to myself. If I could answer those, I would be in a position to disprove or validate Joss's strange story.

- Why did Joss know so much about the royal family, including intimate details that were not at the time public knowledge?
- Did Joss indeed suffer from porphyria, as he announced, and could this have been inherited from the royal family?
- What explained Joss's unerring English accent and manners, and his unusually secretive private education?
- How could I account for the valuable art and furniture of which Joss was indisputably the custodian? And
- Why did Baroness Jean Tromp (née Jean Playfair, cousin of the Queen Mother and frequent childhood guest at Glamis Castle) unequivocally validate Joss's claims?

I will discuss Jean Tromp's support for Joss's story later. Georgina already knew Jean socially and I got to know her well because she and Joss were living together throughout most of the period I knew Joss, and she certainly came across as a completely genuine, kindly woman with no side to her. Joss seemed to intuit that, for us, Jean's endorsement was crucial to his credibility, and she never ever seemed even to wonder if Joss could be anyone other than the son of Wallis Simpson and the Duke of Windsor. But then Jean and Joss clearly needed one another, for at that time they were both equally alone in the world, although it was obvious that Joss sometimes found her exceedingly irritating.

Joss was aware that people would be unlikely to take his account seriously and although he did not go around boasting about his self-proclaimed heritage, he did raise the point that it was obvious that he came from 'the right side of the railway line,' so clearly was from a privileged background in any case. Why then might he have invented another set of parents?

My father, Dr C. J. Molteno, and Baroness Jean Tromp
relaxing at Vyeboom, Cape.

There is no question that Joss had grown up among, or been
educated by, highly cultivated people. His formidable knowledge of European art, architecture and furniture, and his lan-
guid gossiping about people in high places was decidedly more
Mayfair than 'Capefair.' Again, his distinctive upper-class
English accent was inconsistent with a conventional South
African upbringing, for virtually all white South Africans have
some trace of an accent in their speech, even if they try to
suppress it. If he were not who he claimed he was, who could
he have possibly been? His somewhat alien speech pattern was
complemented by his desire to remain unobtrusive. He never
sought to engage in work of any kind, to gain educational
qualifications or to build a career; his financial support came
from the proceeds of various trusts.

Though he did not wish to press his case publicly, Joss was
adamant that his putative father was not legally entitled to
abdicate on behalf of his son and that the coronation of Queen
Elizabeth II should never have taken place. While the then

King Edward VIII more than likely composed the wording of his intention to abdicate, which was broadcast over the radio and in which he took full responsibility, lawyers almost certainly compiled the actual statement or 'instrument' of abdication in which Edward VIII renounced 'the Throne for Myself and for My descendants.' Joss asserted that the inclusion of the reference to his descendants was significant and probably constitutionally suspect. If the instrument was legally flawed, should Joss have been crowned King of England on George VI's death? In other words, should George VI have been made his regent rather than the King of the United Kingdom and the Commonwealth? Unless Joss was considered a threat to the monarchy why, he argued, was his identity hidden so thoroughly and for so long? As Joss put it:

> I suppose that I have to be kept hidden now because they went to a lot of trouble to hide me and cannot unhide me now. I mean it is going to cause endless complications – and I am sixty years old – so it is quite pointless to produce me now. What purpose would it serve? Well, it would serve no purpose for me or for them.

From time to time, Joss worried about having brought me so closely into his confidence and asked me again and again to respect his wish to retain his anonymity until after his death. This could have been a way of 'playing me,' but I think not as I detected real anxiety in his manner and voice when he mentioned that he knew for sure that he 'would never be allowed to testify in a court of law' because, as he put it, 'I just would have an accident before the time. I know that.'

* * *

Much has been written about the Duke and Duchess of Windsor. The public in the UK and Commonwealth, particularly the older generation, is well informed about their romance, extravagant lifestyle, Nazi sympathies, and exile in France. In this book I provide a fuller international and social context to the period but am not seeking to deliver a fundamental critique of earlier accounts. Rather, my account centres on the subjective observations and experiences of their self-proclaimed son, the hidden prince, the bypassed monarch, and, if we are to believe Joss, the royal family's most closely guarded secret. Whether Joss's account of his life is credible, possible, or even the ravings of someone suffering from a prolonged delusion, it is his story and, as such, I have tried to evaluate it as faithfully as possible.

2

The Motherless Child

Joss's story opened in 1936 in an England that was vastly different from the one we know today. Eric Hobsbawm, the eminent British historian who arrived as a refugee to the UK from Germany in 1933, described England in the 1930s as

> a self-contained island where life was lived by unwritten but compelling rules, rituals and invented traditions: mostly class rules or gender rules, but also virtually universal ones, usually linked to royalty. The national anthem was played at the end of every performance in theatres and cinemas and people stood for it before they went home. Wherever you were, you did not talk during the two minutes' silence on Armistice Day, 11 November. The 'right' kind of accent bonded together the upper classes (but not parvenus who could thus be recognized) and ensured deferential behaviour from the lower orders, class-conscious or not, at least in public. In the 1930s these things were obvious. But, of course, they were not expected to apply on the other side of the seas which separated us from the foreigners. Britain was insular in every sense.[1]

The United Nations, the European Union, globalization, cheap air travel, traffic congestion, mass immigration, package holidays, the Eurostar, the sexual revolution, bankers' bonuses, British politicians who fiddled their expenses, Brexit, and the Covid-19 pandemic were all a long way into the future. Very few English people had travelled abroad or met any so-called 'foreigners,' let alone even encountered a black person; and everyone knew exactly where they stood in the rigidly proscribed class structure. Being born out of wedlock was a source of deep shame and if an unmarried woman was unfortunate enough to get herself pregnant, she would usually go into hiding until after the birth when the baby would be taken from her for adoption by a childless married couple. However, in the 1930s, according to Eric Hobsbawm, 'by continental European standards, Britain was still a rich, technically and economically advanced and well-equipped country,'[2] albeit one with some disturbing clouds on the horizon.

This was the decade of the Great Depression, which followed the Wall Street Crash of 1929 and ushered in a period of extreme poverty and high unemployment. It was also the decade that saw the rise of Hitler and of Nazism in Germany, the polarization between left and right that preceded the outbreak of the civil war in Spain, and the election of France's first socialist prime minister.

For the purposes of Joss's account, however, it really started with the abdication crisis following King George V's death on 20 January 1936 and his son Edward VIII's accession to the throne. As older readers are probably aware, the abdication of Edward VIII occurred because the king wanted to marry Wallis Simpson, which, for a range of reasons, Britain's Conservative government under Stanley Baldwin's leadership refused to condone. The reasons given at the time now sound rather trivial and reeked of narrow-minded intolerance. Wallis had been married twice before, was American, disrespectful of authority and nobody who really counted liked her. Given that King Henry VIII kept his crown despite having had six wives, two of whom he divorced and two of whom he beheaded and had established the Church of England to do so, one wonders why some arrangement could not have been made to accommodate the situation.

However, in those highly conservative times in England, there were other, mainly social and political, reasons why the Establishment found the king unacceptable. For a start, Edward VIII was keen to modernize the monarchy so that it would become more accessible to the general population,[3] a form of mild populism that enraged the British Establishment. Although many members of the public seemed keen on the idea of a more open monarchy, in his memoirs King Edward VIII records a conversation he had with George V's Keeper of the Privy Purse, Sir Frederick Ponsonby, in which the latter said, 'If I may say so, Sir, I think there is a risk in your making yourself too accessible. ... The Monarchy must always retain an element of mystery. A Prince should not show himself too much. The Monarchy must remain on a pedestal.'[4] King Edward openly disagreed with this advice and the discussion between them became quite heated.

The king's relative youth, strong views and determination were unappreciated in certain inner circles. Also, various MPs were worried about him wanting to meddle in politics, which monarchs were not expected to do. The British government of the day felt concerned about the king, and Wallis in particular, getting too close to members of the Nazi regime in Germany. Baldwin told Edward VIII that if he married Mrs Simpson the government would resign, to which he replied, 'if the Government opposed the marriage, as the Prime Minister had given me reason to believe it would, *then I was prepared to go.*'[5] On 24 November 1936, after consulting Winston Churchill, Clement Attlee (leader of the opposition at the time) and the Liberal leader, Sir Archibald Sinclair, Baldwin started to initiate preparations for the abdication. Although Churchill had gone along with the government's decision, he wanted the king's reign to continue, as did many others, including the fascist Oswald Mosley, the Communist

Party of Great Britain, and former Prime Minister David Lloyd George.[6]

A popular view, held especially by readers of the tabloid press, tended to approve of the idea of the king entering a morganatic marriage with Wallis, which would mean that he could continue as king but could not pass his title on to his wife or offspring. In fact, the country was rather split over the matter with the more right-wing newspapers owned by Lord Kemsley, such as the *Daily Herald, Daily Telegraph, Morning Post* and *The Times* tending to oppose the marriage, and the *Express* and *Mail*, which Lords Beaverbrook and Rothermere owned respectively, tending to support a morganatic marriage.[7] The latter two newspapers, which supported the marriage, were reported to have had four million more readers than the former group.[8]

* * *

Joss maintained that on 3 December, during this turmoil, Wallis fled to France and, on 16 December 1936, gave birth to a baby son. It was a difficult time for her. The royal family and some of the British public had made it clear that they disliked her and considered an already twice-married American divorcée to be an unacceptable marriage partner for their king. She had literally been forced to flee from the wrath of the British press and certain outraged members of the public. Though there had been rumours at the time that Wallis was pregnant, these were never confirmed publicly and, given that a child never materialized, the subject was soon dropped. When I challenged Joss about the photograph of Wallis that appeared in the *Daily Express* on 8 December 1936, in which she clearly does not look pregnant, he wriggled out of the question by stating that:

There are millions of photographs of my mother and there are no dates attached to them, so why should it be dated December 1936? She did not refute anything else. She used to say, 'Well, if it is true then you are guilty and if it is not true it does not matter' – and she was very arrogant. That is the only thing that she ever refuted.

Joss then reinforced his point by emphasizing that so keen had she been to keep out of the newspapers and the public eye that when she became the victim of a jewellery theft immediately after the abdication in 1936, she grossly underestimated the value of her loss by saying that it was worth £2000 when in fact it was closer to £2 million. Joss claimed that his own knowledge of the circumstances surrounding his birth were patched together from disparate sources. He said he thought, but was not sure, that Ladbrook[9] had told him that Wallis had been pregnant when she had to leave England, but went on to say that:

> I know for a fact that Perry Brownlow[10] went with her and Ladbrook drove them. I think even the old dame at La Pyramide,[11] where she jumped through the window, told me that she did not want them to see her pregnant. That is why she was hidden in the back of the car under rugs. I do not know how pregnant she looked. I cannot imagine my mother ever looking inelegant, so she probably managed to conceal it, I do not know.

In addition, as Joss explained, 'it is mentioned in Diana Mosley's book and in a few other books that a gynaecologist arrived on 10 December accompanied by an anaesthetist and some other doctors and her attorney to Villa Lou Viei.'[12] When that claim was later denied, Joss mockingly retorted that 'I suppose the solicitor had a bad heart and the gynaecologist he brought with him was actually a heart specialist and the other one was actually a clerk.'

Nonetheless, quite apart from all the fuss and hysteria at the time over the abdication, a pregnancy at that time would have placed the couple in an awkward constitutional and personal position. As Joss explained:

> They could not marry before my birth because the divorce with Simpson had not come through and did not come through until the following year, so I was to all intents and purposes illegitimate and they could not postpone George VI's coronation indefinitely. Under English law, I was legitimated when they married. The monarchy was very fragile at that stage, so General Smuts was called in to advise, and Churchill, and I do not know who else, advised that I should just be hidden somewhere.

Apart from the arrival of a legal and medical team at Villa Lou Viei, another indication that a child may have been expected or had been born was the inclusion of a crucial clause in Edward VIII's speech that he was also abdicating on behalf of his heirs. According to Joss, when legal doubts were raised about whether Edward VIII was entitled to abdicate on behalf of his heirs, it became even more necessary for them to hide their new-born son. Then, when George VI died, he just remained hidden. Joss suspected that his forthcoming birth may have triggered the timing of Edward VIII's abdication because until the doctors and lawyer arrived in France, he had given 'no indication that he was going to abdicate.'

* * *

Joss believed that his parents moved to the Chateau de la Crôe in Antibes when they left Katherine and Herman Rogers at Villa Lou Viei. Although Edward VIII and Wallis already had a house of their own in Paris at the time, Joss was under the impression that they were most likely to have been living at the Chateau de la Cröe during his early infancy. Obviously, Joss had no recollection of those early days: 'I cannot remember a thing, but I must have been with my mother. It was probably down at la Cröe.'[13]

* * *

Meanwhile, if Joss's account is to be taken at face value, and from now on in this chapter I have decided to give him free rein, Wallis and Edward VIII, who was by now the Duke of Windsor, must have found it excruciatingly painful to go along with the various arrangements that needed to be made to piece together the new and secret life of their child. South African statesman and former prime minister, General Jan Christian Smuts, who had worked so hard and effectively to promote Anglo–Boer reconciliation during the aftermath of the Boer War, took responsibility for organizing practical matters, such as issuing Joss with a false birth certificate – Joss's birth had never been recorded in France. Though Winston Churchill and the Queen Mother were also purportedly among those consulted, Alexander, Earl of Athlone (1874–1957), the governor general of South Africa at the time, and his wife Princess Alice, Queen Victoria's granddaughter, were largely responsible for making the arrangements for Joss to be brought up in South Africa. Their first task was to select suitable foster parents for the young child. What was interesting about their decision was that they did not choose a couple who were already married. They purportedly chose Mrs Billy Graaff to be his foster mother and Joseph de Wahl to be his foster father. Joss said that 'during the war she, Mrs Billy Graaff, was out here in South Africa, but she lived mostly in London. She had a house in Clarges Street.' He also said that she did not know de Wahl all that well and suspected that they had only met one another on a couple of occasions. He also claimed that she only married him to give Joss a name, for he was well connected.

That his father 'Frederic de Waal[14] was the only South African to be made a Knight of the Command of the Garter' seemed to matter to Joss, and, as he went on to explain, 'she was a friend of my father's, so that is basically why it happened that way.' Joss was given his foster father's name, Joseph de Wahl, and the appropriate documents were carefully drawn up to conceal what Joss insisted was his 'true' identity.[15]

At the end of 1938, when he was two years' old, Joss, under the care of two English nannies and a male household comptroller called Mr Smithers, held that he was sent to the Cape along with a large sum of money to fund his upbringing. However, instead of moving in with one or other of his foster parents, Joss, Mr Smithers and the two English nannies occupied a house called Waterhof at the upper end of Hof Street in Cape Town. Hof Street is a pleasant, leafy, residential road that meanders from the city centre up the lower slopes of Table Mountain before turning sharply right to meet the hustle and bustle and, at that time, jangling trams of busy, commercial Kloof Street, which also runs up the mountain. The houses in Hof Street, particularly the ones higher up the mountain, tend to be large and well-built with spacious gardens; Waterhof was one such house.

Waterhof, the property in Hof Street, Cape Town, where Joss stayed as a toddler.

However, although 6000 miles away from war-torn Britain and from the risk of creating a constitutional crisis, the Waterhof household soon began to face troubles of its own. One day, while Mr Smithers was out shopping in Kloof Street, he was knocked down and killed by a bus. For the two distraught nannies, this was the last straw. Probably concerned about developments back home in Europe, they decided to return to Britain to serve as nurses in the war. A housekeeper from the Eastern Cape called Mrs Pringle and various attendants were then apparently hired to look after Joss.

* * *

At this point, I move from what Joss had been told about his early life to what he claimed to remember; and he remembered loathing Mrs Pringle. She clearly had rather primitive notions about how to look after young children, for she used to force him to sit on the pot for hours and beat him if he wet his bed. Joss was convinced that she had scarred him for life because, as he rather frivolously put it, 'I have never liked anyone from the Eastern Cape since.' Mrs Pringle may well have coped badly with the situation, but a young child who had not only lost touch with his natural parents but had also suddenly been deprived of all three of the people with whom he had recently become most familiar could not have been easy to manage. In fact, the commotion he set up in trying to resist Mrs Pringle's child-rearing practices caused enough of a racket to attract the attention of a doctor living in the house on the opposite side of the road. The public-spirited doctor then took it upon himself to peer furtively with a telescope through the windows of Waterhof. On observing how roughly the woman from the Eastern Cape was handling such a young and clearly distressed child, he decided to make enquiries about the ownership of the house. His enquiries led him to a Mrs Wessels who lived on a farm in Somerset West called Parel Vallei. Mrs Wessels was the mother of Joss's foster mother, Mrs Joseph de Wahl, alias Mrs Billy Graaff. She was asked to rescue the child.

The house opposite Waterhof, then occupied by a
public-spirited doctor.

Joss moves to Parel Vallei

Thus began a new and much happier period in Joss's life in which Ouma (Afrikaans for Granny) Wessels was the central pivot. By the time Joss moved to Parel Vallei to live with Ouma Wessels, her husband Danie (Daniel) Wessels had already died. Danie, Joss claimed, had been a direct descendant of the old Cape governor, Simon van der Stel (1639–1712), who came to Africa in 1679 as 'Commander' of the Dutch India Company's colony at the Cape of Good Hope.[16] Simon van der Stel was an important figure in South Africa's history. He is regarded as one of its founding fathers, and both Simonstown and Stellenbosch are named after him. Parel Vallei had originally been 'a van der Stel farm; François van der Stel built it,' but according to Joss, for some unknown reason the van der Stels had changed their name to Wessels. Nonetheless, it was a well-established Cape family that owned several farms, as well as a fine collection of paintings. Joss claimed that 'François van der Stel's mother was the daughter of Baron Schickler and that Baron Schickler had been Rembrandt's patron; hence, all those Rembrandts and other exceptionally

26

good Dutch Masters.' He also noted that the van der Stels had what he referred to as 'some really good stuff' and that 'a lot of parks around there belonged to them.'

Ouma Wessels, who was of French descent, was a member of the Bourbon-Condé family. Since the House of Bourbon ruled Navarre and France as far back as the sixteenth century, she too came from a family that could boast a long and distinguished history. By the eighteenth century, members of the Bourbon dynasty ruled Spain, Naples, Sicily and Parma and, at present, Spain and Luxembourg have Bourbon monarchs. Ouma Wessels had met her husband Danie in Europe and, after their marriage, Danie Wessels brought his bride to South Africa for a two-week trial period. On her arrival at Parel Vallei as a young bride, Ouma Wessels 'thought that the main house was the lodge, but she was a strong woman and made the most of it, for this was where she was to spend the rest of her life.'

The house in question, is a pretty, eighteenth-century Cape Dutch farmhouse surrounded by vineyards on the gentle southern slopes of the Helderberg range on the northern outskirts of what was then the small English-looking town of Somerset West, a sleepy hollow about 30 miles southeast of Cape Town and overlooking False Bay, but now a sprawling metropolis and dormitory town for Cape Town.

Low, whitewashed walls surround the farm, which is approached through an avenue of flowering gums, now huge and stately, but Joss remembered when they were first planted. Within easy walking distance of the local facilities of a small safe town, yet with spacious grounds and wild unspoiled countryside, mountains, and beaches nearby, Parel Vallei must have seemed like paradise to a little boy.[17]

The Wessels family had a lot of landholdings in the area and apparently owned other farms on the estate, including Paardevlei, Rhone, Buzenval (now called Fleur du Cap), Erinvale, Spanish Farm and several others. Joss claimed that they were a well-off family with a lot of property and he grew

Gated entrance to Parel Vallei.

Parel Vallei farm, a substantial property containing
several houses.

to love the woman he took to be his grandmother. In recollecting his time with her, he claimed that 'Ouma Wessels was rather a wonderful person. She was an outstanding woman and had this wonderful brain. She loved Danie and she just lived within herself. I mean she was the most antisocial person I ever knew.' He also said that 'Ouma Wessels surrounded herself with an odd collection of people.' He spoke of a

28

Mrs Lillianveld, who was a member of the Stocks family of 1820 settlers and of how Ouma Wessels had set up Mrs Lillianveld's two Stocks nephews to make their fortune. He also mentioned that she had a companion called Dolly Roussouw, a secretary named Baby Voigt, a service maid (*diensmeid*) called Marie Haasbroek, a chauffeur called Pete Gayness, and a housekeeper called Mrs Bredenkamp. These were the senior members of her household staff, though Joss believed that Mrs Lillienveld was generally in charge of the numerous servants lower down in the household's hierarchy. Among them, Joss especially remembered Das, Elizabeth, Emily, Simon and Simon's son, though he had forgotten his name.

Ouma Wessels's own house on the farm.

Joss' playmate Sophie arrives

So, after his fraught and distressing period under Mrs Pringle's iron hand at Waterhof, Joss moved into the care of a reserved, elegant, intelligent widow with numerous servants. He does not know exactly when it was that he moved to Parel Vallei, but it was certainly shortly after the outbreak of the Second World War. In any case, it coincided with the period during

29

the war when General Smuts invited the Greek royal family, King Paul, Queen Frederika and their three children to seek refuge in South Africa. During this period, Joss and Princess Sophia of Greece (born 2 November 1938), later the wife of Juan Carlos I of Spain, who was a couple of years younger than he was, became firm friends and playmates. After a period in the Transvaal, Sophie (as Joss called Princess Sophia) and her family moved to Westbrook, a large house near Groote Schuur (the prime minister's official residence) in the Newlands/Rondebosch area of Cape Town. It was also where Princess Alice had lived when her husband, the Earl of Athlone, had been serving as governor-general of the Union of South Africa.[18] However, Sophie used to spend holidays with Joss, and they saw a lot of one another.

* * *

Mrs Wessels engaged a Mrs Brinton as Joss's first governess and she attempted to educate both him and his rather spirited companion. Joss said that it 'was just an honorary position; I do not suppose she was paid to do it, but she was there every day. She probably lived in Somerset West.' He claimed never to have visited her house, though he said that she often used to take him with her when she visited her various friends. Joss referred to these early attempts to teach him to read and fail to teach him to spell as 'Mrs Brinton's war effort.' Joss was scathing about his early tuition.

> I am sure my education was quite wrong because I can still recite the whole of the *Ballad of Reading Gaol*,[19] which I think is really unsuitable for a seven-year-old or six-year-old child. I suppose Ouma Wessels wanted me to be able to read and write. I can read, but I cannot write because I cannot spell. My spelling is monstrously bad. My education is terribly sketchy because I was never

taught the alphabet. Mrs Brinton had this modern method, which they use now, so she was fifty years ahead of her time. She just taught Sophie and me. You used to read cat and dog, so we never learnt the alphabet. I cannot look up a number in the telephone directory because I really do not know the alphabet. Ouma Wessels used to read balance sheets to me because she was busy structuring Anglo-American then.[20] That is of course why I do not know any fairy tales. I could read a balance sheet when I was five years old.

Quite apart from struggling to learn how to read and write using the wrong method, Joss has many other memories of those often-carefree years. Because they were living on a farm, it was possible for them to have numerous pets. This prompted Joss to recall the rather tragic story of Sophie's pig.

Sophie used to go and buy crates of tins of gherkins. It [the pig] lived on gherkins chiefly and then eventually died from overeating. It really did. She fed it to death. And then we were not allowed to see it because it was dead. Dolly[21] came and told us it was dead. Then Sophie started weeping over her pig because it was now dead. And Dolly said, 'Well now do not worry because it has gone to heaven.' And Sophie said, 'do not talk nonsense at me.' She said, 'How can it go to heaven? What about the law of gravity?'

They also had several dogs, which the children insisted had to have surnames. Joss remembers two, Rubbish Viljoen, which the owner of Oak Valley farm, Anthonie Viljoen, had given to them and Hawker Stuttaford, which was

a spaniel that old Ada gave to us. And Rubbish really was such rubbish – he was a lovely dog but used to sneak into Thomas Milton[22] and go and lie in the window. Miss Cooks used to lock up the shop and then by 7 o'clock Sophie would start looking for Rubbish. And there was Rubbish! Rubbish would be sitting either on a chair or a sofa because Miss Cooks always put a chair or a sofa in the window. Of course, Miss Cooks would then have to come and unlock the shop. It never did not happen. I mean one would have thought that one day Miss Cooks might have checked, or Sophie would have noticed that Rubbish was missing, but it never did not happen.

There was also a wire-haired terrier called Cheeky 'who was madly protective of our Hupmobiles, of which there were two.' When these Hupmobiles – American motorcars that the Hupp Motor Company built between 1909 and 1940 – were taken to Benjamin Droomer's father's garage to be repaired – it was wartime, and one could not readily get hold of spare parts – Cheeky would always find his way there and threaten

> to bite the mechanics when they tried to get near the cars. Everybody was astonished that Cheeky should be so clever as to be able to walk down to the Main Street in Somerset West and find the cars, but Sophie could not understand why they were so stupid. She said, 'Of course Cheeky knows the numbers of the cars. It is easy to find the cars, because he could read the numbers, you see.' We used to have a lot of fun actually.

They engaged in quite a lot of visiting, both with and without Ouma Wessels's approval.

> We knew everybody. I mean it was a tiny town. Our favourite person, who of course we were not allowed to go and visit, who of course we did go and visit regularly, was Charles Anderson's wife. She was an alcoholic, and

they lived at Buzenval, which they have now renamed Fleur du Cap. We adored Muriel Anderson. Muriel was the nurse, and she could swear. Sophie timed her – four minutes without using the same swear word twice, which impressed us no end. We loved Muriel and Muriel was very fond of us. We were not allowed to visit her, but we did.

They sometimes went a little further afield, far enough afield to need to secure the services of a chauffeur, of which they had a choice of two, to drive them to their destination. They were Pete Davidson, who Joss claimed, 'had been sec-onded from Scotland Yard as a sort of bodyguard cum chauf-feur and, of course, Simon'. Joss then went on to explain what a good organizer Sophie was and how, because she liked fish pie, especially the one that one of the many servants at Parel Vallei, in this case Mrs Brendal, made she devised a scheme to ensure that they got to eat it at her house despite not being allowed to visit her. In Joss's words:

Sophie was so dishonest really when you come to think of it now. We would go and visit Mrs le Roux at the Old Pastorie,[23] which was then still the parsonage. She would tell Mrs le Roux that the car was collecting us before lunch and the car would be ordered to collect us after lunch. So, we used to go round the corner and eat our fish pie with these people and walk back to the Old Pastorie, be collected outside and nobody was any the wiser.

Joss then went on to recall how Sophie could always get Perel, whom she also seemed to have under her control and who owned the Helderberg Hotel in Somerset West, to lend her his car and chauffeur to further their far-fetched ambi-tions, one of which 'was to sit outside the *pissoir* in the Strand[24] and smoke cigarettes.'

Die Ou Pastorie/The Old Parsonage,
where Mrs Le Roux had lived.

Interior of the Old Pastorie.

However, on this occasion they got caught out because, it happened to be on the one day when Mrs Brendal had got the day off because her sister was dying somewhere in the Strand. Simon was driving her to her sister's house and, as Joss said,

The Helderberg Hotel, Somerset West, Cape.

She nearly fell out of the car because there were the two of us smoking away madly. We had got money from Friedman and bought the cigarettes from across the road. We could not get cigarettes from him. We tried; Sophie tried. She said she wanted to give them to somebody, but he smelled a rat, but he did give us some money to go and buy some. I can understand why Sophie is so popular today because she was much loved in Somerset West and in the Strand.

While Joss was the older of the two children, he clearly looked upon Sophie as the more daring of the two. It was she who devised the pranks and who showed little deference to the adults around them, and this was a quality that Joss seemed to admire:

Sophie always bullied me. I remember we had to eat our supper before we could leave the table. I do not know who made the rule, not Ouma Wessels. She would never make a ridiculous rule like that. It was probably Mrs Brinton. Then Sophie used to chuck her food in some large Ming vase, which was standing in that day nursery

35

of ours. But then old Mrs le Roux got hold of her and told her that it is a terrible sin to waste food, so then she forced me to eat her leftovers. Sophie is very funny actually.

* * *

While Joss was living with Ouma Wessels in a servant-filled household that provided him with food, shelter, at least one regular playmate and some rudimentary, albeit rather informal education where, one might ask, was his mother, or at least the woman he eventually came to refer to as his 'foster' mother? And what role did she play in his life? In fact, Joss saw relatively little of either of his 'foster' parents and seemed to have little contact with or much regard for them. He anachronistically described his foster mother as a 'society flapper,' his foster father as a 'crook' and his foster mother's former husband, Bill Graaff, as a 'playboy.' However, in one way or another, these people played some part in his life. For a start, a firm founded in 1905 to provide discreet financial services and to set up and administer trusts, Graaffs Trust Ltd, took care of his money and, of course, there was a family connection there – not all Graaffs were playboys! And, as I mentioned earlier, his purported 'foster' mother (whom Joss claimed never had a child of her own) was Ouma Wessels's daughter. Joss did not know why Bill Graaff's marriage to his 'foster' mother had failed, or why, after Bill had remarried, he chose to come back to her house – Sonnekus – to commit suicide. As a young boy, Joss would have neither understood nor known about such complicated family dynamics. Unfortunately, Bill's suicide occurred just as Mrs Brinton and Joss were about to pay a visit.

I arrived at Sonnekus, which is that house my foster mother built – Le Corbusier actually built it for her. It is the only Le Corbusier house in this country.[25] De Villiers[26] kindly pulled it down; only the stables remain now. And it was on the island alone and of course it had this wonderful view of Table Mountain, and the lawns went right down to the beach. It was a real Gatsby house. It was a sort of Long Island Sound house.[27] I arrived there with Mrs Brinton and jumped out of the car before the chauffeur could open the doors, as little boys do. And I ran towards the house. I remember the butler, Mathews, coming out and trying to stop me from going into the house, and I ducked under his arm and ran in. The house had three storeys with a staircase going up all the way. And there was this man hanging. He had tied a rope to the banister of the top floor and jumped down and they could not cut him down until the police arrived. We turned up in that split second before the police did. The butler did come out to stop us. I mean he did not wait at the door. He was on his way to the car and tried to block me, but I ducked under his arm. Then, of course, I was immediately taken away. My foster mother never went back there. She then went to Buzenval. Dolly Roussouw went to pack her personal effects. I remember Dolly Roussouw telling me that there were 570 pairs of shoes. I do not know why that stuck in my mind. My foster mother lived there. The house belonged to her, but Bill had married somebody else by then. He divorced her and married somebody else, but he came and committed suicide in her house. A lot of that property that the Graaffs now have was Wessels property. I do not know why they were divorced. I did not really know my foster mother very well.

Arriving at the house immediately after Bill Graaff's suicide must have upset Joss more than he realized, for he erased the whole episode from his memory and it only came back to him when, by chance, he saw the house again. This happened because a photographer called Ben Burger, with whom Joss was friendly and who lived in the Eastern Cape, would come to Cape Town to visit his cousin Breyten Breytenbach who was serving a seven-year prison sentence. Breyten Breytenbach, who was born in 1939 and who is a South African writer and painter living in France, was a staunch opponent of the apartheid regime and this, of course, was all happening when the apartheid regime was still in full control. Breyten had married a woman of Vietnamese descent and, because cross-racial marriages were deemed illegal under the terms of the South African Immorality Act, he had been banned from visiting the country. In 1975, however, while on an illicit trip to his home country, he was arrested and sentenced to seven years' imprisonment on a charge of high treason. He returned to France on his release from prison in 1982. However, as Joss explained, Ben Burger's loyalty to his recalcitrant cousin, served to jog Joss's memory of a childhood trauma:

> I forgot about this incident until many years later. Ben Burger, a photographer, a good photographer because Cecil Beaton[28] chose him as his assistant, reminded me. He was Breyten's cousin and when Breyten was put in prison he came back here to be with him every Saturday; Breyten was allowed visitors. But he said to me that there was a Le Corbusier house at Milnerton.[29] And I said, 'Oh do not be mad, Le Corbusier never built anything in this country' and he said, 'Well, I will drive you out there.' And he drove me out there and as I came up to the house it all came back to me. I had completely blocked it out. But I never knew Bill Graaff.

While Joss never knew for certain why Bill Graaff chose to take his life, he presumed that it was probably for financial

Graaff House in Milnerton as it now stands,
after having been rebuilt.

reasons. He believed that the fortunes of the Graaff family had suffered badly in the aftermath of the Depression and rather pompously assumed that 'they did not understand finance because they were too new to the scene.' Ouma Wessels, however, whose financial acumen Joss clearly idealized, 'sort of steered them through' that difficult period.

The British royals visit South Africa

In 1946 Sophie and her family returned to Greece. Joss was unaware at this stage that the halcyon days of his carefree childhood were numbered and that, during the royal visit to South Africa in 1947, they would be brought to a rather rude and sudden end.

If we continue to take Joss's narrative at face value, one of his first memories of the royal tour of South Africa was of being driven in a Lagonda[30] to visit the king at a farm called Yonder. The Wessels family owned the farm and Joss and Sophie had spent holidays there. It was near Kimberley, which is the capital of the Northern Cape and renowned for its diamond mines.

On this occasion, King George VI had gone there to recuperate after having collapsed from fatigue while on a visit to Mafeking (where the most celebrated siege of the second Boer War had taken place at the turn of the century). Joss said that he remembered staying with King George VI in the farmhouse, which had a wide, wisteria-clad veranda and a beautiful garden, and that the king had made him a kite out of tissue paper and bamboo. Joss thought that he was a kind man and clearly liked him. As he recalled, 'he was very gentle. He made me a kite, which would not fly. It was hopeless. I think the kite was probably all right. It was probably my fault. He was a nice man. I liked him.'

According to Joss, on returning to Cape Town after his sojourn at Yonder, arrangements were made for him to meet Wallis for the first time since his infancy. Joss said she had travelled to South Africa on the HMS *Vanguard* when it set sail from Portsmouth on 1 February 1947 for the royal tour of South Africa. This, however, seems exceedingly unlikely, for the risk of someone identifying her would have been far too high. Her name certainly does not appear on the 'nominal list of all persons aboard during the voyage,' but even if she had been left off the official lists, with 1179 passengers and crew aboard and with the journey lasting two weeks, someone would have noticed and commented on her presence. At least one rating would have sold the story to the gutter press. When I challenged his account, Joss insisted she came to South Africa at that time, whether on the *Vanguard* or by some other means. My own recollection of that time is of excited schoolchildren, of which I was one, lining the sunny streets of Cape Town to wave their little Union Jacks at King George VI, Queen Elizabeth and the Princesses Elizabeth and Margaret Rose as they flashed past in an open limousine.[31]

From Joss's viewpoint, however, preparations were afoot for his visit to the most luxurious of all the Cape Town hotels at the time, the Mount Nelson in Orange Street, which was

Mount Nelson Hotel, Cape Town.

where, he claimed, the meeting had been planned to take place. According to his account, it was not a particularly happy experience. In his own words:

> Well, I remember that quite well. It was at the Mount Nelson. We had the top floor closed off for us and I remember we sat there. There were several sitting rooms, a private dining room, as well as bedrooms and things, and we sat on that one balcony, which has now been closed. She told me that she was my mother and that I did not really belong. And I remember I ran away. I ran down the passage and down the stairs. There was a Scotland Yard man on the stairs, so I ducked under his arm, and ran down, right down and I went and hid myself. There was a seat, a plaza seat, I think it is still there, on the way to the swimming pool, which is sort of cut out of the bougainvillaea. There is a seat in there and I went and hid myself there and they searched for me until quite late. Eventually, I was persuaded to come back upstairs. The following day I went and hid myself in one of the cellars. I am quite an authority on the cellars of the Mount Nelson.

The plaza seat near the swimming pool at the Mount Nelson
Hotel, behind which Joss claims to have hidden.

It is not difficult to imagine how distressing this experience
must have been for Joss and Wallis. Joss claimed to have taken
the revelation that she was his mother to mean that he no
longer belonged with his beloved Ouma Wessels, which is
probably a predictable response, irrespective of whether she
put it that bluntly. He said it was devastating for him to have
to hear such news from a stranger from another country, let
alone such an imperious and rather brittle one. On her part,
however confident or arrogant a woman she may have been, it
could not have been easy to know that her child regarded
her as a stranger. She would have reflected on her own past
and compared the warmth she felt for her Aunt Bessie
Merryman, the person to whom she felt closest in Baltimore,
with the more difficult relationship she had with her 'natural'
mother, Victoria Colonna. In some respects, history was being
repeated. She must have been nervous about how best to
approach Joss and about how he would react to the news. One
wonders at what point in her life she had learnt about her own
parentage and how easy or difficult it had been for her at the
time.

When it became apparent that their sojourn at the Mount Nelson Hotel was going so badly, however, Wallis (who was planning to spend six months with Joss in South Africa before taking him back to Europe) decided to try another venue. This time it was to be at a more family-oriented hotel at a small seaside fishing village called St James, which is located on the main road that runs along the coast between Muizenberg and Simonstown. With a railway line on one side of the road and buildings on the other, there was an unobstructed view of the sea.

St James Hotel, St James, Cape Town.
Now a retirement home.

I was very distraught actually, but then my mother decided to take me to the St James Hotel. I think we spent a few days at the British Embassy, which they cleared out. I did not like it and my mother could not cope with it either, because things had gone wrong. I mean, really the trouble we caused everybody! They cleared out the St James Hotel. I mean the people staying there were just thrown out. Then we stayed there for a few days, but she did not like it, so we went to the Leisure Isle.

Location of the former Leisure Isle hotel in Knysna.

The Leisure Isle was a hotel at Knysna on the south coast of the Western Cape approximately 265 miles east of Cape Town. The hotel has now been demolished but at that time it was a pleasant private establishment with a swimming pool and separate thatched-roofed bungalows for the guests. The hotel was on one of the Knysna Heads, the two hills on either side of a somewhat treacherous channel that separates the Indian Ocean from a large lagoon at the mouth of the Knysna River. It is pertinent that Wallis chose to take Joss there because when George Rex,[32] then believed to be the illegitimate son of King George III, was shipwrecked in Knysna in 1804, he bought an estate on the shores of the lagoon from which the settlement grew.

Knysna Heads.

44

I do not know how long we stayed there, possibly six months or a bit longer. The idea was that I would still be able to talk to Ouma Wessels and it would be quite peaceful, but it was not because I rejected Ouma Wessels and my mother. Ouma Wessels loved me, and I think my mother loved me very dearly, but I just could not cope with either of them. Although I felt instinctively fond of my mother and adored Ouma Wessels, I rejected them both. I do not think I hated them, for I used to go and stay with my mother and even became quite friendly with her. When I think back on it from a psychological point of view, which I had not done before because I never thought I had any psychological hang-ups – I thought I was above that sort of petty thing – I suppose I did resent her having rejected me. She was enormously rich. She had enormous self-confidence. As a princess of money, she was far more important than the Windsors ever were or ever would be, and she should not have allowed herself to have been talked into rejecting me. It is only today that I have thought about it in that way. I never thought about it before because I considered myself above such ordinary human resentment, but apparently, I was not. Of course, I was a child, and I was insecure, which I suppose I still am and perhaps that is why I cannot accept responsibilities. I really cannot!

It cannot have been easy for such a young boy who had already experienced abandonment as a baby and as a toddler to have to accept that the one person with whom he had at last felt secure had also betrayed him. To compound the situation, during this period Wallis made it clear to Joss that she hated Knysna with its unfathomable, bottomless lakes and that she found Africa wild and dangerous. She did not like it at all. She was also clearly finding it difficult to cope with her son's distress. He too must have seemed wild, unfathomable, bottomless, and dangerous. Nonetheless, Wallis persisted in trying to establish a relationship with him, as did Ouma Wessels, but it was never ideal. The one woman to whom he did claim to feel close was Diana Duff Cooper. It is odd that Joss should suddenly have mentioned his fondness for one of Wallis's friends at a time when he was speaking about the loss of trust he had experienced as a young boy, long before he could possibly have met, let alone grown fond of her. Perhaps he felt an affinity with Diana because, although the 8th Duke of Rutland brought her up as his own daughter, she was the biological daughter of the politician and editor, Henry Cust (whom Joss always referred to as Perry Brownlow), so she, like Joss, had a complicated and concealed parentage. Cust also had lots of affairs and was rumoured to have fathered many children. He was a friend of the Duke of Windsor and appears in a photograph with Wallis in France, just before she supposedly gave birth to Joss. Was he aiding them? Incidentally, he fell out both with Wallis and with Elizabeth (the Queen Mother), who summarily excluded him from the court. Did he know too much?

To return to Lady Diana Duff Cooper, née Lady Diana Manners (1892–1986), who was said to be the most beautiful woman in England in her day and was an actress, writer, and socialite. In June 1919 she married Duff Cooper (1890–1954), a Conservative MP, author, and diplomat. From 1944 to 1948 he was ambassador to France where Diana became a popular hostess. The Duff Coopers and the Duke and Duchess of Windsor maintained a friendship that lasted for many years and, according to Joss, she was 'probably the one person who did get through to me. I was very fond of Diana, and she was the one who rang me up when my mother died. I think of them.' Two months after that fateful phone call, Diana also died at the age of 93.

* * *

The royal visit to South Africa marked a sea change in Joss's life and from that period onwards, his world started to broaden. Though still a child, the innocent, carefree part of his childhood, the days of Mrs Brendal's fish pie and the sense of security he had felt in the loving care of his adored Ouma Wessels, had gone forever.

3

Wallis: Princess of Elegance

WHAT WAS THE shape of Joss's imaginary construction of Wallis Simpson, this enigmatic woman about whom so much has been written and yet, according to Joss, so little of the truth is known? He asserted that her 'whole identity' had been hidden and that everything that people claimed to know about her were the mere speculations of those who did not really know her. In fact, he even went on to say that 'nobody who knew my mother personally, or who had ever spoken to her, has ever written a word about her.' However, that is not true because Diana Mosley, who knew the Duchess of Windsor extremely well and was clearly part of her inner circle of fashionable, elegant, clever, forward looking, rich and beautiful people, wrote a book about her, which Sidgwick & Jackson published in 1980. However, Joss had a point in that, despite the great volume of words written about her, quite a lot of it is not especially revealing.

For a start, the descriptions of her private life are particularly contradictory. How, might one ask, did a supposedly sexually promiscuous young woman from an ordinary family in Baltimore come to acquire the contacts and friends that she did? By the early 1930s, when Wallis and her second husband Ernest Simpson were living in a flat at Bryanston Court in George Street, near Marble Arch in London, their social world already knew few boundaries. Why was she only one step away from entering the revered portals of British royalty?

Simply at the level of self-esteem she would have had no fear of the British aristocracy if, as Joss claimed, she was the grand-daughter, albeit the illegitimate grand-daughter, of J. P. Morgan (1837–1913) who, by 1901 had become the most powerful private banker in the United States and one of the richest men in the world. If his son J. P. ('Jack') Morgan Jr (1867–1943) was indeed Wallis's natural father, then it might help us understand how she gained entry to the British upper classes. It might also have made a difference if it had been hinted that Wallis's natural mother had been an aristocrat, and a Colonna no less, rather than Alice Warfield, whose class, financial and social credentials were insufficient to gain her daughter access to the British aristocracy, let alone to royalty. Wallis was presented at court at Buckingham Palace on 10 June 1931, so presumably she would have needed more credentials than those of a twice married commoner without any visible means and, purportedly, loose sexual morals.

From Joss's viewpoint, Wallis was clearly a stylish lady who mixed in very fashionable moneyed circles. In the absence of the Morgan connection, it would be difficult to explain her friendships with people like Bunny Mellon. Joss averred several times that Bunny remained close to Wallis and was to play an important part in the final years of Joss's life. Wallis's close friends included prominent personalities of the day such as Pauline Rothschild, Diana Duff Cooper, Margot Asquith, Thelma Furness, Gloria Vanderbilt, Primrose Cadogan, Margaret Argyll, Jacqueline Kennedy, Doris Duke and many more. Her association with the then Prince of Wales would of course have given her access to the British royal family, but some of these people were friends she had made in her own right in the United States. They were the heiresses to great fortunes who became iconic figures in décor, lifestyle, appearance, and standards of taste. As a group, they were profoundly confident, even disdainful at times, and inhabited a world of people who were largely untouched by the insecurity of the period.

While the masses in the United States and Britain bore the brunt of the Great Depression, Wallis and her friends were turning to Givenchy and Mainbocher to design their clothes, and to Fulco Santostefano, the Duke of Verdura, to make their jewellery. 'Charming Billy,' namely Billy Baldwin (1903–1983) who decorated the interiors of their sumptuous houses, provided a crucial connecting link, for he, like his two friends the Duchess of Windsor and Pauline Rothschild, had grown up in Baltimore. These rich women were setting the trend in taste and style and their brand was new, bold, adventurous, and full of fun. They were the celebrities of their day, and their allure was irresistible. When Thelma Furness (1904–1970), twin sister of Gloria Morgan Vanderbilt (1904–1965) and aunt of fashion designer Gloria Vanderbilt (1924–2019), introduced Wallis to her friend the Prince of Wales in the early 1930s, he was captivated, and it was not long before Wallis was being ushered into the hallowed world of British royalty. While the Prince of Wales was immediately smitten by Wallis's quick wit, style, and self-assurance, some of the other members of the royal family, most notably the Prince of Wales's parents, King George V and Queen Mary, as well as some of the more traditional members of the British Establishment, found her presence distinctly uncomfortable.

At that time, as we have seen, the United Kingdom was insular, class bound and traditional. In the United States, however, despite the Great Depression having cast a damper on much of the 1930s, the heirs and heiresses of some of the great railroad and banking fortunes amassed in the nineteenth and early twentieth centuries were ready to step out into the world and make it their own. Everything about Wallis served as a reminder that the United States was on the ascent and Britain on the decline. She had the audacity to mock their values and traditions. They, on their part, found her brash, irreverent, and American. But then, as Joss explained, she was far too arrogant to care what they thought.

Wallis's provenance, according to Joss

As already mentioned, Joss claimed that Wallis was the child born of a love affair between J. P. ('Jack') Morgan Jr (1867–1943), the son and successor of the railroad, steel, and banking baron J. P. Morgan (1837–1913), and the Italian aristocrat Victoria (Tia) Colonna. At this point, we need to bear in mind that the story Joss recounted about the romance between Jack Morgan and Tia Colonna is three generations old. Consequently, like many family legends, it is likely to contain innumerable inaccuracies, exaggerations, and distortions, especially since, like Joss, Wallis purportedly lived with a false identity and, in her case, the shameful stigma of illegitimacy. In the absence of a formal adoption, records would have been fudged, destroyed, or never kept.

It is known that neither Wallis's birth nor the marriage of her adoptive parents was ever registered,[1] so the dates of these two events are unclear. It is also known that there was a business connection between the Warfields and J. P. Morgan, for Solomon Warfield's association with the Seaboard Air Line Railroad brought him close to J. P. Morgan & Company and Jack Morgan could well have approached him with a view to helping him arrange a home for his illegitimate daughter. It is interesting that Alice and Teackle married after Wallis's birth and, like Joss's foster parents Mrs Billy Graaff and Joseph de Wahl, seemed to have married only with a view to providing a home for an unacknowledged child. It is also interesting that Wallis was sent to the United States rather than allowed to remain close to her natural mother in Rome, which seems to suggest that J. P. Morgan either took his paternity more seriously than Tia Colonna did her maternity or that they had their own reasons for wanting Wallis brought up in the United States.

Nonetheless, Joss said that Jack was infatuated with Tia and desperately wanted to marry her, but that the strong expectations in such circles that members of the aristocracy consolidate their position meant that 'Tia's father would not allow her to marry Pierpont Morgan because he wanted her to marry Catania.' I have been unable to establish how much time Jack Morgan and Tia Colonna spent together, either in Rome or the United States, but it is interesting that his father died in Rome in 1913 when Jack was 46 years old, so perhaps the Morgans retained a base there. In any case, according to Joss, Tia had been in love with Pierpont Morgan, but her father had refused to sanction the match and insisted she marry an aristocrat called 'Catania' instead. Apparently, she 'just walked out of the wedding breakfast' in protest, but then found that 'she could not divorce Catania unless she gave up her Italian citizenship, which she refused to do.' Joss then quoted someone he referred to as Princess Esteva (I failed to establish who she might have been, though Joss thought that she was a Colonna cousin of some sort), as saying that, 'Your grandmother was worse than Cleopatra really. The Roman scandal has made spick, spoke, spire and set the Nile on fire.'

Although, according to Joss, Wallis disliked and had little time for her natural mother, Joss clearly liked his 'real' or 'imagined' maternal grandmother's style and even seemed to admire some of her outrageous conduct. As Joss described her:

> She was great fun actually. My mother was quite unlike Victoria Colonna, except that she had a little of her style – not even all of it. Victoria Colonna was exceptionally beautiful, and undoubtedly the best-dressed woman I ever knew. She was outrageously extravagant, and such style as my mother had she got from Victoria Colonna, except Victoria Colonna had so much more of it. My mother had an American dullness. Victoria Colonna had great *joie de vivre*. There was something special about

her. Her flat in Rome is not really a flat. It is a house. In the eighteenth century, whoever owned it, probably the Colonnas, turned the ground floor into shops, but the shops are about 200 years old, so are terribly interesting. There is a roof garden and the bathroom fittings in the house are made of solid gold. They are still there.

Although Joss claimed to have known his Colonna grand-mother well, he was vague about the other members of her family.

There is Bimbo, and I do not know where Bimbo fits in. Bimbo I think is the cousin. Victoria Colonna had a sis-ter. I have got a vague idea the sister became the Princess of Monaco, but I am not sure about that. It may have been a distant cousin. It may not have been the sister. I am not sure where the sister fitted into the picture.

On another occasion Joss asserted with more confidence that Victoria Colonna's sister had married the Prince of Monaco, the eleventh Duke of Valentinois, Louis II (1870–1949), who ruled the principality of Monaco between 1922 and 1949. It is established that Prince Rainier III's mother was Princess Charlotte, Duchess of Valentinois, Countess of Polignac (Charlotte Louise Juliette Grimaldi (1898–1977), so Joss may have been muddled. However, since he never revealed his grandmother's full name or any details of her genealogy – I am not sure how, or even if, the Colonna and Grimaldi families are related. Given that the likelihood of intermarriage between such families is presumably quite high, Joss could be forgiven for thinking that, 'the Princess of Monaco was Rainier's mother, who was Victoria Colonna's sister, so in other words Rainier was my mother's first cousin, which is another thing that nobody knows. Mind you, his daughter Caroline has got the Colonna style.' In any case, however close or distant Victoria Colonna's association with the Grimaldi family of Monte Carlo, she appeared to have had few compunctions or inhibitions when it came to getting what she wanted:

> She pushed poor Bimbo out of the Colonna palace in Rome. She lived there. Bimbo lived in some tatty little flat down the road, but considering the vast size of that palace, one should have thought she could have given Bimbo a little wing of it. Poor Bimbo, who had an awfully long name – I did once know it – is such a goof. He just went and lived in this flat because Victoria chucked him out. Bimbo was the rightful owner of the house, but she just took it upon herself to go and live in it. I think Bimbo is still alive. I have not seen him for years.

Bimbo is clearly a nickname and since Joss failed to recall his real name, his identity must remain a mystery. I do, however, know that the Colonna and Barberini families merged during the seventeenth century and that the family's direct descendant, the Prince of Palestrina, Don Augusto Barberini, died in Rome in 2005. Bimbo, however, would probably have been at least one if not two generations older. The present Prince of Palestrina is HE Prince Benedetto Francesco Barberini who was born in 1960. The history of the royal houses of Europe is long, complicated and, at times, difficult to follow. There is a lot of intermarriage between the various royal houses because in the choice of marriage partners, pedigrees and dynastic lines take precedence over personal preferences. For example, Queen Elizabeth II was married to a Greek prince until his death; and the Greek princess who used to play with Joss as a child married the king of Spain. There are of course many other examples, but when a monarch chooses a spouse from outside this almost deified circle of royal personages, the match is almost certainly met with disapproval, or at least was in those days. One such case was in 1956 when Prince Rainier III of Monaco married the Oscar-winning American film star Grace Kelly. Prince Rainier, of the House of Grimaldi, and of Dutch, English, French, German, Italian, Mexican, Scottish, and Spanish ancestry, was under some pressure to marry because unless he could produce a direct heir, the Principality of Monaco would revert to France. According to Joss, in these royal circles, the marriage was not well received, but as he put it, 'Rainier was unstoppable.'

To the wider public, however, the marriage was a spectacular fairy-tale romance, and the attention of the whole world was suddenly focused, for the first time in a long while, on this tiny principality wedged between France and Italy on the northern coast of the Mediterranean. It is only 0.78 square miles in size and its population of 39,511 (in 2021), includes numerous wealthy people who, by residing there, can avoid paying taxes in their own countries.

Joss saw an opportunity to gain some street cred for himself when his longstanding South African friend Viscount Barrington expressed a desperate wish to meet Grace Kelly. And this, Joss boasted, was something he could deliver. Henry, born Henry Petersen, had grown up in South Africa and had South African nationality, but he acquired a baronetcy through the untimely death of an English relative.[2] Henry had a cousin called Frances, for whom he had little affection and for whom he later had even less. Joss recounted the story of Henry's brush with the famous film star Princess of Monaco, Grace Kelly, but I suspect it included quite a few embellishments for effect and might well have been wholly fictitious. Anyway, as he recounted it:

Henry's one ambition was to have Grace to tea at Marlow Castle, which is this cardboard castle – a big Edwardian house made from little bricks – that they own on the

Viscount Barrington's family home in Knysna.

Thames at Marlow. So, I said to Grace you must go and have tea with poor Henry. She was not very keen on the idea, but eventually agreed, and Henry went down a week before to prepare the flowers and groom the garden and clean the castle. On the morning in question, Frances sent her two children down with their nanny and a dog, so he pushed them into the furthest corner and thought he was safe from them. And then when I was getting Grace out of the car the dog stormed out and bit her and I had to put her right back into the car and take her to the cottage hospital, because I was frightened the dog might be rabid or something. So, she never had tea with Henry, and she died before I could ever arrange another meeting.[3] Henry will never recover from that, and he has hated Frances ever since.

* * *

Prince Rainier had clearly got away with his marriage to a commoner, for Princess Grace carried out her role faultlessly and was extremely popular, but that was in 1956. Times were quite different when Jack Morgan declared his love for Tia Colonna in the late nineteenth century. The royal houses of Europe had powerful interests to defend and a long and proud history. The Empress Eugénie (1826–1920), wife of the last monarch and first titular president of France, Emperor Napoleon III (1808–73) and mother of the Prince Imperial, had been a Colonna and through her link with the family Joss eventually acquired the treasured Colonna pearls. As mentioned earlier, Julius Caesar had purportedly been wearing these pearls when he was murdered and, as legend has it, they are supposed to bleed from time to time. Joss insisted that they still did, but here again it looks as if he might have been playing to the gallery:

> You know it is interesting because every time you put those pearls on silk then one pearl bleeds and makes a black mark on the silk. Well, I thought the pearl just had a hole in it and that damp got through onto the silk. Then Bill Torbitt, who is the most educated person I ever knew and was also a medical doctor decided that it was blood on the silk. So, he took the piece of silk and had it analysed and they could determine the blood group. And we did it again and the tests showed the same blood group again. There is no sign on the pearl. We assume that it must be Caesar's blood. He was a Colonna.

Joss is referring here to Bill Torbitt, a senior lecturer at the School of Information Technology at the Polytechnic of Namibia, but the story is so improbable that one certainly must put it down to Joss being fanciful. In any event, Joss went on to say that the pearls passed into the hands of 'the Empress Eugénie and they went in her dowry to France when she married Napoleon Bonaparte. Eugénie wore them at her wedding and that is why pearls are considered unlucky, because everything went wrong. They were deposed and the Prince

Imperial was murdered in Zululand.' Their son Louis Napoleon (1856–79), the Prince Imperial, had indeed died from assegai wounds while serving with the British Royal Artillery in the 1879 Anglo–Zulu War, which after several bloody battles and heavy casualties, especially on the Zulu side in which more than 10,500 lives were lost (against Britain's 1727 deaths and 256 wounded) brought an end to the Zulu nation's independence. In any case, to get back to the pearls, Joss thought that the Empress Eugénie, who died in 1920 aged 94, had passed them on to Wallis, on the understanding that she, in turn, would pass them on to her son. Nonetheless,

> Everything went wrong. It was that self-same row of pearls that caused the tradition. Empress Eugénie died years before I was born, but I think she gave them to my mother, and she passed them on to me. I always realized their value somehow. I always looked after them. I always had them with me and that is how Jean Tromp knows them so well, because I was never without them. They are enormous; it is a long string, and they really are exceptional pearls. It did have a clasp with the 13 stars of the Colonna crest, an exceptionally good diamond clasp, a large one. The clasp itself is, I suppose, valuable, but quite modern. I do not know who made it, probably Fabergé.[4] I think it must have been Fabergé because it can also be made into a double string, and you can wear another row with it. Because there was another row of big pearls, but they were not Caesar's pearls. I think there were 73 Caesar pearls – or 75. They came to me as Marie Antoinette's pearls.

If they did indeed come as Queen Marie Antoinette's pearls, then they were exceedingly unlucky. Marie Antoinette (1755–93), the wife of King Louis XVI of France, was executed by guillotine after a sham trial on the charge of high treason on

16 October 1793. Yet, despite all the bad luck associated with them, in some strange way Joss clung to his string of pearls as if his very being depended on their existence and their presence in his life. 'I wanted those with me,' he said, 'because I am very fond of jewellery. I am Victoria Colonna's grandson and she not only believed in but also banked in jewellery.' Joss also claimed that 'Victoria Colonna was very anti-Mussolini and stayed in Rome right through the Mussolini regime and gave him a lot of opposition in her own sort of way.' Benito Mussolini (1883–1945) was, of course, the Italian prime minister and leader of the National Fascist Party who brought Italy into the Second World War on the side of the Axis powers, so it is reassuring to know that at least Joss's grandmother was standing up to him.

* * *

Meanwhile, with so much history and legend pitched against him, Jack Morgan was forced to accept that the love of his life was not going to be his bride and by the time Wallis was born he was respectably married to Jane Norton Grew (Jessie), whom he had met in 1889 and married in 1890. I have been unable to lay hands on any firm evidence of Pierpont Morgan's romance with Victoria Colonna. Ron Chernow describes him as 'courtly with women, and … absolutely faithful to Jessie, a pretty, somewhat matronly woman,'[5] so it may well have been to protect her that he decided to pass off his illegitimate daughter as the natural child of Alice Montague (1869–1929) and the sickly Teackle Warfield. Teackle Warfield, who had contracted consumption at the age of 18, was the younger brother of Solomon Warfield, who became the postmaster general of Baltimore and, through his connection with J. P. Morgan, the financial adviser to the Prince of Wales. Alice and Teackle married on 19 November 1896, 17 months after Wallis had been born and only a year before Teackle died.

There is some dispute about Wallis's official birthdate. In the general census of 1900, the Warfield household lists it as 19 June 1895,[6] whereas other sources hold that she was born in 1896. 'Not only was the birth the only Warfield or Montague advent that was never featured anywhere in print, but the baby named Bessie Wallis Warfield was the first Warfield not to be baptized'[7] and no birth certificate for her was ever issued. Thus, the combination of the timing of Alice and Teackle's marriage, the confusion over the date of Wallis's birth, the absence of a birth certificate and the fact that Wallis was the only member of the family not to be baptized would tend to point to the possibility that Joss's claims about her could be credible.

Although there were good personal and family reasons for wishing to conceal Wallis's parentage on both sides of the Atlantic, Joss held that the real reason was to protect Wallis from the stigma of illegitimacy. As he explained, 'You see, it was terrible for a child to be illegitimate because she could never be presented at court. She could never have "come out" or anything.' The stigma of illegitimacy aside, not to mention the humiliation of not being presented at court, Joss never met his self-claimed maternal grandfather Jack Morgan. This was because, although Joss was already six years old at the time of his death in 1943, it was another four years before Wallis broke the news to him that she was his mother. Jack Morgan thus died without ever having met his grandson, but then, as Joss seemed keen to emphasize, he did not make the money, he merely inherited it from his father.

* * *   .

Meanwhile, back in Baltimore during Wallis's early childhood, Alice Warfield ran into financial difficulties and was reduced to letting rooms in her house. Her circumstances changed in 1902, however, when her sister Bessie Merryman came to her rescue shortly after her husband, the auctioneer David B. Merryman, died of pneumonia in 1901. As a kind and warm woman who loved both Alice and Wallis, she generously turned her large brick house in West Chase Street into a comfortable and prosperous home for them. Aunt Bessie became the person to whom Wallis always turned at difficult moments in her life. But, Joss insisted, Wallis had been a Morgan and that it was through the Morgans that both Wallis, who was taller than the Duke of Windsor, and he got their height, which Joss ascribed to their 'high protein diet.' Joss seemed to think that 'the only good photograph of them together ever taken was the one that Cecil Beaton took in which she kneels on a chair, and he stands looking down at her, because there you cannot see that she is taller than him.'

Wallis's marriages and sexuality

If we are to assume that Joss's claims about Wallis's heritage had any validity then it is uncertain how much Wallis knew about her own background while she was growing up in Baltimore. However, by the time she met the Prince of Wales, her true background had certainly begun to stand her in good enough stead to gain her access to royal circles. Meanwhile, as is well documented, she had married twice, the first time in 1916 to Lieutenant Earl Winfield (Win) Spencer (1888–1950). As Joss described it,

> I do not know why my mother married him. I once asked her, and she did not give me any reply. She said it was a mistake. I think he probably talked her into it. People can talk us into things. When she found herself married to Spencer she did not like the idea and understandably so. She just left. Then, he had it annulled because he said that it was never consummated. Of course, it was not. She was not going to consummate it. She just wanted nothing to do with it.

Wallis's second marriage, in 1928, after her divorce a year earlier, was to a shipping executive named Ernest Aldrich Simpson (1895–1958) who, though born and brought up in the United States, became a naturalized British citizen. He, however, had apparently developed a serious alcohol problem during the First World War and 'she never consummated the marriage with Ernest Simpson either.' Contrary to her popular image, Joss explained that she, like him, was disinterested in sex. He said that 'she was the one woman in whom one felt no sexuality because there was none,' and then continued, 'my father explained to me that she was completely anti sex.' If that were true, I asked, was there any basis for the widespread rumours that she had learnt some tricks in a Shanghai brothel? 'Why', retorted Joss, 'should the most eligible bachelor in the world marry an ex-inmate of a Shanghai brothel? I mean it does not make any bloody sense.'

That sensational rumour, however, had been widely circulated at the time, but it seems improbable that someone in her position would have subjected herself to such accusations, whatever she might have hoped to glean from her tuition in such matters. Nevertheless, irrespective of the alleged spell of sexual tuition in a Shanghai brothel, the question of Wallis's sexuality loomed large during the abdication crisis and numerous rumours were circulated over all the possible affairs she may have had or was having. She was widely regarded as a *femme fatale* who managed to entrap a gullible prince with her erotic powers. Contemporary feminists will recognize such statements as a common misogynistic trope.

Conversely, later there were rumours of quite another sort and 'then, the next sensational book gets put on the bookshelves of the world.' The book to which Joss was referring here was by Michael Bloch,[8] assistant to Maître Suzanne Blum (1898–1994), a French lawyer born in Niort who devoted the later years of her life to taking care of the Duchess of Windsor and attending to her legal affairs. Michael Bloch claimed that

Wallis suffered from a rare condition known as Androgen Insensitivity Syndrome (AIS) and that she was incapable of having normal sexual relations. The *Daily Mail* of Saturday 11 May 1996 was predictably quick to ask, 'Was Wallis Simpson really a man?' The idea clearly annoyed Joss who disputed the suggestion that

> the Duchess of Windsor was a man because it has been proven that neither of her first two marriages was ever consummated. I know they were never consummated because Ernest Simpson told me that and old Earl Spencer had the marriage annulled because she refused to consummate it. That I do know for a fact. She was completely asexual, like I am. I am just not interested in sex. Jean Tromp knows that too, because she says one inherits things, just like her family inherited the insanity from the Strathmores. She does not seem to realize she inherited it, but poor old Jean. In any case, so you know it all just does not tie up. I can understand shop girls reading these books and finding them sensational, but I cannot understand that intelligent people cannot work out for themselves that there must have been more to it than what the world has been presented with so far. My father was not asexual. My mother was asexual and I am.

While it is futile to speculate about the sexual proclivities of a person one has never met, in Joss's case I did gain the impression from evidence of a few close and intense relationships with young, but not openly gay, men during the course of his life that it was more than likely that he had been sexually active at some point, but that he had downplayed it because of the stigma that homosexuality carried during most of his adult life. By the time he reached his sixties, however, the state of his health would likely have dampened the libido of any man, irrespective of his preferences.

Joss often wondered why the Duke of Windsor and Wallis had decided to marry when Wallis had clearly been reluctant to do so and, he claimed, had not loved him. Joss felt that Wallis's money may have been a motive.

> Does anybody really think the King of England would have given up his throne to marry somebody who was not special? Of course, my father did have a great weakness, he was totally money hungry, which is a terrible weakness to have (thank God I did not inherit that) and so that attracted him. I should think that apart from my mother, and perhaps very few other women, there was nobody who was not prepared to be his mistress because he was extremely good looking and extremely glamorous and so he had it all, so she must have been incredibly special.

So, whatever hold Wallis may have exercised over the Duke of Windsor, it was never, according to Joss, a sexual one, despite the British Establishment's views to the contrary. In fact, so great were the suspicions about her sexuality that Dr Alan Campbell Don, the Archbishop of Canterbury's chaplain, wrote that he suspected that Edward VIII was 'sexually abnormal,' for why else would she be able to exercise such a strong hold over him?[9] One cannot help but wonder quite what the good chaplain might have had in mind!

However, it clearly exasperated Joss that so many people had got away with casting Wallis in such a negative light when the likelihood of these stories being true was, as he saw it, blatantly ridiculous:

> After all, the world has been presented with a little girl from semi-nowhere whose mother ran a boarding house in Baltimore. Have you been to Baltimore? Most dreary little town and, by fluke [she] lands herself in London

and sort of persuades the most eligible bachelor the world has ever known, not of his time, the world has ever known, to marry her because I mean do not forget he had it all. He had all the Bs, every single one. Well, he had brains; he had beauty. He was terribly good-looking, unbelievably good-looking, the best-looking man I ever saw. He had great benevolence and he had breeding. And he had bread. He still had money; he had what was left of the Windsor money. I really think she married him to get him away from the throne because he was too pro-Hitler and because he was terribly anti-Semitic. I think perhaps that she was also just coerced into it. I do not really know. I should not make statements like that because perhaps they were genuinely attracted. They were two terribly outstanding people. Who else could either of them really have married?

Wallis's links with the Roman aristocracy and royal houses of Europe on one side of the earth and with the world's most powerful financial dynasty on the other – the Morgans, Rothschilds and Drexels were all related – gave Wallis access to whatever she wanted in the world. It also made her very arrogant. In fact, as Joss expressed it, 'my mother was the most arrogant woman of all times; she really was.' Joss claimed that he shared this quality with her because, in 1996, when he was being systematically stripped of his belongings, he believed that it held him together at a time when he might otherwise have felt that his life was falling apart. 'I suppose I am armour plated by my arrogance,' he said, 'which I inherited from my mother, because I am still not cowed; I am still not broken; I can still tell everybody to go to hell.' Although Joss often described himself as arrogant, he did not really come across as such. Granted, he was elitist insofar as he never questioned the superiority of the aristocracy, and he had the kind of bearing that made people wonder who he was, which could only have come from a strong sense of his own worth. However, I never witnessed him belittle other people, which perhaps is arrogant because it suggests that he did not feel threatened, but he seemed too gentle to be called arrogant.

Portrait of Wallis Simpson, 1936, by Samuel Johnson Woolf.

Joss's tales of his parents

The following reminiscences, though bearing the distinct marks of well-worn society myths, perhaps better depict the arrogance of Wallis and the people with whom she associated, especially in the early years of her adult life. Wallis and Margot Asquith (1864–1945), Countess of Oxford and Asquith, and wife of Herbert Henry Asquith, prime minister of the United Kingdom from 1908 to 1916, were travelling on a ship on which Jean Harlow (1911–37), the famous American film actress and sex symbol of the 1930s, also happened to be a passenger. As Joss explained:

Jean Harlow insisted on addressing them all by their Christian names. She attached herself to them and called Margot Asquith 'Margotte.' At the end of the journey, Margot said how nice it was to know her, and that she appreciated the fact that she did not stand on ceremony. 'But, for future reference,' she said, 'please remember that the "t" in Margot is silent, like it is in Harlow,' which is a shitty thing to say.

Joss then recounted another story about Margot Asquith, this time getting the better of Winston Churchill.

He once said to her, 'If you were my wife madam, I would poison you.' I do not know what she did; she was probably laying down the law. Anyway, she apparently looked him straight in the eye and she said, 'Sir, if you were my husband, I would drink the poison.' My mother had a whole repertoire of these sorts of stories in an age when it was fashionable to be witty – they had the gift of repartee.

Though these amusing reminiscences depict a carefree world of fun and laughter, Joss felt that the members of Wallis's circle had begun to lose touch with reality.

They certainly made a mess of everything, so it was not a lovely world perhaps. I suppose everybody, the beautiful people, had lost contact with reality. It was because they were so privileged. That is why my father was so refreshing. Despite being part of that set at that time, he still had enough compassion to make a remark like 'something must be done.'

The Duke of Windsor made that remark while visiting a mining village in Wales during the Depression and, in his, the

Duke of Windsor's own words, he describes the incident in his personal memoirs as follows.

> An incident occurred that momentarily brought tension into the atmosphere surrounding the journey. I was quoted as having said, in the midst of some dismal scene of ruined industry, that 'something must be done to repair the ravages of the dreadful inertia that had gripped the region.' The statement was the minimum humanitarian response that I could have made to what I had seen. The Liberal Press naturally took approving note. But certain Government circles were not pleased. It was intimated that by saying that 'something must be done' I had suggested in effect that the Government had neglected to do all that it might have done.[10]

So, here we see Joss distancing himself from the arrogance of the extraordinarily rich and identifying with the more grounded response of the Duke of Windsor who had been brought up to fulfil a role in society, albeit a role he was to be denied. Nonetheless, he greatly admired many of Wallis's qualities. For a start,

> My mother was generous to a fault. I used to be – in fact, I still am with my time. I no longer have money to be generous with. Even without her background or money, she would have been outstanding because she did every-thing with great style. She was a personality in her own right and had a wonderful brain. She is a chatterer like me; we are not doers. She had unbelievable self-confidence and was very stimulating. For instance, she had not visited Buck House for about forty years and then she noticed that the arrangement of pictures in one of the upstairs passages had been altered and that there were two pictures missing. This was when the Duke of

Windsor died, and she went to stay there for the funeral. She had a photographic memory and knew her furniture. I remember going with her to the Grosvenor House antique dealers' fair and her objecting to one piece of furniture as not being what it pretended to be. All the experts were up in arms and eventually when they brought in enough of them, they had to concede that she was right. Anyway, why should I defend her? I mean she did not want defence. She was sufficient unto herself.

To Wallis, money was not something she earned, acquired, or inherited; it was something she *was*. It was an integral part of her being. As Joss saw it, 'that you have money makes you the person you are. It gives you the confidence you have and the tastes you have; it is all part of your makeup; you cannot separate yourself from it.' When it came to the question of taste, money was clearly no barrier for Wallis, though the Duke of Windsor did not necessarily feel the same way. Joss claimed to have recalled how when:

Elsie de Wolfe[11] painted the library at Boulevard Suchet, she charged a vast price for it and my father, who was very mean about money sometimes, objected. I do not know how he found out; perhaps the secretary told him. He said, 'it is ridiculous. She could not conceivably have used more than £50 worth of paint, and a painter I suppose costs ten pounds a day, so how did she get to that price?' Elsie de Wolf never charged hundreds, always thousands. Even in those days, it would never occur to Elsie to send less than a five-figure account.

Wallis apparently responded to the Duke of Windsor's objection by telling him a story about a famous milliner in London called Lilly Daché.[12] Joss said,

I do not know if the story was true, but my mother claimed it was and she did not tell lies, but she perhaps made it up to amuse my father. A Bolivian lady came in to Daché's establishment requesting a sensational hat because she had been invited to an important party, for this was the age of cocktail hats. Daché took a piece of tulle and a piece of cotton, draped the tulle, and secured it with three stitches, all with one piece of cotton. The Bolivian lady was ecstatic because it was exquisite. 'What is it going to cost?' she asked. Daché said, 'five hundred guineas', which was a lot of money for a hat in those days. So, the Bolivian lady said, 'Well the piece of tulle is not worth more than five bob and the cotton I do not even count.' So Daché carefully undid the stitches and handed the piece of tulle and the piece of cotton and said, 'You may have these for nothing.' So, you must pay for expertise, you see.

Joss seemed to infer that because Wallis was so much richer than her husband, she had better taste and was more discerning than he was and, to illustrate his point, he told me a rather sad story about how the Duke of Windsor had bought Wallis a second row of pearls for the large pearl necklace she often wore, if she was wearing jewellery, but had been 'ignorant enough to have bought cultured pearls for it.' Thereafter, 'she mainly wore it to please him.' Joss then went on to explain that:

> When we were sorting out the jewellery, I said to her (this was a strange bit of loyalty on her behalf), 'well you know I'll have those pearls.' And she said, 'no' and just chucked them with the junk. When they were sold, I realized why; it was because the one row was cultured. But she would not tell me that he had made that *faux pas*.

No doubt, for many of us who only recognize the distinction between real and fake pearls this would have been a natural mistake to make. Among those in the know, however, the real distinction is between natural and cultured pearls. The valuable pearls, those that occur spontaneously in the wild are extremely rare, for most pearls are farmed from pearl oysters. Wallis must have felt some affection for her husband to have protected him so sensitively from his unappreciated gift.

* * *

Joss had an unshakeable faith in the power of genes to determine not only how people looked but also how they thought, behaved, and felt. If he had ever, which I suspect he had not, engaged in a debate about the relative importance of nature versus nurture in determining how people turn out, he would have come down heavily on the side of nature. Consequently, he held Wallis responsible for his failure to appreciate music.

> It is strange really because I went through a phase when I was completely allergic to music. My mother hated music of any kind or description. It was physical pain to her. Now I am indifferent to it. Some tunes quite appeal to me, but I could not listen to a symphony concert. It just makes me very restless. I said it was because we were uncultured, but my mother said no, it is because we are further evolved. I asked why? This is a most supreme bit of arrogance: she said music is the sound of the sea and when creatures first ventured onto land during evolution, they would listen to the sea coming in, so we are that far removed. She hated all music. She really did. I suppose music either appeals to you or it does not. It is strange because I enjoy the beautiful things in life, yet I have always had this deaf ear for music. Well, I suppose

nobody else in this world knows my mother was allergic to music. My father always said you enjoy the visual arts because you and your mother cannot carry a tune in a bucket.

* * *

Joss also held his mother's genes responsible for his extreme laziness and that is a quality he had for which I can vouch. He would always get other people to do things for him. Other people had to cook his food, wash his clothes, arrange his medical or dental appointments, sort out his accommodation, deal with his finances, ship his furniture in and out of the country, even write personal letters on his behalf, and so the list went on and on. This refusal, even inability, on his part to take any responsibility whatsoever for his life and affairs is probably the single most important reason why his life ended up as it did. Wallis, he claimed, was also very lazy.

You see, what one must also remember is that I am my mother's child. My mother needed 52 servants to keep her going to the day of her death. She always said that if you want a job well done and one servant would do, you must employ two, because then you get jobs better done. She was just a non-doer. So how anybody imagined she had the energy to chase this unfortunate man and trap him into marriage, I mean she just did not have the energy to leave her bed. She never left her bed unless she had to. She did not entertain, but my father entertained a lot. She was like me. She wailed and it made no difference. If I had a thousand million a year, which I should have, I would still wail. I would still be bothered with housekeeping. Everybody claims that my mother was so madly efficient. She was not because I remember Patrick gave notice because she would take no interest in his work. He used to send the menus up to her in the morning and she said he must please not do so; she cannot be bothered; they clutter up her bed. And she really, honestly did not know what was going on in that house and neither did she want to know. She just lived in her bed. She never left her bed if she could conceivably help it. She did not entertain because she was far too lazy. She just had no energy. She had a pendulum that amused her. She read quite a lot. She telephoned. She was a great telephoner, but only to a few people. Maître Blum she rang every day.

Since the mid-1940s, the Windsors had used Maître Suzanne Blum as their lawyer. Although a dedicated member of the French Resistance and opponent of the Nazi occupation of France during the Second World War, a Jewess and a socialist, Maître Blum never let rumours of the Duke of Windsor's Nazi sympathies stand in the way of the firm friendship she developed with the couple, especially with Wallis, for the rest of their lives. During Wallis's declining years Maître Blum became her firmest friend, protector, and supporter, which was something her laziness needed. As Joss explained:

Maître Blum just stood between her and the world squarely and strongly and I suppose she [Wallis] knew a few odd people like Anna Henry[13] like I know Jean, but they are not really terribly important. She was very friendly – actually she was friendly with Diana Duff Cooper, but Diana Duff Cooper was really the Jean Tromp in her life – because she used to ring her every day and Diana was very stupid and used to dole out all her sympathy.

While Joss could perhaps convincingly enough identify with Wallis's idleness and lethargy, he was hardly able to match her style and elegance, but then her declining years were cushioned in a way that his were not. As he explained:

> She did look elegant, I must say. She had natural style and beautiful houses, but it is easy to have a beautiful house if you employ the best interior decorators in the world. It is easy to have a well-run house if you employ good staff, which you do not even have to do yourself because Maître Blum could employ them, and you can get them in Europe. Maître Blum was one of the most wonderful people I ever met. She must have an armchair in heaven for having put up with my mother all those years. Overall, she was quite happy if Maître Blum was around. Maître Blum would arrange for the odd person to come in and chat to her and listen to her endless complaints, but she was her best friend and depended on her completely and absolutely.

In the later years of Wallis's life:

> Maître Blum gave up her practice to look after my mother. Well, I suppose to look after the money basically. I liked Maître Blum. She was one of the most brilliant women I ever met and was terribly clever. She had the finest collection of Impressionists in the world, not the best private collection, just the best collection because she collected Impressionists long before anybody thought of collecting them. She was very well connected, but I do not really know who she was.

* * *

Joss had complicated feelings about Wallis, which was understandable given their history, or what Joss seemed to believe was their history, and would often express contradictory views about her. In other words, he both liked and disliked her, but seemed convinced that both she and the Duke of Windsor loved him and felt concerned about his welfare once they would no longer be around to protect his interests.

> I think my mother felt very guilty. That is why she kept on saying that one has no right to have children because you do not know what is going to happen to them. Little did she know what would happen to me! Perhaps she did realize that it was going to be difficult. She certainly wanted me kept in the style to which I am entitled, to which I was born and that is – I mean let me please be miserable – in enormous comfort. I mean that is what she wanted. Otherwise, I do not think she really bothered.

Joss felt that he was the one person who really did touch Wallis and that she had regretted having agreed to let him go so far from her, which was why, as he put it, she 'dragged me back.' However, having dragged this confused and resentful child back to Europe, nobody seemed clear about what should be done with him. Pushed from pillar to post between the Duke of Windsor, Wallis, and someone he alluded to as 'Nathan' Rothschild, Joss began a somewhat schizophrenic existence as both a moneyed member of the British upper classes and a South African national. If we accept his own account, he mingled intermittently with royalty, with the British aristocracy, with the Windsors' friends and with the various personalities of the day, yet nobody could or would openly acknowledge what he imagined to be his real identity.

4

The King and I
and Other Royals

ACCORDING TO JOSS, while still reeling from the shock of discovering that he was not the boy he thought he was, he was suddenly catapulted into a wholly alien world. It was not only far from the sunny, carefree existence he had only recently enjoyed as an affluent child on a South African farm, but it was also quite different from the world of privilege into which he believed he had been born before the devastations of the Second World War. The war had touched every family in Britain, and everyone had to come to terms with a new order. Now that it was over, things would never be the same again.

Following the Labour Party's landslide victory in the 1945 general election, Britain acquired a welfare state, a National Health Service, and free and compulsory education for all children. On the other hand, the heyday of the British Empire had passed and its slide towards extinction had started to accelerate, especially once India gained independence in 1948. The empire was shrinking, and British politicians were looking inwards to repair the damage at home.

The democratic impulses that the war and its aftermath had unleashed hit the wealthy upper classes especially badly, for they were now made to carry a much heavier tax burden. Also, they could no longer expect the sort of deferential subservience of the lower classes to which they had been accustomed. Many aristocrats were hard-pressed to find either the staff or the cash they needed to continue living in the style to which they had grown accustomed before the war. A number found that if they were to remain in their homes, their only option was to sell them to the National Trust, which had been set up in 1895 to preserve buildings or other places of historic interest. The National Trust would buy up and maintain stately homes, but in exchange their owners, who were allowed to continue living in them, would have to make their properties available to the public on certain days of the week or year. John (Ian) Russell (1917–2002), the 13th Duke of Bedford, inherited Woburn Abbey in 1953. The property, which had been in his family since 1547, was in a bad state of disrepair, but rather than sell it to the National Trust, he decided to commercialize it himself and embarked on a massive restoration project, which his successors have continued. The property now includes a safari park and various other attractions for visitors. Joss found the idea of allowing the public to wander arounds one's house and grounds quite appalling and an affront to one's self-respect. He considered it much 'more dignified to sit in one room and starve than to open your house to the public.' He then ranted on about having once gone to Woburn after the Duke of Bedford had 'turned it into a circus' and claimed that it was 'just like the rose show at Elgin.'[1] In an open display of snobbery, he then carried on about how 'every Tom, Dick and Harry' turns up 'and all they want are lavatories; I mean, every person who arrives asks you where they can find a toilet. They call them toilets! No, there is more to life than that.' Perhaps, his reduced circumstances made Joss want to cling to what little sense of class privilege he still could!

Although a few stoical efforts were made to maintain or recreate the elegance and glory of former times, other aristocrats felt sufficiently defeated to let their houses go completely and some were lost forever. Spencer House, a private mansion in St James's Place, London, built for the 1st Earl Spencer in 1756, was one exception. It was restored to its original glory, though only in 1986 when the Rothschild family company, RIT Capital Partners PLC, bought the leasehold. Joss described it as 'a beautiful Palladian house' and 'the last of the great town houses left.' He said he remembered the Duke of Windsor pointing out where places such as Lansdowne House and Devonshire House had once stood but were now replaced by what he called 'tacky 1930s blocks of flats.' He therefore concluded that Jacob Rothschild[2] did well to restore Spencer House because it is probably 'one of the last of the great houses left.'

So, all in all, it was into a somewhat diminished Britain that about a year after his supposed first meeting with Wallis Joss said that he had arrived in London with one of his tutors, a Mr Calitz, in tow. If indeed this is what happened, it must have been a confusing period for him because he never seemed to stay anywhere or with anyone for long enough to feel entirely at home. And, as he reminded me, precautions needed to be taken to ensure that his presence did not attract outside attention.

Joss arrives in London

Although the Windsors had supposedly been exiled from England since the abdication, it was to London that Joss was brought and it was there, he claimed, that he first became acquainted with the Duke of Windsor, who was staying at York House at the time.

The Duke of Windsor's association with York House had gone back a long time. It had been his family home during his childhood. Then, shortly before setting off for Canada in August 1919, the then Prince of Wales decided, with his father's permission, to move out of Buckingham Palace, which he had never liked.

He preferred the sprawling red-brick property in St James's Palace that 'King Henry VIII had built for his second queen, Anne Boleyn, on the site of a hospital for "leprous maidens".'[3] Frances Donaldson described York House as 'old and rambling' with largely Victorian furniture.

> Here and there were some very fine pieces, however, and with the aid of these … the Prince made it all that he wanted. A reasonably large room on the first floor became his sitting room, off which he had a bedroom and bathroom. … The Prince's cousin, Lord Louis Mountbatten, occupied some of the rooms at York House for a time, and when he got married the Prince's younger brother, Prince George, took these over.[4]

Then later, Donaldson continued:

> In the early part of his reign the King did not wish to disturb Queen Mary, who, before moving to Marlborough House,[5] had to pack or dispose of the accumulation of a lifetime. The offices of his secretariat therefore remained at Buckingham Palace, but he continued to occupy York House and to spend much of his time at Fort Belvedere.[6]

However, a lot of water had flowed under the bridge since those days, so it was surprising to learn that the Duke of Windsor still maintained a *pied-à-terre* there well over a decade after his abdication and exile. This seems to suggest that political considerations may have played a greater role than personal animosities in determining the royal family's public attitude towards the Duke and Duchess of Windsor. At that time, it may have been considered necessary to demonize the Windsors to stabilize what was then an insecure and fragile monarchy tainted with rather too much enemy blood. While the legends surrounding the abdication imply that there was a complete split between the two brothers and their families, Sultan Mahommed Shah, Aga Khan III, 48th Imam of the Shia Ismaili Muslims, witnessed a softer side to relations between the two brothers.

The Aga Khan (1877–1957), who comfortably straddled the divide between East and West, had mixed freely with royalty between the reigns of Queen Victoria and the present Queen Elizabeth II. He had been active in founding the All-India Muslim League in 1906 to safeguard the political rights of Muslims in India and was its first president. He was also president of the League of Nations, the precursor to the United Nations, between 1937 and 1938. Educated at Eton and Cambridge, he became an important player in the British Empire and on the world stage. On meeting the Duke and Duchess of Windsor in Berlin during the autumn of 1937, he wrote,

> I called on them and we had a long, extremely intimate, and extremely revealing conversation. I was deeply affected by the obvious and transparently sincere loyalty and devotion with which the Duke talked of his brother, speaking of him always as the King; the whole tenor of his remarks was that of fidelity from a devoted subject to his sovereign. Later that year when I was in London, I had an audience of King George VI. … Before I left, the King asked me, 'You saw my brother?' I then told him the substance of the Duke of Windsor's conversation with me, and I stressed the warmth and the obvious sincerity of the Duke's loyalty. The King was clearly most deeply moved by his elder brother's willing and complete acceptance of the new situation – so moved in fact that I myself was equally stirred.[7]

* * *

If for the moment, we accord Joss's account a status other than pure fiction, then, given their mutual affection, King George VI would probably not have denied his brother a place to stay in London in which to meet and get to know his son for the first time. After all, as we were led to believe in Chapter 1, King George VI had already met Joss during the royal tour of South Africa in 1947 and had even made him a kite. Anyway, Joss was in no doubt that the Duke of Windsor sometimes stayed at York House when he was presumed to be in exile in France and, as Joss put it, at that stage York House was one of the places into which he, Joss, 'just drifted' and stayed for a relatively short while, 'about six months, if that. It is where Prince Charles is now living, at St James's Palace.'[8]

Although a relatively brief stay, Joss claimed that this was where he first got to know the Duke of Windsor. He also said that his most overriding impression of him was of a deeply unhappy man. Joss was unlikely at that time to have known much about the Duke of Windsor's personal circumstances and would have been unaware of how bitterly he resented being exiled to France, or how difficult it was to have to watch his younger brother carry out the duties for which he had been groomed and was destined to fulfil. Also, from 1940 to 1945 the Duke of Windsor had served as governor of the Bahamas,[9] but the appointment had been a disaster. The Windsors, who should have kept a dignified constitutional distance from the islanders, got too close to disreputable businessmen and too embroiled in the islands' political clashes. Michael Pye went so far as to say that they had 'brushed too close to treason, riot and murder'[10] ever to recover their shattered hopes of royal respectability. Little did Joss know that the Windsors

> would leave the islands, in a bare five years, in utter disgrace. ... [Instead] of the lovely legend, there would be a bickering middle-aged couple, furiously beating back age and boredom in a shallow little world of rich people, trivial

times. Instead of royal dignity, there would be a Duke dis-qualified from any public position except that of mourner or celebrant at great family occasions. In Nassau, the main settlement of the Bahamas, their legend would die away, and their chances of public life would finally be wrecked.[11]

After his disastrous spell as governor of the Bahamas, the Duke of Windsor would more than likely have been feeling misrepresented, belittled, frustrated and sad. It was little wonder then that Joss, the perplexed, displaced child he was meeting for the first time since his infancy, and with whom he purportedly stayed at York House, would have picked up the unhappy atmosphere. Since children as a rule tend to assume that everything revolves around them, Joss probably felt responsible for the Duke of Windsor's misery, so:

Every day I used to drag Mr Calitz all the way from York House to Grosvenor Chapel[12] to pray for my father's happiness; he was such an unhappy man. I used to pray for him in Farm Street[13] too, because I thought if I prayed in two churches it would work twice as fast, but nothing ever happened.

Joss then, as was his wont, trivialized his comments by say-ing that, 'talking about praying,' neither Farm Street nor Grosvenor Chapel were any good at yielding results, but he could definitely guarantee the efficacy of the Dutch Reformed church in Bredasdorp.

According to Joss's version of events, about a year after the initial shock of having learnt that he was the son of the former King of the United Kingdom and British Dominions and Emperor of India, a member of the royal family and perhaps even, at a stretch, the rightful heir to the throne, Joss said he was discreetly introduced to certain members of a family that would never publicly acknowledge his existence.

Dutch Reformed Church, Bredasdorp.

Joss meets the royals

At this time King George VI was still alive and the present queen, then as Princess Elizabeth 'had just married and was out in Malta with Philip.' Joss was therefore not introduced to her, and he suspected that she might have been unaware of his existence, either then or even later when she succeeded to the throne. In any case, Joss certainly had no recollection of having met 'her before her coronation.'[14]

However, he does claim to have remembered that his purported paternal grandmother, Queen Mary, had expressed concern about the way in which the question of the succession was being handled. Joss argued that perhaps it was because members of the royal family were not of one mind about how to handle the matter that he continued to be hidden, for at that time, he asserted, not all of them disregarded the possibility of him succeeding King George VI. However, since as Joss himself put it, he was 'only 15 years old when King George VI died in 1952,' that would have weighed against any claim Queen Mary may have wished to exercise on his behalf.

* * *

According to Joss, who was light years away from being a constitutional expert, the Duke of Windsor had been mistaken in assuming that he had a legal entitlement to abdicate on behalf of his heirs, which, of course, is what he had done. Whether or not Joss's supposition was correct, however, is a matter for others to decide. The legality of the waiver was, of course, never put to the test because Joss's existence, if he was indeed who he claimed to be, was never made public. Had Joss presented himself at that time and made a claim to the throne, then no doubt numerous lawyers would have been brought into the fray, all hell would have broken out and the monarchy would have had to face yet another damaging crisis, which at that time it could ill afford to do. As it was, the public had always assumed that the Duke and Duchess of Windsor were childless, and it clearly was easier in every respect just to leave it that way.

However, Joss felt that things might have turned out differently had King George VI lived longer and he, Joss, been that much older. Joss claimed to suspect that he had been kept out of the picture because by the time the Duke of Windsor got married, 'I suppose he had discovered that he could not constitutionally abdicate on my behalf. Otherwise, it would not have mattered, would it?' In other words, if the abdicating king had been legally entitled to deny his son's claim to the throne, there would have been no good reason to conceal Joss's identity. Joss would merely have been the Windsors' son, and nobody would have thought too much about it one way or another. Even if some members of the royal family felt that his rights were being overlooked, Joss was certainly devoid of the disposition required to exercise power or influence. In fact, he insisted that the notion of being king had never appealed to him in the least. Also, as he pointed out, when George VI died the royal family could hardly suddenly produce him out of wraps as if they had merely forgotten to tell the world that there had been an heir in waiting when Edward VIII gave up his throne.

Queen Mary, however, had especially strong feelings about the monarchy and found it impossible to comprehend that her son should for one moment consider putting his personal emotional needs and feelings before his duty to his country. Greg King claimed that, for Queen Mary,

> love for the throne came first; her feelings for her children, second. The majority of her life had been spent sacrificing personal desire for the sake of public duty. Her world was one of dignity and tradition; love was a personal emotion, completely separate from a royal marriage. She had been raised in a world in which one married for duty first; love, if it also existed, was to be appreciated, but the idea of disregarding one's sacred obligations for the sake of a frail human emotion was anathema to the elderly Queen. She could not even bring herself to consider such a union as her son now proposed; it was simply beyond her comprehension.[15]

According to Joss, she had wanted to stop the second coronation because 'she believed that the monarch had a divine right,' which 'should not go to somebody who was not legitimately in line.'

Queen Mary survived George VI by only 13 months[16] and, or so Joss claimed, had during that period expressed a wish to see him, but, as he explained, the meeting 'just did not happen' before she died. If she were meddling, Joss contended, her death 'was very convenient. I do not know how else to put it!' Although, by these remarks, Joss seems to be implying that some members of the royal family may have wished to see his purported grandmother dead because of her unwillingness to overlook his claim to the throne, it would be irresponsible to suggest that her death may have been unnatural. After all, she was 85 years old when she died, which by most counts is an advanced age. Joss claimed to have been very fond of her. 'I got on very well with her actually. She was a woman of great taste. The Earl of Athlone, the old Cape governor, was her brother.[17] I remember when she died. I was at York House and my father[18] came and stayed with me there.'

Unfortunately, Queen Mary's death on 24 March 1953 did nothing to ease the antipathy that some members of the royal family still showed, at least in public, towards their banished king. Although he had sailed all the way from New York to attend his mother's funeral, it was made perfectly clear to him that he was not expected to attend the family dinner at Windsor afterwards. The Duke and Duchess of Windsor were also deliberately excluded from the invitation list for Queen Elizabeth II's coronation only a couple of months later, on 2 June 1953. Might Joss's shadowy presence have played some small part in prolonging the show of family tension at this time?

* * *

86

On a lighter note, Joss recalled a memorable occasion when he was having tea with Queen Victoria's granddaughter Marie Louise[19] when Queen Mary paid them an unexpected and not altogether appreciated visit.

> We were having tea at Marie Louise, who at that stage was living in that shop at Shepherd Market where she kept moving the staircase from the left to the right side of the room. Arthur Brotherfield, who was an architect friend of hers, put the staircase on the left side of the room, which was, I suppose the best place to put it. Then she wanted it on the right side of the room because she thought it would be better. Then, when he moved it to the right side of the room, she said she wanted it moved back to the left side and then he said he could not do it. She was disenchanted with him and indignant that he was so unhelpful. But I think the building would have fallen down if he had moved it yet another time.

Joss got diverted at that point by the problematic placing of Marie Louise's staircase, but he did eventually return to his story. He continued:

> I cannot remember who took me there. Somebody must have because I was too young to have gone on my own. Perhaps I did. Perhaps Edward Winfield[20] took me, I do not know. We were sitting drinking tea when suddenly a car stopped outside, and one could look out through the window and see the car and who it was. So, Marie Louise handed me this nice melon-shaped teapot and said, 'put it under the sofa!' which I did. I put it under the skirt of the sofa. Then Queen Mary walked in and looked around the tea table and did not see a teapot, and she said, 'Where is the teapot?' – not hello or anything. Marie Louise said, 'It is in the kitchen being refilled,'

which is nonsense because one makes tea at the tea table, but apart from that nobody believed her. Then she looked straight at me and said, 'Joss, where is the teapot?' And I just could not tell her a lie, not because I could not tell a lie, I was quite capable of telling a lie, I told many lies, but at that stage I was in complete awe of her. She was the sort of person I could not easily deceive. And so, I just produced the teapot, and was not popular with Marie Louise. She gave the teapot to the lady-in-waiting, and I think stayed a little while. She chatted to us a while and then left and Marie Louise was then truly angry.

Queen Mary had taken it upon herself to reassemble all the various bits and pieces of crockery and tableware to which Queen Victoria had carelessly allowed her numerous children to help themselves. In Joss's opinion, this had been allowed to happen because 'Queen Victoria did not really value things as she should have.' As he put it, 'I am being polite now, but she just did not know.' She had allowed her children to take whatever they needed without any regard for whether they were breaking up sets. Now, Queen Mary had taken it upon herself to restore these original collections to their former state. Apparently, it was a quest in which she succeeded because she did eventually manage to reassemble most of the sets. However, according to Joss, 'she really was quite ruthless. She went around taking things because, quite rightly, nobody wanted to give up their teapots, candelabra, and candlesticks, so they used to hide them from her.'

Queen Mary clearly had a strong sense of wanting things to be where they were originally intended to be, and if we have any inclination to believe Joss, this included her wanting to see him as the rightful heir to the throne. Also, according to Joss, she was not the only member of the royal family to object to the way most of them were sidelining him.

Dicky Mountbatten[21] was very outspoken about how badly I was being treated. He was very much on my side, but I did not like him because he behaved so badly to Edwina.[22] He was a homosexual and he married Edwina, who was an heiress, because he had no money. All the things he did to her he objected to everybody doing to me and then, of course, he was blown up.[23]

At this point in his narrative, Joss entered a rather conspiratorial frame of mind and reverted to a tendency he sometimes displayed of placing himself centre stage when he was unlikely to have been anything of the sort. Joss claimed that at the time Mountbatten was killed he was threatening to go public about him and that 'there is no doubt that people would have believed him.' He even went on to say that his granddaughter India[24] thought 'he was blown up because he tried to defend me,' but then tried to soften it by saying that 'what India thinks is not a fact, but just an opinion.' Although I am in no position to speculate on the motives of any would-be assassin, almost certainly the IRA was simply looking for a high-profile victim and Lord Mountbatten's murder was unlikely to have had anything to do with Joss.

What is more interesting, however, is what it says about Joss, about his ever-present sense of the kind of consequences that might ensue should someone reveal his identity. One is left to wonder whether this display of egotism stemmed from an unrequited yearning to be included, acknowledged, and valued, or from a genuine fear of what might transpire if he were to step out of line. However, irrespective of whether Mountbatten was prepared to defend Joss's interests, Joss disliked him intensely and could not imagine that anyone might like him. 'Well, to quote my father, "he had an unfortunate manner." I never came across anybody who knew my father who did not like him, and I never came across anybody who knew Dicky Mountbatten who liked him.' He felt quite differently about Edwina, whom he described as 'lovely, terribly, terribly attractive and a very agreeable woman who died mysteriously in India a long time ago.'[25]

Joss also claimed to have known some of the Mountbatten children and grandchildren. Among those he mentioned were the present Countess Mountbatten of Burma, Patricia (Pat) Knatchbull, who he claimed not to know very well. He described Pamela Hicks as nice but not 'nearly as nice as her mother,' but seemed to have adored Pamela's daughter India, who 'has all that Hicks charm.' He also claimed to have known her sister Edwina,[26] but could not remember the name of the third one. He said he rather liked David Hicks. Well, as he put it, the Mountbattens 'were always there.'

In contrast to his negative opinion of Louis Mountbatten and perhaps unexpectedly given the known and well-documented animosity that was supposed to have existed between the Windsors and the Yorks, Joss claimed to have rather liked the Queen Mother and to have enjoyed a relaxed and pleasant relationship with her, albeit one tinged with a little disdain. He said that he went to Buckingham Palace quite often, but used to see the Queen Mother, whom he rather disdainfully referred to as Cookie, at Clarence House on a more regular basis. She seemed to remind him of Jean Tromp. He said that they were rather alike and that she irritated him just as much in that they were both always so eager to please him. This strikes me as odd given that the Queen Mother was a member of the royal family who had been particularly hostile to the Windsors' marriage. Perhaps she was feeling a little guilty about harbouring such uncharitable feelings!

The Queen Mother and Jean, being cousins of the same generation and both descended from the Strathmore family, knew each other well. Jean had spent a good part of her life in South Africa, predominantly at Westminster (east of Ladybrand, which is close to the western border of Lesotho), in Durban and Cape Town. During her marriage to Baron

Tromp she had lived in Zimbabwe (then called Rhodesia). However, as children she and the Queen Mother had spent holidays together at Glamis Castle[27] in Scotland. Jean recounted that, at Glamis, they would overhear the servants gossiping about the monster in the castle, to which nobody but the Duke of Westminster had access. Jean held that this 'monster' was none other than 'poor Eddy,' the elder brother of George V to whom Queen Mary had initially been engaged and who had ostensibly died of pneumonia in 1892. Jean explained that rumour had it, 'and you know how servants talk,' that poor Eddy, the Duke of Clarence, had had a homosexual relationship with a doctor whom some people suspected of having been the notorious Jack the Ripper.[28] According to Jean, on hearing of poor Eddy's death and funeral (presumably the coffin was empty), the doctor under suspicion committed suicide and Eddy, Jean held, was kept hidden at Glamis Castle for the rest of his life.

More royal gossip

Another of Jean's stories, and this she said she had always just known, was that her uncle, Pip Playfair,[29] who had been the head of the Royal Air Force during the war, had had a hand in 'doctoring' the aeroplane in which George, the Duke of Kent (1902–42), had been so tragically killed on 25 August 1942. The Sunderland flying boat, with 11 other people on board, crashed while *en route* from Invergordon in Scotland to Iceland. As Higham[30] pointed out, questions were asked about the crash at the time. For example, the pilot, Wing Commander Moseley, was known to be an excellent navigator and the best pilot in the squadron he commanded. The weather conditions were good. He had flown that route on numerous other occasions and his compasses were in perfect working order, yet he inexplicably crashed into a hill. Everyone bar one member of the party was killed instantly, and the cause of the accident remains a mystery.

Who might have wanted the Duke of Kent out of the way and why? Though hardly qualified to speculate on the first half of the question, the Duke of Kent had on more than one occasion been a source of acute embarrassment to his family and to the British Establishment.

For a start, there were political reasons why the Duke of Kent may have presented difficulties to the government of the day. For example, in January 1935, when Hitler was well into his ascendancy in Germany, Baron Wilhelm de Ropp, whose loyalties remain controversial, came from Berlin to London to meet the Prince of Wales and the Duke of Kent with a view to persuading them of the virtues of Rosenberg, Hess and other Nazi leaders. This was the 'double agent and emissary of the Nazi theorist Alfred Rosenberg who, during a visit to London in 1933, had placed a swastika wreath on the cenotaph to the war dead.'[31] After the meeting, Sir Robert Bruce Lockhart wrote in his diary that the Duke of Kent was 'strong in the German camp.'[32]

Then, in August 1941, the Duke of Kent's scheduled official visit to the United States created a further source of anxiety, particularly given that it would correspond with the presence in the country of his favourite brother, the Duke of Windsor. At the time, such was the popularity that the two brothers enjoyed among the public that the British government feared that they might succeed in swinging 'their weight behind the various senators and congressmen who wanted to keep America out of the war.'[33] His arrival in the United States confirmed his popularity. President Roosevelt took a great liking to the young duke and when Prince Michael of Kent was born on 4 July 1942, the president of the United States became one of his godfathers.

Were his close personal ties with the highest office holders in the United States government and with the German Reich creating difficulties for the wartime Cabinet? Given that the duke was adamant about wanting to serve in the war, this might have been a consideration. As John Wheeler-Bennett explained, although at the outbreak of war the Duke of Kent was governor-general designate of Australia, he immediately asked to be allowed to play a more active role in the war effort. Finding employment for the king's brother during the war, however, presented certain difficulties, not least of which was that his status automatically gave him the rank of air marshal. He himself suggested a way out of the conundrum by accepting the rank of air commodore and for a while he performed the normal duties associated with his new position. In time, however, his horizons broadened and to great effect he extended his interests to looking after 'the welfare and comfort of the Royal Air Force at home and abroad.'[34] It was during this phase of his career that he met his death.

The Duke of Kent's personal life, however, had also brought pain and concern to his family. In his *Diaries*, Sir Robert Bruce Lockhart mentions rumours circulating around London of Prince George's affair with a young boy in Paris in which blackmail was involved.

> According to several sources, Prince George gave the boy magnificent, personally inscribed, Tiffany and Cartier cigarette boxes and lighters. The Prince of Wales had to make a disagreeable journey to France to pay money to retrieve these damaging items, but the boy sold the Prince of Wales copies, retaining the originals.[35]

There were also rumours in circulation that he had had affairs with a black actress, with Noel Coward[36] and with a Latino youth. He was known to have had a drugs problem, especially with morphine and cocaine. It was therefore no doubt a great relief to everybody concerned when he eventually decided to marry the beautiful and highly suitable Princess Marina of Greece.[37] However, did the problems surrounding his personal life stop there?

For a start, there is evidence of quite a lot of family tension surrounding the Duke of Kent and Princess Marina's continued and close relationship with the Duke and Duchess of Windsor. Although George was eight years younger than his eldest brother, the two became close when they stayed together at Sandringham[38] in the winter of 1911. From then onwards, the two brothers spent a lot of time in each other's company. While the most powerful members of the royal family took a hard line over the abdication and exile of the Duke and Duchess of Windsor, the Kents and Windsors never lost their soft spots for one another. Wallis too had developed a particularly close relationship with the Duke of Kent in her own right in 1934, when she was still married to Ernest Simpson, and they all spent time together at Fort Belvedere, colloquially referred to as the Fort. He was an artistic, introspective young man and Wallis grew very fond of him. However, other members of the royal family felt that it was important to keep the Windsors ostracized and there were times when pressures were brought to bear on the Kents not to fraternize too freely with the disgraced former king and his unacceptable wife. The family clearly wanted to distance itself from the Windsors' Nazi sympathies. Did it wish to distance itself also from those of the Duke of Kent?

Joss had his own views about the Duke of Windsor's relationship with his younger brother, or more pertinently his wife. In his early days, the Prince of Wales was known to have had relationships with several young women. Thelma Furness, the twin sister of Gloria Vanderbilt,[39] is widely believed to have had a sexual relationship with the Prince of Wales. In fact, it was through her that the Prince of Wales initially met Wallis. Contrary to popular myth, however, Joss claimed that this was untrue. He said, 'I asked my father once whether he had an affair with Thelma and he said "no".' Of course, in the light of Thelma Furness's later description of the Prince of Wales as a 'little man' and the consensus that their sex life had been unsatisfactory, the Duke of Windsor may well have preferred to deny that he had ever had a sexual relationship with her. However, Joss went on to say that 'as he admitted to having an affair with Marina, I do not see why he should have denied having an affair with Thelma.'

Joss then said that he thought, and had always thought, that Michael[40] was the Duke of Windsor's son and I must say that, from their photographs, they seem to bear a rather close resemblance. Joss claimed that Wallis also thought so, which was why she had always taken a close interest in him. This was rather a scandalous admission to have made given that Marina was his sister-in-law, but with George homosexual, Wallis asexual and he and Marina heterosexual, they might well have formed a very amicable foursome. Joss said that he and Michael's sister Alexandra were practically twins, for she was born on 25 December 1936 only nine days after he was, and he remembered the two families being close.

* * *

Joss seemed much less certain of his ground on the widespread allegations in circulation during the build-up to the Second World War that several members of the royal family had been Nazi sympathizers. He said that it was a pity that his tutor Edward Winfield was no longer alive because he had been in Intelligence during the war and would have known which members of the British aristocracy had supported Hitler. However, he poo-pooed any suggestion that 'senior members of the British aristocracy would have been pro-Hitler' because, as he put it, 'there would have been a class clash.' He certainly dismissed any idea of Queen Mary sending signals from Marlborough House on the grounds that she was too arrogant to send signals to anyone. Also, to counter the accusation, he reminded us that 'Hitler deposed Wee Willie[41] and Wee Willie was the first cousin of Edward VII' and that 'the Dowager

Empress of Germany[42] was Queen Victoria's daughter.' However, as Joss reminded us, he was not around at the time, so did not have much of an opinion on the subject.

Though there is no doubt ample evidence that the Duke of Windsor and many of the people with whom he associated closely were pro-Nazi and anti-Semitic during the build-up to the Second World War, Joss was not alone in pointing out some inconsistencies in the accusation. Higham noted similar contradictory behaviour. As he put it when

> King Edward was lending his personal support to a government that was totally committed to Hitler … he seemed to find nothing untoward in the fact that he and Wallis visited one of the most prominent figures in the Jewish financial community, Baron Eugene Rothschild, and the baron's American wife, Kitty, at their Schloss Enzesfeld residence. … To increase the irony, [they also] … visited Heinrich Neumann (the Jewish professor [and physician] who had refused to attend Hitler) for the king's ear trouble.[43]

Nonetheless, as I mentioned earlier and as we see in the next chapter, Wallis's family had close connections with the Rothschilds and, if Joss's claims are to be believed, she entrusted his care to a member of that family.

Joss certainly knew a lot about the Mitford family, all of whom had been great friends of the Duke of Windsor, and some of its members were openly pro-Hitler. The most notorious of these was Diana,[44] whose second husband, Sir Oswald Mosley, whom Joss described as 'mad,' became the leader of the British Union of Fascists. In fact, their wedding in 1936 took place at the home of Joseph Goebbels with Adolf Hitler as guest of honour. Diana's first marriage, which ended in divorce, had been to Bryan Walter Guinness, with whom they had two sons, Jonathan, and Desmond. The latter was the father of Patrick Guinness, whom we meet later in the book when he tried persistently to set up a trust to support Joss in his hour of need. Joss particularly liked Patrick's mother Mariga (1932–89), an architectural conservationist and co-founder of the Irish Georgian Society, who he said was 'a lovely person' and 'a great friend.' He could not understand why she married Desmond because he treated her so badly, but 'then their son Patrick,' he averred, 'has got all the Mitford charm, all the Guinness charm, and all the Irish charm.'

Joss spoke of knowing the author Nancy Mitford (1904–73) especially well and said that it was she who told him that her younger sister Unity (1914–48), who was an openly anti-semitic fascist, had committed suicide in 1948, though the family did not officially acknowledge it as such at the time. The other members of the family Joss mentioned were 'Mrs Pamela Jackson who lives in Gloucestershire and is the least published of all the sisters, and Debo who is the Duchess of Devonshire and the one I know least well.' Joss called them 'a decidedly odd family' and said that their 'blue Mitford eyes' made them look 'insane.'

* * *

In any case, by the mid-1950s, the old wounds, scandals and schisms that had so very nearly torn the royal family apart shortly before the Second World War were now firmly in the past. King George VI and his charming wife had, so to speak, 'pulled it off' and their daughter Elizabeth had already embarked on her long and honourable reign. The royal family was widely considered to be solid, firm, relevant and respect-able. They were playing their parts impeccably and there was virtually no anti-royalist dissent. Though the Queen Mother was, according to Joss, kind to him and concerned about his welfare, he in turn still felt the stab of his purported father's disappointment. Joss was sorry that he had been denied, or had denied himself, the opportunity he craved to fulfil his potential. Joss had no doubts in his mind about which of the two brothers was the better equipped for kingship, which had the better brain. He clearly felt that George VI and his wife were wanting and had been pushed into a situation they were not 'bright enough to handle.'

Though the people of Britain and the Commonwealth seemed to agree that George VI and his wife Queen Elizabeth were doing an exceptionally good job, Joss felt that the Windsors would have brought considerably more style to the role and that the Queen Mother and George VI had stripped the office of any 'dignity' that it might otherwise have had. In fact, Joss got quite heated over the issue. 'Just look at how Cookie used to do her hair in little Shirley Temple[45] curls,' he railed, and 'look at those unbecoming clothes she wears!' He said that if you have a meal with them, you realize that 'that Scottish lot just do not know how to set a table!' In his usual way, Joss ascribed these shortfalls, as he did everything, to heredity. He then rather mockingly said that Jean Tromp and 'Cookie' were 'related to the Menzies' family, a fairly common surname in South Africa, but that they pronounced it 'Mainyees.' He then said that 'it must take sheer genius to create that sort of slummy feel.' He also said that it must have irritated the Duke of Windsor no end to see the job so badly done. However, given the 'slummy' conditions in which Joss and Jean had descended at the time, I found these remarks a little inappropriate. Joss then tried to rescue himself a little by saying that he did not want to sound as if he were making a plea for recognition because, he insisted, 'I really do not want any recognition.'

Although Joss insisted that he had never craved recognition for himself, or at least he persuaded himself that it had never been anything he had ever wanted, he was nonetheless con- vinced that the Duke of Windsor would have made a better king than King George VI.

My father, I think, was an outstanding man. He was one of those rare things that England seems to spew up. They spew up the right man at the right time and they always have. History has always done that. It produced the greatest pop star of all time because he was quite unlike the rest of his family who were singularly dreary and very ordinary.

In fact, so convinced was Joss of the Duke of Windsor's exceptional ability and suitability to reign that he even went so far as to say that he would have been able to prevent the outbreak of the Second World War, would have created the welfare state much earlier than it was, not allowed 'the trade unions to bankrupt England,' and that 'the whole of Africa would have been saved.'⁴⁶ These are clearly ridiculous assertions that suggest that Joss was incapable of employing any critical distance on the subject. Joss described the Duke of Windsor as 'a fashion setter' and assumed that the rest of the world would have followed his example because 'it was the fashionable thing to do.' He was clearly impressed by the Duke of Windsor's 'unbelievable presence' and by how people used to give 'up their tables at Maxims'⁴⁷ for him without even being asked to do so. Joss then contrasts this glittering star with his younger, less gifted brother whom he branded as 'dim' and dismissed as 'sad because he tried so hard.'

Although not wishing to deny that the Duke of Windsor may well have been highly intelligent and had a strong presence, it seems a bit far-fetched to assume that he could have prevented the outbreak of the Second World War, let alone the dissolution of empire and the rise of the trade union movement. It is even further fetched to think that he might have introduced the welfare state before the war. All he really succeeded in doing was to disqualify himself from being king. Joss clearly idolized him and felt sympathy for his frustration, even bitterness, at being denied the job he had been born and groomed to perform. Joss felt that he had been treated shabbily because he had been 'brought up to do his job' rather than as a member of the idle rich. He had taken his role seriously and, according to Joss, 'played left-handed golf because his right hand was crippled from greeting people.' Joss said that it irritated him to see it done so badly and regarded 'Bertie[48] and Cookie' as 'so *ordinary*.' As Joss put it:

> It is all right 'to walk with kings and yet retain the common touch'[49] but nobody wants a king with a common touch. And that is what they achieved in the end. I remember my father, with his very British sense of humour, once looked at Cookie and said all she needed was two candles and she would be the only mobile Christmas tree in the world.

How Joss acquired his snobbery

The Duke of Windsor may well have been brought up to serve his country rather than to indulge his fancies, yet barring his unfortunate spell as governor of the Bahamas, he had effectively been forcibly retired since his early forties. He was therefore left with little option but to join Wallis's world of the idle rich or, as Joss called them, the 'non-doers.' He had little choice but to cavort with the other wealthy, beautiful and stylish people who crossed their paths and much of their snobbishness rubbed off on Joss. Joss, for his part, had never even considered doing any work of any kind, voluntary or otherwise, not even when he was destitute. He had spent a good part of his life in South Africa where deprivation is acute, yet, though he was a kind person, the idea of doing anything to help alleviate the poverty around him never crossed his mind. With a few notable exceptions, such as Edwina Mountbatten in her later years, the people in Joss's world tended to live mostly for their own pleasure and cared little about what the poor people surrounding them either thought or had to endure.

For example, when Joss and his friend Rab Cecil, about whom there is more later, acquired a house in what was then considered an unfashionable part of Chelsea, he felt answerable to no one. As far as he was concerned, 'it was a lovely house, one of those perfect Georgian houses that you usually only find in Islington or somewhere out of the way; it was even more beautiful than Argyle House,[50] so we bought it.' As far as Joss was concerned, that he had bought a house in a part of London that others considered 'slummy,' immediately raised the status of the area. We 'set the fashion,' he said, 'we do not follow it.' Apparently, Chelsea had not been a success though because 'the servants would not live there – they did not know where to shop,' so they abandoned it. These were people who made their own rules and formed their own opinions about themselves and everyone else. They were superior, class conscious and elitist. Joss claimed that the Duke of Windsor loathed members of the middle class, irrespective of whether they were 'middle-middle class, lower-middle class, or upper-middle class,' though he did not seem to object to the working classes, perhaps because they granted him more deference. Joss, however, said that Wallis 'always maintained that when you associated with people who did not come from your background, you agreed with them on everything except the things that mattered, which I think is true really.' Joss often said, though usually somewhat self-mockingly, that he had absorbed much of the snobbery and sense of superiority of his parents and their associates. He referred to himself as a self-professed snob and claimed to be among 'the last of the great snobs. Not only me but also old Jean, and the few others of us who still exist.'

Whether through snobbery, slothfulness or self-abnegation, Joss certainly felt no need to keep up appearances with respect to his dress. This had once, he said, occasioned comment from the Duke of Windsor's only sister Princess Mary (1897–1965), the Princess Royal, who had married Henry,

Viscount Lascelles (1882–1947), the sixth Earl of Harewood, in February 1922 and who Joss described as 'a sweet woman who had such a dreadful life.' Anyway, she had apparently once asked her brother, though not unkindly, 'Why is Joss always so poorly dressed, David?' (which is what the family called the Duke of Windsor) and he had replied, 'Well you see Mary, Joss can afford to dress badly.'

If indeed Joss was already in those days dressing as badly as he did in later life, Mary clearly had a point. In fact, during the years I knew him Joss dressed so scruffily that one could not help but assume that he was trying to make some sort of statement. To get back to Princess Mary, however, Joss failed to explain why he thought she had 'such a dreadful life,' unless of course she had been unhappy in her marriage, but I have found no hard evidence of that. She and her husband, who was about fifteen years her senior, shared a love of horses and country life, though a rumour had been circulating at the time of their engagement that his proposal to her had been linked to his having lost a bet. In any case, apart from some tension in March 1936, when the Earl of Harewood made a controversial speech to the British Legion, which the new king stingingly denounced by saying, 'How can I make my contributions to foreign policy if my own relatives make irresponsible statements?'[51] Mary's relationship with her disgraced brother and his wife had been one of steadfast loyalty and kindness.

Mary was brave enough to take a stand against other members of the royal family if she felt they were being unjustifiably cruel to her eldest brother and his wife. Although Elizabeth Bowes-Lyon (later the Queen Mother) had been a bridesmaid at her wedding and she a godmother at Princess Elizabeth's christening in the private chapel at Buckingham Palace on 29 May 1926, she refused to attend her goddaughter's wedding to Prince Philip in November 1947 because neither of the Windsors had been invited. As Greg King explains:

Certain members of the Royal Family … felt that this ostracism was the last straw. In protest at the lack of an invitation for her brother and sister-in-law, Mary, the Princess Royal, deliberately stayed away from the ceremony. To the public it was simply announced that she was ill; but privately her protest was made quite clear, although it failed to have any effect on Buckingham Palace's continued war against the Windsors.[52]

Princess Mary had been with her brother when he broke the news to his mother Queen Mary of his intention to marry Wallis. Mary also frequently visited the Duke and Duchess of Windsor whenever they happened to be in New York. In fact, she accompanied the Duke of Windsor on the ship from New York to London when their mother Queen Mary was dying.

When Princess Mary suddenly died of a coronary thrombosis on 28 March 1965 at the age of 65 while she was taking a walk through the grounds of Harewood House, her home in Yorkshire, the Windsors were in London but were too ill to attend her funeral in Leeds. This distressed the duke, but he and Wallis, along with 2500 invited mourners, did go to her memorial service at Westminster Abbey on 1 April. Greg King describes

David [the Duke of Windsor], looking frail and his eyes guarded by dark glasses, was helped by Wallis, clad in a black coat and hat, down the aisle of the transept; seeing them, the congregation rose spontaneously in silent respect. It was the first time the Windsors had ever appeared together at an official function in England.[53]

However, it took more than this to heal the family rift. Although, as they were nearing the ends of their lives, Elizabeth II granted the Duke of Windsor and Wallis permission to have their funeral services at St George's Chapel at

Windsor and burial afterwards at Frogmore,[54] the gesture was not wholly generous. In fact, when the Duke of Windsor died in 1972, his beloved sister's eldest son George, Lord Lascelles (born 1923), the first grandchild of King George V and Queen Mary, fourth in line of succession and a prisoner-of-war in Germany in 1944, was not allowed to attend his uncle's funeral because he too had suffered the disgrace of a divorce. His younger brother, Gerald Lascelles, did however attend.

The Duke of Windsor dies

Cruel as it may have been to deny a nephew the right to attend his uncle's funeral, Joss called his own exclusion from the Duke of Windsor's funeral plain 'inhuman,' though he did assert that he had been allowed to go to Buckingham Palace at the time.

* * *

Although Joss said he had informal access to the various members of the royal family, as well as to their friends, associates, attitudes, and values, many of which he shared, he was nonetheless kept firmly on the outside. He claimed to know for certain that he was the son of the Duke and Duchess of Windsor, and that this had imbued him with a sense of entitlement, even superiority, but that the royal family's refusal to acknowledge his existence formally meant that he could never participate fully in their lives.

Joss affirmed that since he did 'not exist officially,' he had never attended social functions or enjoyed a 'social life' with the people who were otherwise available to him. He seemed to think that attending a formal dinner party, for instance, would have 'caused terrific embarrassment' because he 'would have had to have gone into the dining room after the last sort of knight, not even nobility. A knight would take precedence over me!' The things that some people consider important! He did, however, concede that he had some 'sort of obscure baronetcy from old man de Waal,' which suggests that he was assuming his South African 'de Wahl' identity.

If Joss's claims were false, the question that continues to niggle is who else could he have been? If he was the natural son of his so-called foster parents and had no genetic relationship with the royal family or with the super, super-rich, how did he gain access to them, get to know so much about them and to acquire so many of their valuables and such a lot of money? We know that royals like to mingle with the celebrities of the day and vice versa, but by no stretch of the imagination could Joss have ever been able to pass himself off as a celebrity. There was nothing glamorous about him at all. He had no claim to fame other than that he thought he was born of parents willing to deny his existence. Did they regret his presence in this world? Joss was not entirely sure about that, but thought not, though he did say that he thought that they (the Windsors) felt 'guilty and genuinely concerned' about his welfare once they would no longer be around to support him.

Despite having expended so much of his childhood energy praying for the Duke of Windsor's happiness, Joss was left with a sense of his disappointment with life. He was less resigned to his fate than Wallis had been. She was too lazy, too rich, and too arrogant to care much about anything, but the Duke of Windsor, who Joss claimed busily 'used to go around opening up houses so that they would feel lived in,' felt underused, stripped of a proper role in life, and exiled from his country and people. According to Joss, he 'did not like France. He was essentially an Englishman and should have lived in England.' Of course, as Joss pointed out, 'the London he knew,' the London in which he had been happy, no longer existed.

Once again, we find Joss, while often quite critical of Wallis, totally in awe of the Duke of Windsor, for whom he seemed to have nothing but praise. 'I think everybody loved him. I never came across anybody who did not love him who came within touching distance of him. It was not difficult to love him.' Joss waxed on about how 'he did not come over as being so nice – he really *was* so nice. It was not an act.' He had 'no guile,' he went on, was never dishonest and 'was enormously compassionate.' This was warm praise indeed, but surely there were things that annoyed and irritated him. Well, Joss conceded, 'he hated Victoriana and corny literature,' though not in an 'ugly way;' his pet hate was Kipling.

* * *

As the reader might recall, earlier in this chapter I spoke of how touched Aga Khan III had been by the fond sentiments that the Duke of Windsor and King George VI expressed for one another. Although, as head of the Ismaili Muslims and directly descended from Shah Fath Ali Shah of the Persian Qajar dynasty, the Aga Khan was firmly entrenched in the Eastern world, he was also very much part of the West. His son Prince Aly Khan moved right to the centre of the British aristocracy when he married Joan Yarde-Buller, daughter of the 3rd Baron Churston of Churston Ferrers and Lupton in 1936. Joan had recently been divorced from her first husband Loel Guinness, with whom she had a son, Patrick Benjamin Guinness, who was born in 1931. In her marriage with Aly Khan, she had two children, Sultan Karim Khan IV, the present Aga Khan, born in 1936, and Amyn Mohammed Khan, who was born in 1937. She and Aly Khan divorced in 1949 and she married, John Seymour Berry, 2nd Viscount Camrose, in March 1986. A year before her death aged 89 in 1997, Joss recalled how Joan, whom he described as 'older than God,' had lived in a lovely house in Berkeley Square, in which her youngest son Amyn started a small business, which Joss said, 'lost a great deal of money.' Joan had apparently told him about how 'Camrose kept on complaining that her son and his business were costing more and more and taking up more and more of the house.' The last time Joss visited Joan in that house, she had been pushed right up into 'the gods' because Amyn's business, 'which kept on costing Camrose such a lot of money,' had taken over the whole house and Camrose was still asking 'how could one business lose quite so much?' Joan eventually moved to a large house in Belgrave, which Joss described as 'very unfair because she loved her house.'

Joss had by then lost contact with those people 'because it was a long time ago,' but he remembered being the same age as 'the present Aga Khan,' who he said had been 'such a nice-looking young man,' but now had 'no hair and looks too awful.' Joss then explained that Yasmin, 'Aly's daughter by Rita Hayworth',[55] was still around, though he had also not seen her for years. Joss then recalled that Yasmin, whom he described as 'very handsome' had caused a scandal by having had 'an affair with the wife of that Canadian prime minister.'[56]

Joss also claimed to have known Joan Aly Khan's two sisters. One was Primrose Yarde-Buller, who married the 7th Earl of Cadogan, and the other was Lydia. Lydia Yarde-Buller had been married to Ray Lyle, or more accurately Sir Archibald Moir Park Lyle, who died in action in 1942. She then married John Russell, who subsequently became the Duke of Bedford. In fact, they had farmed in South Africa until he inherited Woburn Abbey, which was when he returned to England to turn it into what Joss described as 'a circus.'

* * *

Joss loved to gossip about all the various people he had known during his life and, given that he never had access to the information technology we all now take for granted and was not a serious reader, he seemed to know an awful lot about them all. He said that meetings with his purported 'father,' whom he claimed to have visited intermittently for the rest of his life, usually took place in France, either at the Windsors country property 15 miles southwest of Neuilly outside the village of Gif-sur-Yvette called the Moulin de la Tuilerie, which they referred to as the Mill, or at their splendid town house at 24 Boulevard Suchet in Paris. He said that the last time he saw the Duke of Windsor 'was in that yellow sitting room on the first floor of the Boulevard Suchet, and the last time I spoke to my mother was in that red sitting room at the Mill.'

* * *

To retain the secrecy of his identity, by his account, Joss had to keep moving, for no one could be allowed to deduce who he really was. Thus, after his initial stay with the Duke of Windsor at York House, Joss maintained that he moved to Ascott, which was a Rothschild property. This would be a new and important phase in his life and his first exposure to high finance. Joss said that regular contacts at York House between a member of the Rothschild family and the Duke of Windsor preceded his move to Ascott.

5

Rothschilds and Ashrams

F ROM JOSS'S ACCOUNT, and this is his account alone, as a ten-year-old boy he was introduced to the fragile aristocracy of post-war London and got to know the Duke of Windsor, the unhappy man he had come to look upon as his natural father. He also established a tentative relationship with his purported ageing grandmother, Queen Mary, and various other members of the royal family. However, since there was no place for him as a member of *that* family, some other solution had to be found and an elderly man, whom Joss called 'Nathan' Rothschild, agreed to take him under his wing. Consequently, Joss then moved to Ascott, a Rothschild property at Wing near Leighton Buzzard, in Buckinghamshire.

I must admit that I found Joss's recollections of this period particularly difficult either to authenticate or to believe. For a start, I was unable to determine with any degree of certainty exactly who this 'Nathan' was. I consulted several Rothschild biographies and autobiographies, but never established for sure exactly to whom Joss might have been referring. He just called him Nathan, but then Nathan (or Nathaniel) is among the names that lots of Rothschilds bear. Could he have meant Anthony Gustav de Rothschild (1887–1961), who owned Ascott at the time, or could he perhaps have been another more obscure member of the family? When I challenged Joss on this point, he seemed taken aback and said that he would ask Miriam Rothschild, who was still alive at the time (she died in 2005), but I doubt he ever did. He would have been too lazy to have done that and probably did not even have a record of her phone number. From Joss's viewpoint, he was just Nathan and he had never questioned his identity beyond that.

After paying a visit to Ascott (which was donated to the National Trust in 1949), I felt none the wiser. However, on a visit to Waddeston Manor, another Rothschild property donated to the National Trust in 1957, I came across a genealogical chart containing one possible candidate. This was Louis Nathaniel de Rothschild[1] who lived in England and Vermont after leaving Austria, so may have lived at Ascott for a while during the period Joss claimed to be there. It is plausible that his name was contracted to 'Nathan' (Nat, Natty and Nathan were all used in the family's history). Joss always spoke as if 'Nathan' owned Ascott, but on this point he could possibly have been mistaken.

To compound my own uncertainty, Joss then admitted to being vague about where the various members of the Rothschild family fitted in, so it seems highly likely that some of his facts about them are inaccurate and that, apart from one or two of its members, he did not know the family at all well. Though Joss believed that Wallis had some sort of vague genetic link with the Rothschilds, he seemed to know little about them. Since 'some of the Austrian ones live in England, some of the English ones in Austria, some of the French ones in England, and some of the English ones in France,' he said, it is all 'very confusing.' He claimed to know the Windsors and Morgans but was much vaguer about the Rothschilds because 'they never talk about themselves.' He knew 'that the Earl of Rosebery, who was prime minister of England, had married a Rothschild,' but then that was a long time ago.

The Earl of Rosebery (1847–1929), who briefly succeeded William Gladstone (1809–98) as prime minister of the United Kingdom in 1894/5 had indeed married Hannah de Rothschild (1851–1890), the only daughter of the banker Mayer de

Rothschild. It was an unlikely marriage because, although she was the richest woman in England, it was rare for the anti-Semitic British aristocracy to allow a Jewish woman to gain entry to their circle. However, as Niall Ferguson[2] argued, by the mid-nineteenth century the Rothschilds had risen so high in European society that they felt themselves to be the equivalent of royalty. Such self-regard was not necessarily reciprocated. For example, Queen Victoria openly expressed her anti-Semitism on more than one occasion and certainly balked at the idea of elevating prominent Jews to the peerage. Once, having agreed to dine with Lady Rosebery's cousin, the Liberal MP and art collector Ferdinand de Rothschild, she insisted on eating in a separate dining room from the Jewish guests. Other members of the royal family, however, felt more relaxed on that front, but, as Joss pointed out, that was all an exceptionally long time ago.

A Rothschild closer to Joss's generation and one he admired greatly – among other things they shared a taste for simple clothes – was the admirably eccentric British entomologist, zoologist, and author Dame Miriam Louisa Rothschild (1908–2005). He said that he knew Miriam 'terribly well,' but although 'about 90 now' (she was 88 at the time of this interview in 1996), she was the generation below Nathan. 'Miriam is still alive,' he said,[3] 'and she lives in that house in Northamptonshire,' though he could not recall its name.

Joss was almost certainly thinking of Ashton Wold, the Tudor-style property at Ashton, near Oundle in Northampton-shire, which was built for the Honourable Charles Rothschild in 1900. Joss might have forgotten the name of the house, but he remembered that it had wisteria growing through the walls, which is interesting because, apart from being the world's foremost authority on the flea, Miriam Rothschild was also passionately interested in conservation, especially of wild-flowers, and had apparently advised Prince Charles on what to plant when he moved to his country home, Highgrove House, in Gloucestershire. Joss thought that allowing the wisteria to grow through the wall was 'her way of bringing her garden into the house.' However, 'it is a strong house made of stone,' he conceded, so could withstand 'the six-inch gap' that the wisteria had created. He did not find the house particularly attractive – 'the Rothschilds own such ugly houses,' but 'mind you,' he conceded, 'she has made a pretty garden; she just stopped mowing her lawn and it turned into a meadow garden.'

After saying how much he liked her and what a nice person she was, he mentioned how she 'and Primrose Cadogan had been among the Vera girls' who cooked for and fed the East End of London after the war. Joss said that 'the average East Ender is two inches taller than before the war because they gave them such good food. They taught them how to eat.' Miriam, he said was the only one to survive into old age. Joss's reference to these women as 'Vera's girls' was probably an allusion to the forces' sweetheart, the popular singer Vera Lynn, born in the East End of London in 1917, who worked tirelessly during the war to raise the morale of the British troops. She thus exemplified the spirit of the women who were doing their bit for the war effort, for the war gave young women opportunities they would never otherwise have had. Primrose Cadogan, née Yarde-Buller, was a close friend of Wallis's (and presumably also of Miriam's).

Although unaware of what contribution Primrose Cadogan might have made to the war effort, Miriam for her part is known to have been actively engaged in it. She strove to help decipher German secret codes and cyphers. When German bombs destroyed the laboratory in which she had been working, she returned to help at Ashton Wold, which had been converted into a military hospital and airfield for the duration of the war. After the war, she did a lot of work trying to locate refugees and took many into her own home. She was clearly a 'Vera's girl' *par excellence.*

Joss's move to Ascott

Joss obviously knew nothing at the time about what arrangements and discussions preceded his move to Ascott, but he and 'Nathan,' as Joss called whoever this person may have really been, were given enough time to make one another's acquaintance. Joss described how Nathan used to come and see him while he was still living at York House, intermittently at first until they got to know one another better, and then daily. Joss said that 'strange as it may seem,' he 'used to ask my opinion about things.' This made Joss feel that 'he must have thought that I could be of assistance to him because he then invited me to stay with him at Ascott.' It was sensitive of Nathan to make Joss feel that he could be 'of assistance' to him and that he valued his opinions. Presumably, the timing of the decision that Joss should stay at Ascott with Nathan and a small staff of retainers corresponded with the Duke of Windsor returning to his exile in France.

Strangely, Joss claimed to have maintained contact in later life with the grandson of a member of Nathan's staff, whom he simply referred to as Parker.[4] Perhaps the members of staff were the people with whom Joss interacted the most because he said that, apart from Nathan, there were no other Rothschilds at Ascott while he was living there. He presumed that Nathan's wife had already died and here again the story gets confusing. Since the wives of both Anthony Gustav and Louis Nathaniel were still alive until 1977 and 1981 respectively, one wonders why Joss knew so little about Nathan's nuclear family, let alone his wider family.

The only reference he made to Nathan's wife was that she had collected 'beautiful boxes' and that he had lost them. He remembered putting them into the boot of a car and then failing to retrieve them and they got lost. Losing things, he said, was the 'story of his life,' which he described as 'biblical' insofar as he seemed to think that everything happened 'for a purpose' beyond his control. By the time he reached adulthood losing things had become a pattern in Joss's life and one cannot help but wonder why. There is ample evidence of him being the beneficiary of copious amounts of beautiful and valuable possessions, and he claimed that they were of great personal as well as financial value to him. In fact, his main interest in life seemed to be in *objets d'art*, so why did he need to lose them? Did he perhaps feel that he did not deserve them? Or, conversely, did he subconsciously resent the fact that they were accorded such value, when his own existence was of so little value that not even his own parents, whether real, imagined, foster or otherwise, seemed prepared openly to recognize *his* value to them?

Joss described Nathan as 'a difficult man' and 'terribly mean,' so at least he was one person who saw no need to spend money needlessly on either Joss or anything else. Indeed, it is on record that when Anthony de Rothschild inherited Ascott in 1937, he went to great lengths to simplify the house so that it would be easier to manage, which might explain why, from Joss's vantage point, there were surprisingly few servants there. While Joss undoubtedly noted an austere side to Nathan's character, if we are to take Joss's claims at face value, he also seems to have had a caring side in that he was willing to help his royal friends out by giving Joss refuge. In that rambling old house in Berkshire, Joss would have been one removed from royal circles, so less likely to attract attention than he would have been in the bosom of his own family. Joss recalled one of the staff explaining to him how clever it had been to keep him incognito and how much work had gone into it, but that it had been 'much easier after the war' because there were a lot of war orphans around 'and people asked fewer questions than before the war.'

The reference to war orphans strikes a chord because the Rothschilds (particularly Lionel and Anthony) played active roles in supporting the *Kindertransport*, which brought approximately 10,000 children to Britain, usually by train, to escape the Nazi death camps to which German Jews were being sent. Lionel and Anthony de Rothschild were among the 11 founding members of the Central British Fund for German Jewry, which

> attempted to bring together the various elements of the Jewish community for the purposes of relief work and fund raising. … These men represented a wide spectrum of religious and political thought and, though some brought with them antipathies and quarrels that had been long in the making, the plight of their German coreligionists bound them together in a common purpose.[5]

The number of Jewish refugee children far exceeded the number of places available to them in orthodox Jewish homes and any attempts to assimilate them into wider British society created tensions in the Anglo-Jewish community. 'While … the Zionist president of the Board of Deputies, for example, saw assimilation as "an abandonment of a [Jewish] sense of history", Anthony de Rothschild believed that assimilation was not only the "civic ideal" but also the "true fulfilment of the Jewish ideal at its best".'[6] The Rothschilds (along with the Sainsburys, the actor Lord Attenborough and the celebrated pianist Dame Myra Hess) fostered more than 26 children between them. That, however, was immediately before the Second World War and Joss claimed to have come to Ascott after the war had ended.

The Rothschilds and the royals

How plausible was this supposed link to the Rothschilds? It is worth pointing out that this was not the first time the Rothschild family, which had been breaking bread with royalty for at least 200 years, had been summoned to help resolve an awkward royal situation. One example is given by

Frederick Morton,[7] who described how, in 1825, Salomon Rothschild, the founder of the Austrian branch of the family, had been called upon to handle Europe's most delicate love affair. Marie Louise, wife of Napoleon Bonaparte and daughter of the Austrian emperor gave birth to two children in 1817 and 1819 respectively while her husband was in exile on the island of St Helena. Her lover was a young major-domo called General Albert von Neipperg. The children's births were not registered, and their existence was kept secret, even from their own grandfather, the emperor, until after Napoleon's death in 1821 when the couple entered a secret morganatic marriage. Salomon Rothschild's delicate role here had been to guarantee a secure inheritance for the children without loss of any of their mother's land and without drawing attention to the illegitimacy of their claim.

Then, on the English side, the Prince of Wales[8] had formed a close and intimate friendship with Leopold Rothschild while the two were students together at Cambridge in the 1850s. The families remained close from then onwards without any religious compromise on either side. Frederick Morton[9] has described how the Prince of Wales braved a shocking blizzard to attend Leopold's wedding at the Central Synagogue in Great Portland Street on 19 January 1881 and mentions how much the prince loved the kosher food and roared with laughter at the Jewish jokes.

Perhaps, then, it might have been perfectly fitting that when King Edward VIII was on the point of abdication, he should turn to the Rothschilds; in fact, it was to Salomon's great-grandson, the Baron Eugene de Rothschild (1884–1976) that he fled at the height of the abdication crisis. Eugene and his wife Kitty (1885–1946) extended a hand of friendship to the troubled king at their castle, Schloss Enzesfeld near Vienna in Austria, irrespective of whether he loved the wrong woman or held the wrong political views. Joss claimed that his parents turned to the Rothschilds because Wallis was related to them.

Be that as it may, in providing discreet and loyal services to Europe's leading monarchs over many years, the Rothschild family had shown itself to be adept at and experienced in dealing with the political, social, financial, or sexual embarrassments that arise from time to time.

*　*　*

While this general background connecting royalty to the Rothschilds lends some plausibility to Joss's account, the details provided, particularly on the mysterious 'Nathan,' are vague or inconsistent. Nonetheless, in the spirit of allowing him his voice, I recount Joss's recollections of Ascott, his supposed next home. Spread across approximately 100 acres of farmland, with views extending across the Vale of Aylesbury to the Chilterns and with a large, formally laid out garden, this sprawling old building had seen many alterations and extensions since it was first built as a timber-framed farmhouse in the early seventeenth century. Joss thought that 'Ascott was a hideous house.' Although, he conceded, it might have started as 'quite a pretty little manor house,' they kept on adding to it and 'it ended up as an elephantine Edwardian mansion full of junk.' Nonetheless, it was an ideal place in which to conceal a growing boy in the years following the Second World War. Joss explained that by the time he first went there, wartime austerity had already taken its toll and the once beautiful garden that the distinguished Chelsea nurseryman Sir Harry Veitch had originally laid out, was a mess.

As mentioned earlier, Joss depicted Nathan as notoriously mean and, in describing this aspect of his character, rather amusingly evoked what is surely a well-worn cliché to the effect that when someone once asked him why he always travelled third class on the train to London that his reply had been 'because there is no fourth class.' Joss said that Nathan and Wallis got along well together and that he respected her opinions and regarded her as 'a good sounding board.' None-theless, as Joss explained, she failed lamentably in her attempts to cure him of his reluctance to spend money. 'She used to irritate him endlessly,' Joss said, by buying things like sheets, towels, and table napkins, charging them to his account, and sending them to Ascott. He would then send them back on the grounds that they had enough towels and accused her of 'wanton extravagance.' He did not seem to mind that the ones they had were threadbare and full of holes. As far as he was concerned, they were perfectly all right and that if she carried on like that 'she would end up in the poor house.' Wallis had apparently said that his linen 'was poor quality to start with,' and Joss concluded that 'they used to have interesting scraps.' Joss also said that he employed 'a skeleton staff' at Ascott and paid them 'starvation' wages.

* * *

Irrespective of whether he underpaid his staff, or if the quality of the linen was up to scratch, what, one might ask, did Joss and this old man do with themselves and with their time? For a start, unlike most children, Joss had not been sent to school and so had virtually no opportunities to meet young people of his age or to participate in the kinds of activities that most boys are likely to enjoy. Consequently, Joss just entered the spirit of what Nathan enjoyed discussing – banking. Nathan allowed Joss to believe that he was a great help to him in his business and that he relied heavily on his financial expertise.

Thus, from the isolation of their rural retreat, Joss and his mentor played what could only have been a childhood game, for they were single-handedly taking it upon themselves to put Britain and the world to rights. It was as if he had been catapulted into the world of high finance, buying, selling, borrowing, lending, crashing companies and all the other procedures associated with manipulating money markets.

Here Joss's description of his work with Nathan takes on a ridiculous braggadocio that is wholly out of keeping with any likely scenario. His adoption of the royal 'we,' the way he seems to place himself on the same level as Nathan, not to mention his assumption that he is able to judge the wisdom of Nathan's decisions are, in every respect, unconvincing. It is important to remember, however, that we are talking about a boy who in adult life was never capable of managing his own affairs, let alone those of whole nations. Yet, Joss is suddenly proclaiming that he enjoyed a spectacular career as a pretend banker:

> I worked all the bloody time. I worked seven days a week, eighteen hours a day. I mean we financed Japan. We still own 51 per cent of the shares on the Japanese market and we financed Germany. We still own 51 per cent of all the shares in Italy because we financed them after the war. Nathan had this bee in his bonnet that the Second World War happened because the defeated nations were not helped onto their feet again. It was actually a very stupid plan when I think of it now.

Joss did not, however, explain his role in this venture. He nonetheless asserted that, in retrospect, he felt that some of Nathan's methods to raise revenue to fund the post-war reconstruction were immoral and he regretted having been associated with them. One device he said that Nathan pioneered was a form of cheque fraud called kiting. This involves exploiting the time (technically known as the float) between which a deposit is made in the recipient's account and is deducted from the sender's account. In other words, there is a time when the money is present in both accounts and this offers bankers brilliant opportunities for fraud, especially in the days before electronic banking when bad weather or poor communications often delayed the period before cheques could be cleared. From most of our experiences of banks, however, one cannot but suspect that these practices continue, despite the introduction of electronic cheques and the Check Clearing for the 21st Century Act, which the United States Congress introduced in October 2003 to target this kind of fraud. Joss said that they used Pierpont Morgan's methods to keep England afloat and that these made a lot of people destitute, for which Joss claimed personal responsibility. 'It lies on my conscience very greatly,' he said, and 'that is why I am now destitute.' He claimed to have seen people 'queuing up for one egg a week' and then sitting down and weeping 'when the egg was rotten.'

First, it is difficult to believe that Joss witnessed people crying over a rotten egg. How would they have known it was rotten until they took it home? It is also inconceivable that a child of that age would have been allowed a hand in either crashing companies or rescuing the post-Second World War economy. If any of this has any validity at all, Nathan was obviously humouring him rather than relying on his financial expertise, which even Joss eventually admitted by saying that he 'never went to an office or anything' and was never really anything more than 'a messenger boy.' Although such a confession is tantamount to admitting that he tended to overstate his role on the world stage, it did not stop him holding forth about how Churchill had ruined the British economy by spending all the country's foreign assets on fighting the Second World War and by having allowed Britain to lose its manufacturing base. He accused Winston Churchill of spending 'all the foreign assets on this wretched war, instead of simply bankrupting Hitler, which he could have done with the help of Rothschild.' He called Churchill 'an old-fashioned warmonger' who left England without the wherewithal 'to pay for imports' and without a manufacturing base with which to make goods for export. He said that the English used to manufacture 'the best goods in the world for the privileged few and they do not even do that anymore.' He thought that London had become 'a junk shop' and that it could never possibly recover, which was a shame, he said, because the country had been 'enormously rich' and would never again be able to build up the fortune it once had.

Joss emphasized that rich people like the Rothschilds should have used their own money to bail Britain out of its difficulties rather than draw on ordinary shareholders who had already been badly hit by the Wall Street Crash. 'Look at the Gold Coast of Long Island and all those houses that people had to leave because they could no longer afford to live in them!' And this, he carried on, was 'because of what we did to Wall Street,' note the royal *we*. Granted, for the first three decades of the twentieth century, the so-called Gold Coast of Long Island, New York, was the most fashionable place in the United States for rich and famous Americans to build their sumptuous homes and there were hundreds of mansions there, and that now only a few remain, but this was long before Joss's time, so he had no reason to see any of it as his responsibility. 'The truth of the matter,' he continued, 'was that one made a lot of money out of crashing companies. The ordinary rich can only start educational trusts and educate people. When you get to the mega rich you can cause a world depression by picking up a telephone.'

Joss goes East

As Joss was growing up, he said he started to feel uncomfortable about how easily the super rich could change the fortunes of the not so rich. It is difficult to say to what extent this shaped his outlook, but he certainly constructed a mindset in which he viewed his life as something over which he had no control. This was evident in his passivity and reluctance, even incapacity, to take responsibility for anything, or to do anything to ease his own, or anyone else's, path through life. Perhaps because he could not reasonably claim to want what he knew he could never have, which was something as basic as his parents' public acknowledgement of his existence, whoever his parents might have been, he turned in on himself and developed a Buddhist-like acceptance of his fate. Being devoid of greed, hatred, or resentment would make it easier for him to cope with his ambiguous status. If his life was preordained, then it would run its course irrespective of what actions he took. To emphasize his point, he mentioned having had a couple of peculiar encounters in London with a woman he claimed had psychic powers.

He described how in the early 1950s, when 'people still wore stockings with seams at the back,' a woman wearing 'purple stockings,' which was unusual at that time, approached him outside a barber's shop in Shepherd Market, looked him straight in the eye and said, 'your debt is not an ordinary one: it is a national one.' It seems odd that Joss should have given even a second thought to such an incident, which most people would dismiss out of hand as the remark of a deranged or disturbed woman. That Joss seemed to take it as an omen, or evidence of his importance, strikes me as rather sad. He then recalled encountering her again many years later, also in Shepherd Market, and the encounter was equally bizarre.

What was slightly more interesting about this second encounter was that he had remembered that the barber's name was Ivor, and there was indeed a salon at 14 Shepherd Market called Ivor Edwards Hairdressing,[10] and that 'it was where poor old Margaret Argyll spent the end of her life.' The second meeting must have been nearly forty years later because Margaret, Duchess of Argyll only died in 1993. Born in 1912, she had been debutante of the year when presented at court in 1930 and was noted for her breath-taking beauty and extravagant and reckless lifestyle. She was notorious in her day for her scandalous divorce from her second husband the 11th Duke of Argyll in 1963, in which her husband named 88 men, including two Cabinet ministers and three members of the royal family as co-respondents in the divorce proceedings. She was obviously a very sociable duchess. Joss said that 'she used to sit in the barber shop all day' because all the people she knew used to go there 'to have their hair cut or their beards shaved, so she could chat to them all day long.'

It was no doubt a good place to get a haircut, but it is difficult to comprehend why Joss should have attached any significance whatsoever to what an eccentric woman had to say other than to assume that it was because he felt drawn to some or other form of spiritualism. In any case, around the mid-1950s, when he was about 17 or 18, he had a strong wish to withdraw from English society and said, 'I just instinctively felt I wanted to go to this monastery in Tibet.'

According to Joss, the person called upon to secure a place for him in the monastery was none other than Doris Duke (1912–1993) who, like the Duchess of Windsor and Bunny Mellon, was an American heiress backed by a huge amount of money. Doris Duke, who was, among other things, a horticulturalist, art collector and philanthropist, came to Paris after the war, which of course was where the Duke and Duchess of Windsor were spending much of their exile. While in Paris Doris Duke wrote for *Harper's Bazaar* and, in 1947, she married Porfirio Rubirosa (1909–1965), the playboy son of the chargé d'affaires at the Dominican Republic consulate who had been linked romantically to such famous celebrities as Joan Crawford, Zsa Zsa Gabor, Ava Gardner, Judy Garland, Rita Hayworth, Eartha Kitt, Veronica Lake, Marilyn Monroe, Kim Novak, and Eva Peron, among numerous others. Perhaps, not unexpectedly in such a competitive environment, the marriage did not last, and they divorced in 1951. However, given that Doris Duke took a keen interest in Islamic and Southeast Asian art and religions – she in fact paid for the building of the Maharishi Mahesh Yogi's ashram in India (which the Beatles visited in 1968) and bequeathed innumerable pieces to the Asian Art Museum in San Francisco – she was ideally placed to arrange for Joss to spend time in a Trappist monastery in Tibet.

The monastery, he explained, was situated on top of a hill in a rural area near a town. He had liked the experience very much. He said that 'it was really quiet. I can still recreate that, when you just meditate, and things come to you.' Obviously, he did not speak their language, but said that one person there spoke English. This meditative environment suited Joss. There he learnt to detach himself from the materialism of the capitalist world and from the smart circles to which he had been exposed. In the monastery there was no need for pretence or concealment; everybody was equal before a higher spiritual being. What he felt he learnt from this period was that people perform their role in the grand scheme of things simply by being, which is a very Buddhist approach. Joss wished that he had been able to spend longer there, but said that Nathan had summoned him back because, as he pretentiously inferred, 'he could not manage on his own.'

Joss claimed that he had resented being called back to the UK before he felt ready to return, for his exposure to the East had a profound effect on shaping his values. In retrospect, he said, it had saddened him to see Tibet move into the modern world, for he felt that its people lost some of their former wisdom in the process. 'Now it has all become a circus because the Dalai Lama is going around making public speeches.' Here, Joss was referring to the Dalai Lama's political activities in support of the Tibetan independence movement at a time when the People's Republic of China, under the leadership of Chairman Mao Zedong, who was in office from 1943 to 1976, initiated the attempt to incorporate Tibet into mainstream China. Communist China looked upon Tibet as a backward region controlled by feudal landlords and hidebound by religion, whereas the supporters of Tibetan independence wanted to retain their religious and cultural traditions, as well as their distinctive way of life. The Dalai Lama, who is chosen because he is believed to be the reincarnation of the previous Dalai Lama, is the most influential figure in Tibetan Buddhism and, as such, is considered a holy man.

The present 14th Dalai Lama, born in 1935, identified as the reincarnation of the previous Dalai Lama at the age of two, who started his reign in November 1950 at the age of fifteen, had been pulled into the fray by political circumstances. Joss was obviously unsympathetic to both positions, for now barely out of his adolescence he just wanted to be left alone to sort out his own values and religious beliefs – or what he came to refer to as his 'crackpot religion,' which he said was 'based on reincarnation.' 'I believe there is some power' and that everything is preordained, but 'I am certainly not a missionary,' he said, 'and have no desire to convert anybody to what I believe.'

It is interesting, though perhaps understandable, that Joss was so attracted to the idea of reincarnation. Given that he seemed to think that his life would leave no legacy, and I think he felt this irrespective of who he really was, it must have been a comfort to him to believe that he would one day get another chance to be somebody with a proper, acknowledged existence. Also, in a way, his conviction that his life was preordained let him off the hook because it fed into his laziness by allowing him to believe that nothing could make any difference to how it turned out. Although we are all aware of the tension between doing something and the constraints that wider forces impose on our actions, most of us can exercise some agency over at least certain areas of our lives. Joss, however, seemed unusually bereft of this ability. He saw life as 'a gigantic game of chess' that was being played out and that we, the humans, are simply being used as pieces on the chess board. Joss's 'crackpot religion' provided him with a useful crutch, but it did not save him from destitution.

* * *

If Nathan was Louis Nathaniel Rothschild (a faint possibility), his death in 1955 informally marked the end of Joss's childhood and teenage years and, for better or worse, Joss's personality had been formed. He knew what he believed or did not believe and had evolved a set of mechanisms with which to deal with the circumstances of his life. What remained from his Ascott days was the link to Parker, who had been a young child when his grandfather was on the staff at Ascott when Joss first claimed to have gone there. Although Parker's grandfather had worked for the family, 'Parker's father went into business, so was not in service.' Joss said he had later employed Parker as his valet, that he was 'wonderful' and 'when one used good china he would wash every piece himself in a *papier mâché* bowl and could set the table second to none.' In 1966, when Joss was making these remarks, there was certainly no good chinaware to be seen, let alone a table to set, yet it seemed important to him that he had once commanded respect from the most highly regarded servant of the upper classes. 'Parker knows everybody,' he went on, 'and he is the most snobbish person I have ever come across.'

> Rab[11] once stood and watched Parker's stately progress down Bond Street and everybody who was anybody stopped to speak to him. Parker could not live in South Africa – it is not grand enough for him. If Parker says they are redecorating the yellow drawing room at Buck House, you can take it as done. He probably got the information from nobody less than the Queen because she does not speak to other servants.

Joss claimed that he had once been able to employ people to take care of his London households and that another employee of whom he had grown fond was Rogers, whom he had hired as his chauffeur. Rab later employed him, and he is 'still alive,' in fact quite 'young, probably in his mid-fifties.'

One house in which Joss claimed to have once lived was in North Row in Mayfair and he believed that it had previously belonged to a member of the Rothschild family, but here again he seemed confused about who that might have been. In any case he seemed to have ambivalent feelings about it.

> My father described it as a giant lavatory. It had a hall in the centre, which was six storeys high and made from white cipolin[12] and marble and it did honestly look like a *pissoir* built for giants. There is not very much more to say about it other than that it was built in a very awkward period. It was not furnished with beautiful things; just stuffed with things. It was one of those Edwardian town houses that were not vulgar enough to justify themselves.

He then went on to say that he thought that King Hussein of Jordan (1935–1999), who was a contemporary of Joss's, had eventually bought the house and had lived there at one stage, but 'whether they are still there, I do not know. I really have lost contact with London.' Given that the second of King Hussein's four wives, Antoinette Avril Gardiner (born 1941), the daughter of a British army officer whom he married in 1961 and divorced in 1971, was English, the family might well have wanted to keep a *pied-à-terre* in London, but then I was never able to establish the veracity of that claim.

* * *

While Nathan's death ended a chapter in Joss's personal life, according to him it also represented a decline in the Rothschild family's fortunes. Joss was quite scathing about the family's subsequent achievements. While it is possible to concede that there are now more players in the field than they were when N. M. Rothschild & Sons ruled the roost – including a bevy of tech billionaires, property developers and speculators – the Rothschild bank nonetheless consistently ranks among the top ten investment banks in the world, so perhaps we should take Joss's remarks about them with a pinch of salt. He held that, given that 'they had the most enormous reserves,' he found it unbelievable that 'they have now overdrawn at the Bank of England and all over the show.' 'All I can say is that it must have taken great genius to bankrupt Rothschilds,' he railed on, 'they underwrote Lloyds and that went for a bang. They underwrote all the wrong things. The Rothschilds are moneylenders, and you must know who to underwrite otherwise you can lose your boots. I do not know of any Rothschild houses that are left, not even one.' His last remark was not actually true because, as we saw earlier, he had been admiring of the way in which Jacob Rothschild had restored the Spencer House. However, now he was feeling in a more belligerent mood because he expressed outrage that:

> Jacob has now restored the Spencer House, which is the only good thing he has ever done, but he has now opened it to the public. How cheap can one be? It really is one of those beautiful houses of the world and I thought he was going to live there, but he is not. He seems to be turning it into a business. You can hire it for functions and things, which is silly. I hope the money is going to charity. If he is pocketing it, then he really is letting down the side.

Since, as Joss claimed, the Rothschilds were supposed to be bankrupt, one might wonder how poor Jacob was supposed to survive if it was so undignified to run a business.

Between materialism and spirituality

Joss seemed to have emerged from his adolescence as a somewhat fractured young man and in this chapter, we have seen different, often contradictory, aspects of his character. His lack of resolution between what he wanted and felt entitled to have on the one hand, and his disdain for and renunciation of money and material possessions on the other, sent mixed messages to those around him. His incapacity to take responsibility for looking after any cash or assets that would come his way was later to leave Joss virtually defenceless.

We also see Joss making claims that were unmistakably gross exaggerations of the truth, or even pure inventions. No minor would ever be allowed to crash companies or sort out the world's economies. Whatever childish insights he may have been able to bring to bear on a situation could only have been serendipitous. He never had any formal schooling or further education and certainly had no special talent for business. He even failed to acquire simple manual skills like sweeping a floor or making a bed. Yet, Joss frequently implied in conversations that he was held in high regard by people in powerful positions. Remarks like 'Nathan must have thought I could be of assistance,' or 'I made a lot of people destitute in my youth … because of what we did to Wall Street' are clearly nothing more than hollow boasts. For understandable psychological reasons, he seemed to want me to think that he was more central to what was happening in the world than he could ever possibly have been.

Joss obviously had a complicated array of feelings about the Rothschild family. He sometimes appears to believe crude nineteenth-century anti-Semitic tropes about the Rothschilds running the world through their fabulous wealth and control of the banking system. He also expresses feelings of resentment, envy and contempt for their bad taste – 'they always had such ugly houses' and maintains that their fortunes are plummeting. However, he also expresses a sense of admiration for some family members, especially for Miriam who had achieved so much as a scientist and innovative thinker. Above all, he fixates on Nathan who is constructed as a benign uncle – a form of emotional substitution that can be likened to what psychologists call 'paternity uncertainty.'[13] In general, Joss's supposed relationship with the Rothschilds looks far from convincing. From this I must presume that his sojourns at Ascott were either more fleeting or less significant to the Rothschild family than Joss cares to admit, or that this part of his story was exaggerated or fabricated. Nonetheless, in subsequent chapters I will continue to listen to what Joss had to say for himself but warn the reader that the Rothschild connection must be treated with considerable scepticism.

On the other side of the coin, there was an aspect of Joss's character that contradicted his desire for inclusion, relevance, bequests, money, and possessions. He frequently expressed a longing for simplicity – exemplified in his Tibetan experience – and embraced a philosophy of renunciation akin to Buddhism. Joss's blind faith in predestination, his belief that some divine purpose underlies what happens in life, may have made it easier for him to handle his marginal status, but it left him vulnerable to the calculating actions of people who did not believe in predestination but were, on the contrary, on the lookout for whatever opportunities they could find to further their own personal interests in the here and now and on this earth. As we shall see later in the book, Joss's spiritualism, or 'crackpot religion,' was later to turn into self-abasement and abjection.

6

The Uncertain Years

WHILE JOSS WAS based in the UK during his adolescence, he used to visit South Africa on a regular basis and usually remained there for extended periods. At first, his visits were mainly to see Ouma Wessels in the Cape, but later he moved into establishments of his own. Although he regarded London as his spiritual home, Joss always maintained a base in South Africa, for his official identity was that of a South African citizen and South Africa was his domicile. In fact, he spent a good part of his life shuffling backwards and forwards between London and South Africa. He was, in effect, despite being a South African national, living a life much like that of a 'snowbird.'

When Joss was born near the end of 1936, South Africa, or more accurately the Union of South Africa as it was then called (comprising the Cape, Transvaal, Orange Free State and Natal), was a dominion of the British Empire, with a governor-general representing the constitutional monarch. At that time, before the advent of the Second World War, European governments, notably Britain and France, but also Belgium, Germany, Italy, Portugal, and Spain, controlled the whole of sub-Saharan Africa bar Ethiopia and Liberia. In other words, with few exceptions, until about the mid-1950s, Africa was firmly under European control.

In the aftermath of the war, however, during which people from all corners of the British Empire had stood firmly and loyally at the side of the mother country, and in numerous cases sacrificed their lives, the mood changed. Not only had it become unviable for Britain (and of course for other European countries with colonial possessions) to maintain its overseas empire, but many of the inhabitants of these colonies were also growing eager to throw off their colonial bondage.

Thus, with a move afoot to grant independence to African countries, the future political situation was growing considerably less certain, especially for the unyielding white supremacists in the more southerly African countries where white settlement was firmly established.

On 3 February 1960, Conservative British Prime Minister Harold Macmillan, addressing the South African parliament in Cape Town after a month-long visit to several African colonies, gave a now famous speech in which he stated that 'the wind of change is blowing through this continent. Whether we like it or not, this growth of national consciousness is a political fact.' These words made the white National Party government, which had been firmly entrenched in power since 1948, feel distinctly uncomfortable: the British government, and a Conservative one at that, was expressing its willingness to grant independence to its African colonies. This was a message the South African government did not wish to hear. It was a message that the right wing of the British Conservative Party also found unpalatable. Indeed, some of these right-wing factions got together to form the Monday Club, a pressure group supporting white minority rule in southern Africa. Macmillan's 'winds of change' speech had sparked the resignation from the Cabinet of the 5th Marquess of Salisbury (1893–1972) who became the Monday Club's first president in 1962 and whose grandson, Rab Cecil, was later to become Joss's closest friend. In the Reith Lectures of 1961, Margery Perham described South Africa at the time as

the last beleaguered stronghold of white mastery in Africa. Its ruling garrison are Africans, white Africans, who will defend their position to the last, for they are, in fact, a little nation which has built itself over three centuries into this position and has nowhere else to go. They have their backs to the wall, but they dare not turn to read the writing on it. Yet all the rest of the world can read it.[1]

In October 1960, eight months after the 'winds of change' speech, the General Assembly of the United Nations passed a resolution stating that 'unpreparedness should not be a pretext for delaying independence.'[2] Soon thereafter one African country after another began to cast off its imperial legacy and enter a new state of independence. Independence Day celebrations that saw the lowering of the imperial flag and the raising of new flags with bands playing stirring new national anthems became regular events on the calendars of politicians and celebrities in the public eye. For the most part, the transition happened with good humour, a certain amount of fanfare and, despite the forebodings of the doubters, most of the world wished them well for the future. There were, however, some exceptions. These were countries like Algeria, Angola, Rhodesia, and South Africa, where white rule and significant white populations had become so deeply entrenched and had such huge interests at stake that they were not going to hand over control to majority native populations without putting up a truculent fight first – and this was often a fight to the death.

In Algeria, a bitter war was waged from 1954 to 1962 between the French colonial power and various rival independence movements. While it eventually led to Algerian independence being granted in 1962, it was at a huge cost to human life and ultimately caused the collapse of the Fourth French Republic. The Angolan War of Independence, which lasted from 1961 to 1974, was of course much closer to home, and South Africa became intertwined with what white South Africans called the Angolan Bush War. This was a civil war that lasted from 1966 to 1989 in which South Africa and its allies were pitched against the Angolan government and its allies. In cold war terms – remembering that the cold war had not yet ended – this meant a threat to the delicate balance between the West and East, between capitalism and communism, between the United States and the Soviet Union, or between left and right. White Rhodesians, under the leadership of Ian Smith (1919–2007), also fiercely resisted black majority rule and, in November 1965, Ian Smith signed a unilateral declaration of independence from the United Kingdom to prevent Britain recognizing majority rule. Meanwhile, from 1964 to 1979, a civil war waged in the country, which eventually ended in the creation of the Republic of Zimbabwe with Robert Mugabe at the helm.

The South African government, like the Rhodesian government, was for its part going to resist the tide and, in May 1961, a mere 15 months after Macmillan's 'winds of change' speech to the Cape Town parliament, South Africa threw off its dominion status, declared itself a republic and was promptly ejected from the Commonwealth. The country's leaders preferred to go it alone than to countenance the possibility of black majority rule and, in the years that followed, the South African regime grew ever more racist, defensive, authoritarian, inward-looking, recalcitrant, and afraid.

The white elite takes cover

White South Africans, especially those with substantial overseas and/or local assets, were growing increasingly concerned about how the political situation might impinge on their financial security. For a start, along with its newfound status as a republic, South Africa changed its official currency from the British pound to the South African rand. Though still loosely tied to the sterling area, by appointing the South African Reserve Bank to carry out the functions formerly assigned to the treasury, it was indicating that there would be much tighter controls imposed on all movements of money into and out of the country.

The South African government feared that there would be a flight of capital out of the country and its trepidation was justified because, in a climate of uncertainty, people were bound to want to spread their risk. To forestall such an eventuality, the South African authorities introduced official controls over all fiscal transactions involving either the receipt or payment of any foreign exchange. All South African residents were, by law, required to declare all their foreign assets and liabilities, including stocks and shares, investments, mortgages, or fixed property. Cash in foreign banks or in foreign currency notes held in South Africa also had to be declared to the authorities. Provisions were made to allow South Africans to remit foreign assets to South Africa, but they were not allowed to leave them overseas. The purpose of these draconian measures was to ensure that people kept their money firmly in the country. It then became well-nigh impossible for South African citizens to function as they had done before, especially in an international context. Some South African residents with overseas assets resorted to illegal ways of protecting their wealth. They might risk entrusting their money to friends or relatives overseas who were not South African residents or nationals; people travelling to South Africa or abroad might try to conceal bank notes or bullion that exceeded their allowance in their luggage or on their person; or of course they might just lie to the tax authorities and hope that they would never be found out.

Although some of these restrictions were gradually lifted, in the period after South Africa became a republic, the authorities made it illegal for South African nationals to hold either dual citizenship or an overseas bank account. Limitations were imposed on how much money they were allowed to take with them on overseas holidays and exceedingly close tabs were kept on all money movements both into and out of the country. Apart from the heavy restrictions the South African nationals had to face from their own government, they also encountered the opprobrium of people who found apartheid offensive. Consciousness-raising campaigns abroad were drawing attention to the iniquities of the apartheid system and South Africans were being made aware of the withdrawal of international approval. South African Airways was forbidden to fly over parts of Africa and South African nationals were denied entry to several countries. White South Africans resented being made to feel like pariahs and how they responded to their exclusion depended largely on where they stood on the political spectrum. With the focus of the world on them, opinions were becoming more polarised as people questioned their values and grappled with their consciences.

The new situation was especially grave for someone like Joss whose assets were tied up in complicated trusts, which allowed him very little economic discretion in his own right. His carefully constructed South African nationality had now become more of a nuisance than an advantage. Also, because at that time South Africans could only claim British nationality through the paternal line (this law changed in 1983 when maternal descent was given equal status), Joss could not, as many other South African nationals of British ancestry had been able to do, apply to become a British national. Although the person whom Joss asserted was his natural father had a claim to British nationality, his official father, Joseph de Wahl, had none, so that loophole was unavailable to him. He was thus in an awkward position.

Under the South African legislation in operation at the time he could not legally hold assets abroad in his name, yet, during those uncertain years when nobody really knew how things would eventually turn out, people were reluctant to remit their assets to South Africa in case the situation deteriorated into a civil war, in which case they were likely to lose everything. Joss explained that because he was a South African subject and because 'by then the Nats[3] had come to power and were repatriating everything,' he was worried about being forced to bring all his overseas assets to South Africa. He said that 'BOSS, whatever BOSS stood for, went around investigating all South Africans' bank balances anywhere in the world and if you had any money then they demanded that it be repatriated here [to South Africa] and one realized that this country was going nowhere in a hurry.' Joss is slightly confused here because the National Party had been in power since 1948: what had in fact changed was that South Africa had become a republic and left the Commonwealth. BOSS was the South African Bureau of State Security, which was established in 1969 to monitor national security. The National Intelligence Service (NIS) replaced it in 1980 after a scandal was uncovered in which South African government funds were being used to set up an English-speaking pro-National Party newspaper.

Joss claimed that this situation made it difficult for 'his mother,' Wallis, or anyone else for that matter, to register assets in his name. As he put it, 'the Nationalists kept on repatriating' people's overseas assets, and 'we knew it was only a matter of time before it would blow up and then you would not ever be able to get it out again and it would be of no use to anybody.' Joss's use of the word 'repatriation' in this context is clearly a simplification of a more complicated and sophisticated fiscal policy, but it conveys the essence of the new restrictions.

If we take his claims to be true, when Joss was first sent to South Africa no one, least of all General Smuts, purportedly the inspirational force behind constructing his new persona, could have foreseen quite how far the apartheid government would drift away from the Commonwealth or how strenuously it would watch over movements of capital and assets into and out of the country. Because of his South African nationality and residency and because virtually all his assets were overseas, financial complications arose for Joss as the

National Party in South Africa became ever more deeply entrenched.

Apart from the impediments that the South African authorities placed between Joss and the money that would keep him in the style to which he was accustomed and to which he no doubt felt entitled, there was also the question of how to evade various taxes. According to Joss, people with such a lot of money do not write wills in the way the rest of us do, for that would entail paying out far too much in death duties. As Joss explained, when someone from that class dies, their money is, as he put it, 'all sort of quietly transferred.' The two important considerations were therefore to minimize death duties and to prevent the money available to him having to be transferred to South Africa. This left Joss unable to gain hands-on control of his finances. That he would have been capable of exercising such control is, of course, another question altogether.

Joss also faced a third complication in that his foster father, Joseph de Wahl, who lived in Vryburg, which is a couple of hours drive north of Kimberley, had during Joss's absences abroad sold several farms in the Cape, which, according to Joss, the Duke and Duchess of Windsor had bought for him and registered in his name. Not a word had been leaked over the high seas to Europe about these nefarious happenings and it was only when Joss returned to South Africa that he discovered what had been going on, by which time his farms had been sold. They were 'just pinched. It is biblical.' Joss often referred to the loss of his acquisitions as biblical, which is apt given that Mark 4:25 states that 'whoever has will be given more; whoever does not have, even what he has will be taken from him.'

That was certainly Joss's fate. First his property, and later (as I shall document) many priceless material possessions started to slip from his grasp. By the nature of the circumstances in which he found himself, he was always the victim of other people's financial decisions. At the time, though, being young and doubtless a little carefree, he was not particularly concerned about a group of farms in Somerset West. 'It did not seem to bother me,' he said, 'it is only lately that it has bothered me.'

Did Joseph de Wahl Sr defraud Joss and deprive him of a source of independent wealth inside the country? Joss insisted that he did, that it had happened before every South African had to have an identity document, and that he was able to do so because they had the same name and, Joss thought, he had always had his power of attorney. Anyway, he concluded, 'it is water under the bridge' and 'he is dead.'[4]

One cannot help but wonder whether Joss really did own those farms or whether Joseph de Wahl Sr was, all along, the legitimate owner. Irrespective of whether he was his foster father or father, Joss's relationship with Joseph de Wahl Sr, who was an auditor in Vryburg, was complicated. He rarely spoke about him and, although they had kept in touch on an intermittent basis, Joss never seemed close to him. Nonetheless, a few supportive letters, signed 'Pa,' remained in his possession. One is a strong letter to Joss's one-time landlady in Simonstown defending Joss against her plans to raise his rent. He also at one point settled a few pharmacy bills for Joss's medicines. He must have felt some obligation towards him because, as Joss put it, 'he gave me a large allowance and when he died it just stopped.'

Joss's tutor, Edward Winfield

Despite old man de Wahl's occasional presence in his life, it was clear that Joss needed more hands-on support. This came in the form of a tutor, Edward Winfield, who, along with his mother, was shipped out to South Africa lock, stock, and barrel. Joss assumed that this had been arranged because by then it had become clear that the original arrangement was no longer working and that the people he referred to as his 'foster parents' were no longer a couple, and possibly never had been. Joss interpreted Edward Winfield's arrival in terms of giving him 'an English pedigree and background.' Joss seemed impressed that 'his family had plenty of money,' that he was a 'Pennington Winfield and that the Penningtons had lived in the same house for several hundred years,' and that his mother had come with him. 'Why,' he asked, 'should the Honourable Mrs Winfield, who hated South Africa, be trekked out here with her servants, who hated South Africa even more? And why should they go to all the trouble to set up house here?'

So, while his foster parents were gently being pushed out of the main frame of the picture, Joss prepared to move in with Edward Winfield and his mother. Joss said that Edward Winfield had been a teacher at Eton and had been in Intelligence during the war but had been living in Paris immediately before moving to South Africa and setting up house at a property called Faraway in Constantia. 'He stayed with me for the rest of his life' and died in 1969. Constantia is a very old, rather affluent rural suburb approximately nine miles due south of Cape Town city centre. First settled in the seventeenth century, it was noted for its wine farming, with the most famous of its wine estates being Groot Constantia, which the Dutch colonial governor of Cape Town, Simon van der Stel, started in 1684. Beautiful old Cape Dutch homesteads with whitewashed walls and thatched roofs characterize much of the architecture of the area.

Joss had got to know Edward Winfield some years earlier because, as I mentioned in Chapter 3, he thought that he may have been the person who accompanied him to see Marie Louise on that fateful day when he hid Queen Victoria's teapot under the sofa. However, Joss did not move into the Winfield household right away because the Winfield family's arrival happened to coincide with Joss taking a much-needed break in Pretoria, where he had maintained connections with the Smuts family.

Street scene in Pretoria, with jacaranda in blossom.

Jan Smuts and his wife Isie lived in an austere single-storeyed house at Doornkloof close to Irene, which is between Pretoria and Johannesburg in the Transvaal. General Smuts (1870–1950), Joss averred, had fostered his love of Cape Dutch architecture and furniture. Joss recalled going there to have tea with Isie every Wednesday and sometimes staying for supper. General Smuts would sometimes join them and gave Joss his very first kumquat.[5] He also claimed that Smuts 'taught me most of what I know about Cape architecture'[6] and was a 'brilliant man.'

Joss was not, however, alone in commenting on General Smuts's brilliance. In 1970, Lord Todd, the then master of Christ's College in Cambridge, where Smuts had been a student, said that 'in 500 years of the College's history, of all its members, past and present, three had been truly outstanding: John Milton, Charles Darwin and Jan Smuts.'[7] One cannot get much higher praise than that, but it was for his knowledge of Cape architecture that Joss seemed to value Smuts the most.

Joss had always had a strong appreciation of art and had started to develop his own, albeit short-lived in his opinion, talent for drawing. He had, he claimed, taken lessons in Europe, and claimed to have met some of the world's greatest contemporary artists, including Salvador Dali (1904–89). He thought that Dali would 'go down in history as one of the two greatest artists who ever lived,' in 'the same class as Vermeer.' Joss spoke of having attended an exhibition in a 'funny little gallery in 42nd Street in the year dot' at which the only exhibit had been a pair of spoons that Salvador Dali had made with jade and silver and that Joss claimed to have bought. He thought that they 'must be terribly valuable,' but no doubt, like everything else, they had been lost or stolen and he wondered if they had been included on any lists.

In any case, Joss had decided to use his holiday in Pretoria as an opportunity to develop his self-professed gift for drawing but concluded that a combination of poor tuition and a motorcar accident had put an end to what might have been a promising career. Of his lessons with Jan Hendrik Pierneef (1886–1957), a well-known South African landscape artist, Joss could merely say that they destroyed whatever talent he had. While there is no reason to assume that great artists make good art teachers, Pierneef is reputed to be among the best of South Africa's landscape painters. I cannot, however, vouch for Joss's artistic talent because by the time I knew him he had stopped even trying to draw.

When Joss returned to Cape Town after his sojourn in Pretoria, Edward Winfield and his mother had settled into Faraway and were ready to devote the remainder of their lives to his welfare. As important as Edward Winfield had been in Joss's life, and he clearly took impeccable care of him and of his interests, Joss did not see him as being on an equal footing to himself. 'Edward Winfield was a tutor,' he said, and 'a tutor after all is an upper servant.' Did such a patronizing remark convey false bravado or a genuine sense of superiority? Whatever it was it did not show Joss in a good light.

Joss's friend, Rab Cecil

For Joss, the description 'equal' was reserved for his close friend Lord Richard Valentine Gascoyne-Cecil (1948–1978), nicknamed Rab, the son of Robert Cecil (1916–2003), the 6th Marquess of Salisbury. Rab's father had taken over the presidency of the Monday Club from his father, the 5th Marquess of Salisbury (1893–1972) and he, in turn, had been foreign under-secretary, paymaster general and dominions secretary during the Churchill government and later leader of the House of Lords. Rab's family had long associations with, and vast landholdings in, Rhodesia (now Zimbabwe). Its capital Salisbury (now Harare) was named after the 3rd Marquess of Salisbury. As mentioned earlier, Rab's grandfather, a staunch supporter of white-minority rule in Rhodesia, resigned from Macmillan's cabinet in the aftermath of the 'winds of change' speech and became the first president of the Monday Club. Joss met Rab in London in 1971 when Rab was 23 and Joss 34. Rab's career had by that stage taken him from Eton College to Sandhurst and then into the Grenadier Guards, with which he served three tours of duty in Northern Ireland.

Joss could not remember who introduced them – merely that it was an 'extraordinary young man whose name I cannot remember.' He did remember, however, that this 'extraordinary young man' was very friendly with Aly Khan and that they had all met at the Hard Rock Café in London, which at that time was clearly *the* place in London for people of that circle to frequent. Joss also remembered that he, Joss, had brought an ornate dog collar with him, which he claimed had once belonged to Catherine the Great, the eighteenth-century empress who, having deposed her husband Peter III in a coup, ruled Russia until her death in 1796. She was a ruthless woman and during her reign she greatly extended Russia's borders and brought the country into line with the other powerful European empires of the day. She is best remembered for her extraordinary sexual proclivities. Joss held that Wallis had somehow acquired the dog collar of Catherine the Great's Great Dane and that she had passed it on to him. He said it was made 'of gold mesh' and had an enormous square-cut emerald, the width of the collar, in it. They were all apparently looking at the collar when Rab asked whether they thought it would suit him. Then 'everyone suggested that he had better try it on' and it did in fact suit him admirably. Rab was still wearing the collar when Joss realized that he needed to go because he had agreed to meet Pauline Rothschild[8] at her flat in the Albany, 'I particularly say *the* Albany,' Joss said, 'because my father said it was pretentious to say Albany,' and he went off and 'forgot about the collar.'

Joss then deviated into a story about the origins of the first Hard Rock Café, which a couple of American businessmen started in London, and which was eventually developed into a worldwide chain of theme restaurants. Wholly implausibly and pompously, Joss held that the intention of the founders was to keep out the hoi polloi from the East End. He said that in those days, everybody was socialist and 'you could not keep the East Enders out of the right places,' so they made the Hard Rock Café look like an East End café. Consequently, 'even if you paid them, no East Ender would go there; they wanted to go to the Savoy Grill, Claridge's, or the Ritz. They just took one look at it and fled to a better caper in their own part of town.' However, because Rab was still wearing Catherine the Great's collar when Joss left the Hard Rock Café that evening, he made enquiries about where Joss was living and, later that evening, came round to North Row to return the collar and, according to Joss, they 'just clicked' and, despite their 11-year age gap, cemented a friendship that was to endure on both sides of the Equator until Rab's tragic and unexpected death in 1978.

> Rab was one of the nice things that happened to me. He was wonderfully supportive. It is strange really when one thinks of the people one has known. Some people you can say nothing bad about. I can really say nothing bad about Rab, even if I thought to. He was very special.

According to Joss, it was around this time that the two of them bought the Georgian house in Chelsea described in the previous chapter. When that failed to work out because, Joss laconically observed, the servants 'did not know where to shop,' Joss said that Wallis arranged for them to move to a Gothic house, 15 Waverton Street, in Mayfair, which Pauline Rothschild helped them decorate. Joss thought that, although not a decorator by profession, Pauline Rothschild 'was very clever, had wonderful taste,' and really did know what she was doing. He said that her flat at the Albany, which he thought was still there, should be preserved 'as a monument to her.' He went on to explain how she 'had 365 dinner services at Mouton-Rothschild,[9] one for each day of the year,' and that they were all antique and all outstanding. However, he lamented that there was no bedroom for Rab in the Waverton Street house, so he had to sleep on a couch in the library. He also mentioned that Mick Jagger,[10] lived next door.

By this stage Rab had abandoned his military career with a view to pursuing a life in politics. However, when he lost Barrow-in-Furness to the Labour candidate in the 1974 general election – he was, of course, standing for the Conservative Party – he stepped out of politics and turned to journalism. By now he and Joss had formed a close friendship and they were virtually inseparable. Unlike Joss, Rab took to South Africa like a duck to water and the two of them got into the habit of spending the English winters in South Africa and the South African winters in Europe.

Rab had strong family and political connections in Rhodesia, which he was able to evoke to gain special admission to events and places to which other journalists were denied access. Also, by the mid-1970s the conflict between the white settlers and black nationalists in Rhodesia was coming to a head. Consequently, for a swashbuckler like Rab, these were interesting times, but for Joss, the antithesis of an adventurer, his distaste for South Africa amounted almost to a phobia.

As he put it, 'I am one of the few people who has never liked Africa. Whenever the aeroplane wheels hit African soil, I think, "My God what did I get myself into?" I have never *not* felt that. I never ever wanted to come back to Africa.' Joss said that he wondered if Wallis's loathing for Africa had rubbed off on him. To me, he seemed unusually eager to identify with what he claimed were her opinions and it made me wonder if he could have been using it as a ploy to strengthen his claim that he was her son. If Wallis was his mother, perhaps she had fostered his distaste for his adopted country because it evoked unhappy childhood memories. By any reckoning, apart from those enjoyable days playing with Sophie, he could not have had many happy childhood memories.

Then, on the other hand, he might merely have preferred to live in a large, vibrant metropolitan city. Well, that at least was how he saw it. He did not enjoy outdoor pursuits. 'I am essentially a city person,' he said, 'which is rather sad because now I am stuck in Bredasdorp.' Then he again, as was his wont, evoked Wallis by saying that she was also 'a city person' and that neither of them even liked the English countryside and loathed the French countryside. He preferred beautiful buildings to rolling hills. In fact, as he put it, 'I have always preferred man-made things to God-made things. I love New York for instance; New York is very stimulating and super smart.' He also saw 'a lot of beauty in Paris.' So poor Joss never felt at home in South Africa and looked upon being there as a kind of banishment, a poor substitute for London. 'London is like a comfortable coat,' he said, 'I am quite happy there. I know my way around. I can still find my own world in London, but here I cannot. I am just completely shipwrecked.'

* * *

Nonetheless, shipwrecked or not, South Africa was where Joss was destined to spend a good part of his life, especially in his middle and later years. In the 1950s and early 1960s, before South Africa's stringent currency restrictions began to bite, various family friends brought bits and pieces from Europe to make his life in the country he so despised more agreeable. A rich mutual acquaintance of Wallis and Edward Winfield, who lived at Château Vernier in Geneva, in the Avenue Foch in Paris, and in Monte Carlo, used to come to South Africa most years and brought a lot of things for Joss on his yacht.

Rab Cecil also took it upon himself to amass and ship out various artefacts, which Joss claimed were his. Despite Joss's deep knowledge about and refined appreciation of art, furniture and *objets d'art*, he took little interest in how Rab procured the objects or from whom. He supposed, but was not even quite sure, that they were gifts from the Duke of Windsor, mainly pictures at first, but later silver as well, and that they came from a vast warehouse in Paris where they were being stored. Joss trusted Rab unreservedly to bring the right and most appropriate items for him but did not give the same leeway to Edward Winfield who, he said, 'really had no taste at all.' Joss implied that it was Rab rather than the Duke of Windsor who decided what to select from the warehouse because he said that 'the Fabergé was the only thing that my father ever gave me personally.'

Peter Carl Fabergé (1846–1920) was a Russian goldsmith and jeweller who moved from designing and manufacturing conventional jewellery to manufacturing fanciful golden Easter eggs and other ornate objects for the Russian and other royal families. The purpose of importing all these possessions from Europe, according to Joss, was not about the value of the silver and pictures *per se*, but about 'sitting at a table that was properly set or at least eating off plates that did not give one the screaming heebie-jeebies.' He clearly had a low opinion of the quality of goods available in South Africa because, as he put it, 'the trouble is really that I am so tired of the second grade and tawdry because it is not my scene.' Well, perhaps for those with as refined a genetic heritage as Joss was claiming for himself, any assault on their etiolated senses must have felt like torture.

Nevertheless, amid all this toing and froing between Europe and South Africa, Joss maintained his unique blend of utter disdain for worldly possessions and unqualified intolerance of anything that could be branded tatty, vulgar, or tawdry. No doubt, all this took place alongside lots of loading and unloading of yachts and containers, with or without the statutory bills of lading and mounds of paperwork one would normally expect to accompany such transactions. In my final chapter, I raise the question of whether these shipments could have been part of a more elaborate and illegal venture.

In 1972, three years after Edward Winfield died, Joss bought a magnificent, wooded, mountainside property over-looking the sea at Llandudno, a small seaside resort southwest of Cape Town, and there he and Rab set up house in fine style. Sakkie Seldom Inn, Robinson Avenue, Llandudno had acres of land and a magnificent view of the bay. It was later sold to Sol Kerzner (1935–2020), the founder of Sun City, the Las Vegas style gambling town in the former Bantustan of Bophuthat-swana, northwest of Pretoria.

Joss and Rab intended to run the Llandudno house in the grand style to which they had grown accustomed in England, and which befitted the aristocratic backgrounds into which they had been born. Although they 'did not spend the whole year in South Africa,' they still needed to make certain local adjustments. For example, their staff was 'terribly South African.' They had apparently 'once tried to bring Parker out,' but he was far too disdainful to tolerate such a hick backwater. 'We had Jean, who was an exceptionally good chef,' and they 'stole' their man-servant Ronnie from the Mount Nelson by offering to double his wages. Tessa Meltzer[11] secured them their head gardener, who was a Dutch woman and, according to Joss, 'so terribly butch that she made everybody else look like a sissy,' but he could not remember her name. At last, Joss claimed, 'things were just properly done' and even he took an interest in them. 'Rab took great interest.'

In fact, by this time Rab had become the driving force in Joss's life. He seemed able to turn their shared tastes and inter-ests into a mutually agreeable lifestyle, and Joss felt he could really trust and confide in him. A notable feature of Joss's character, however, was that, unless somebody else did things for him, they would be left undone. In fact, he was so unused to doing things for himself that he became virtually incapable

Approach to Sakkie Seldom Inn, Llandudno, Cape Town.

of action. He thought that this was because 'Edward Winfield was so over-protective. I was never taught to do anything and by the time I was expected to it was too late.' This did not matter when the people closest to him, such as Edward Winfield and Rab, had his best interests at heart. Inevitably, however, during his life he was to cross paths with people who went on to exploit him mercilessly. The slightly wider circle of friends with whom Joss began to associate included some who clearly saw in their association with him an opportunity to promote their own social and financial ambitions, about which Joss seemed naively blind. Whereas Edward Winfield and Rab Cecil had been unstinting in their total and unquestioned loyalty to him, they were not always around to protect him from various predators lurking in the wings.

Enter Leonora Pegram, friend of Jean Tromp

One such person was Leonora Pegram (née Schofield), whom Joss always referred to formally as Mrs Pegram, and we shall hear a good deal more about her. Joss could not quite remember when she joined his inner circle, but he seemed to think that it was around the mid-1960s when he was living at Clifton, a smart seaside resort on the Atlantic coast near Cape Town where the sea is bitterly cold, but the sunbathers cut a dash.

150

Joss met Leonora Pegram through Jean Tromp, which is probably why he so readily trusted her. As it turned out, however, their long and complicated relationship went horribly wrong, and Joss lived to regret having ever known her. According to Joss, Mrs Pegram had found her way into Jean Tromp's affections by regularly inviting her to dinner, which was a good ploy because, as Joss so often reminded me, Jean's own catering skills left a lot to be desired. By the time I got to know Joss, he would fume with anger whenever Mrs Pegram's name was evoked and would blame Jean, whom he accused of 'monstrously bad taste' and of being 'the most incompetent and incapable woman I know,' for having introduced him to Mrs Pegram in the first place. I suppose it does not count that Joss ranked among 'the most incompetent and incapable' men I ever knew. Be that as it may, Joss felt that 'being one of my own kind,' as he put it, Jean should have protected him.

It seems unfortunate that poor Jean Tromp, General Smuts's goddaughter, who obviously cared deeply for Joss, should have been so bitterly resented for having been taken in by someone whom Joss himself had trusted implicitly. Joss saw Jean as one of his own kind because, he argued, the association between their two families, the Playfairs and Windsors, had gone back a long way (as far back as the House of Saxe-Coburg-Gotha). He said that Jean's 'great, great grandfather was my great grandfather's tutor,' but then of course he was working on the assumption, or delusion, that he was indeed the great grandson of Edward VII. Apparently, Queen Victoria, whose mother was German and Albert, who was completely German, wanted their son to grow up as an English aristocrat and the prime minister of the day selected Lord Playfair of St Andrews,[12] Jean's grandfather, or perhaps even great grandfather, Joss was not sure which, to be the most appropriate person to assume that role.

Although Joss was a generation younger than Jean – she was born at the end of the First World War – she had clearly shared a lot of details about her private life with him. Perhaps partly because her marriage with Bob Tromp had been unhappy, she tended to cling, not only to Joss but also to various members of her own extended family who were scattered around the world. For example, Jean used to spend holidays in Spain with her aunt Chrissie, who had married into the Scott family, which had made a lot of money and lived in a substantial Victorian mansion in Eastwood near Nottingham in England.[13] She also often used to go and stay with her sister Olive Melrose. Because Jean had been ill with rheumatic fever as a child and been sent to the Playfairs' house in Scotland to recuperate, she would subsequently go there regularly for holidays until, she claimed, 'the war disrupted everything.' Nonetheless, as Joss explained, 'she still speaks to Oliver[14] on the telephone on a regular basis; he calls me the "Elephant Man", and she used to speak to her cousin Raymond, but he is dead now.' She also had close Playfair relatives in Canada. Joss thought that it was her father's younger brother who moved there, but Joss did not think that Jean had much contact with that branch of her family.

Another member of Jean's family was the playwright, Kate Playfair. She was the wife of Patrick (Pip) Playfair mentioned in relation to 'doctoring' the plane in which the Duke of Kent died, and had left Jean a whole lot of jewellery in her will, which Mrs Pegram subsequently tried to sequester out of her. Joss said that it was fortunate that he arrived on the scene just as Jean was about to part with this jewellery because Mrs Pegram had convinced her that it would help Joss.

* * *

Thus, each in their own way – Joss, Jean, and Leonora Pegram – clung steadfastly to whatever memories they could muster of the distinguished people from whom they were descended. Joss, of course, sought to claim the British royal family and if one counts his fictive American relatives, he had a financial advantage over them. Jean, for her part, whom Joss often belittled for being rather stupid, was descended from one of the cleverest scientists of his day. Nobody could have derided Baron Lyon Playfair for being a fool. He was a distinguished chemist, a government minister and one of the organizers of the 1851 Great Exhibition at Crystal Palace. He also had several prominent friends, including Prince Albert, whose son (Edward VII) Joss claimed he tutored. Leonora Pegram was not quite up there with Joss and Jean, but she too could hold her own in society. Her grandmother, who had left her a lot of money in trust, was from a family of successful nineteenth-century manufacturers, and the Schofields on her father's side were proprietors of a well-known department store in Leeds and nearby cities. She was also related to the Kynoch family – she had a Kynoch grandmother – and George Kynoch (1834–91), who had been a munitions manufacturer in Birmingham, emigrated from England to South Africa in 1888.

All three of them had led complicated personal lives and the two women seemed to look upon Joss as a surrogate son.

Jean's father was Henry (Harry) Lyon Playfair from Perthshire who, along with two of his brothers, had fought in the Anglo-Boer War[15] and later bought land from the Duke of Westminster[16] at a place called Westminster near Ladybrand in what was then called the Orange River Colony. There, her father both grew cereals and, on one of his farms, which Sir Herbert Baker[17] had designed for the Westminsters, he also had a dairy herd. As Jean explained, the Duke of Westminster only sold land to his friends. Her father also owned land adjoining that of their cousins, the Bowes-Lyon family at Glamis, where the late Queen Mother had lived as a child.

Irrespective of how she and Joss came to be friends, Leonora Pegram and other members of her circle were to become long-term fixtures in Joss's life in South Africa. Though Joss eventually regretted ever having got to know her, he was largely to blame for the situation. While he seemed to be able to maintain some sort of balance between his appreciation of beautiful objects and a certain distancing from material possessions, many of the people around him clearly felt differently. They found the temptations Joss dangled in front of them increasingly difficult to resist, especially since he was relying on them to make all his decisions for him. As we shall see in the next chapter, Joss had access to important assets, yet the objective circumstances surrounding his situation, the times through which he was living, the people he grew to trust, the arrogance of his class position, and the personality he formed, all worked against any ability he might otherwise have had to protect his interests. By his own admission, he had been poorly educated: 'I am not an intellectual at all, but a typical product of my class. We do not think very much of education, we do not think very much of anything except our own opinion, which is frightening.' He also admitted to being 'a very lazy person by nature' and never doing 'anything unless it is an absolute emergency.' He said, 'it was never considered a virtue in my world not to be lazy.' One hears about people who are not lazy, who are willing to work,' but he was clearly not one of those. Despite his straightened circumstances and the loss of just about all his worldly possessions, and certainly his loss of access to any of his assets, which most people would regard as a humbling experience, he retained all his confidence, arrogance, carelessness, and sense of superiority. He claimed never to have experienced envy or jealousy because 'I always feel that my position in people's lives is secure' and that what others say and do cannot change that. Nonetheless, there were times in his life when he did come close to despair.

While Joss certainly attached considerable significance to the family credentials of these two older women who seemed to be in competition for the position of most significant person in his life, I cannot help but wonder what might have been driving them, especially Mrs Pegram. Jean, who I got to know quite well, was relatively easy to understand and I have already described my impressions of her. However, having never met Leonora Pegram personally, to form any impression I have had to rely on copies of letters or faxes she had written, her taped telephone conversations with Joss, and of course the insights of my cousin Georgina – who had met her – as well as those of Joss and Jean. Needless to say, although they were all in agreement that her behaviour towards Joss was at the very least deceitful, and more than likely criminal, I have never been able to get to the bottom of her real motives. In other words, whose interests was she really trying to serve? Were they her own interests, Joss's interests, or those of a third party? And what had Joss and Mrs Pegram really been engaging in for all those years? Were these valuables with which they seemed so pre-occupied part of some shady import–export business they were operating to protect their wealth from the South African authorities?

Joss's centre falls apart

As the years progressed, the political situation in southern Africa began to seem increasingly more threatening for people like Joss and his circle of moneyed friends. The civil war that started in Angola in 1975 was particularly worrying. Not only was it being waged between pro-communist and anti-communist factions and thus, in the days before the cold war ended, presented a threat to world peace, but it was also a war in which the South African Defence Force became involved and, for the first time since the Second World War, it was faring badly on the battlefield. In November and December 1975, the South African troops in Angola took a bloody nose, inflicted mainly by Cuban forces in alliance with the People's Movement for the Liberation of Angola (MPLA). With conscription into the South African army compulsory for all white males and many being called to the front, levels of anxiety among white South Africans were riding high.

The collapse of white military supremacy was paralleled by a series of misfortunes in Joss's personal life. In the late 1960s and early 1970s, his comfortable world began to fall apart dramatically. The first blow came when Edward Winfield died in 1969 and, with his death, Joss lost his most assiduous protector. Then, in 1972, several blows came in quick succession. Not only did Joss's supposed father, the Duke of Windsor, die in that year but so too did his purported foster mother. These deaths he could somehow handle, but nothing could have prepared him for the sudden and tragic death of his closest and dearest friend, Rab Cecil in 1978.

Rab had gone to what was then Rhodesia to observe the guerrilla warfare that had been raging there since 1971 between African nationalists agitating for an independent Zimbabwe and the white supremacist supporters of the then prime minister, Ian Smith.[18] Rab was planning to make a television documentary about the Second Chimurenga (known to whites as the 'Bush War'), but even though he was wearing a press badge at the time, which Jane Beaverbrook (later Shand Kydd) had given to him, he was tragically shot at short range and killed, purportedly because the soldier firing the gun had been unaware of the significance of a press badge. The news devastated Joss. He was left lost, and ill-equipped to cope. And, to make matters worse, he had shown that he was vulnerable, which Joss regarded as a dangerous precedent. Because he had shown himself to be weak, he said, he believed that he was even more of a threat than he had been before because he had been 'taken in.' He compared his situation with that of wild animals, which destroy their weakest members to enable the herd to survive. 'It is strange,' he remarked, that 'probably the most civilized people use the most primitive methods to cope with their weak.'

Joss went on to describe how, on one occasion when he was having tea at the Ritz with Rab's sister Rose,[19] she described how she had gone to Greece in search of a lost relative, an alcoholic called Sebastian, but had failed to locate him because he had already left his last known address by the time she got there. Rose had apparently been taken aback by the poor impression the Greek people had formed of his family. 'Fancy leaving him there without money and without looking after him! It would never happen to their people,' and, said Rose, 'I dare say they are right.' No doubt, Joss concluded, 'the better one's birth, the higher the price one pays. At least the poor look after their own.'

As we shall see in the next chapter, Joss eventually came to realize that 'one must have a certain amount of aggression to survive – it would appear I have not got enough.' However, he continued, 'I suppose cultivated aggression would be like anything else pseudo; it would not be worth having.'

Joss was clearly struggling emotionally and was too effete to keep tabs on his money and belongings. Unfortunately, there were plenty of people around him who were only too willing to give him a hand in exchange for the vague promise of an eventual reward. This placed him in a demeaning position. Unlike the hero in William Ernest Henley's poem 'Invictus,' which Nelson Mandela had so admired, Joss may have been 'the captain of his soul' but, regrettably, he was never 'the master of his fate.'

7

Riches and Rogues

I HAVE MENTIONED in earlier chapters that at one point Joss appeared to have been the custodian of numerous priceless possessions, including jewellery and paintings, not to mention the named beneficiary in several mysterious, but well-endowed, trusts. As he had asked my cousin Georgina to recover and sell his possessions, I was made aware, with Joss's consent, of the extent of this extraordinary treasure trove. Lists and lists of goods appeared from the paperwork that Joss had squirreled away. Were these riches his, once his, or never his? Did he own the jewellery, furniture, and paintings he recorded, or had they merely passed through his hands? Did they even exist? How was I to evaluate the authenticity of the trusts, holding vast assets, of which he was the named beneficiary? The provisions of the trusts were often framed in legalese, which Joss himself certainly could not have written. Nor, given his limited ability to understand anything technical – a typewriter was well beyond his capacity – was there any way he could have forged the impressive letterheads of various firms of solicitors based in the UK and elsewhere. I spent many hours trying to unravel these conundrums.

Jewellery, furniture, and paintings

Joss's jewellery, his papers indicated, included a string of 75 ten-millimetre regular pearls which, he impressively noted, were the Colonna pearls, once owned by Julius Caesar, and a triple string of graded natural pearls that had once belonged to no less a person than Queen Marie Antoinette. He listed a large silver and platinum jewellery box inlaid with a 400-carat gold sapphire (Bohemian ruby) from Marie Antoinette's collection. There was a platinum and gold key watch fob that had purportedly belonged to his grandfather, King George V, and a brown ruby star sapphire ring set in gold. There was a brooch consisting of three large pink sapphires, four small pearls and one large pearl set in gold and small diamonds, which had belonged to Queen Mary. He recorded a diamond ring surrounded by rubies and 20 odd pieces of Fabergé that had once formed part of Queen Alexandra's collection.

For the benefit of readers who may be losing track of who is who among the various royal personages whose possessions had strangely trickled down into Joss's hands, Queen Alexandra (1844–1925) was Princess Alexandra of Denmark who, at the age of 16, was pinpointed as the future wife of the Prince of Wales, while Albert Edward ascended to the crown as King Edward VII on Queen Victoria's death in 1901. Joss also listed in his possessions a pure gold necklace that had once belonged to the last Empress of China, the Empress Dowager Cixi (1835–1908) who ruled over the Manchu Qing dynasty in China for 47 years until her death in 1908.

It is impossible to say whether these objects were once in his possession, let alone whether he was indeed the legitimate owner of all these valuable jewels with their unparalleled provenances. Much better documented, is that Joss had access to innumerable pieces of exquisite furniture and lots of paintings. Turning first to the furniture, on 28 October 1975, when Joss was still living at his house in Llandudno, which he had acquired in 1973, he received a letter from Chethams of 23 Bentinck Street, London W1A 4WR, saying: 'We have spoken to Mr Senior concerning the Ming thrones and other Ming Lacquer to be sold. Mr Senior has said that the £75,000, which you place as a minimum, is far too low.'

CHETHAMS   23 BENTINCK STREET LONDON W1A 4WR

JOHN A.FRANKS
LESLIE G.T. MITCHELL
PETER WESTLEY
DAVID DAVIES
STUART MONTLAKE
IAN T. EASDALE

Incorporating

Telephone 01-486 2111
Telegrams Chethams London Telex
Telex   24932 Chethams London
Cables   Chethams London W1

Your Reference

Our Reference JAF/JP/19908   28th October 1975

J. de Waal, Esq.,
Sakkie,
Robinson Avenue,
Llandudno,
Cape Province,
SOUTH AFRICA.

Dear Sir,

Sale of Furniture

We have spoken to Mr. Senior concerning the Ming thrones and
other Ming Lacquer to be sold. Mr. Senior has said that the
£75,000 which you place as a minimum is far too low. He is
of the opinion, in view of recent sales, that the items as a
whole are worth considerably more. As regards these items, before
we make any attempt to sell them, we think it advisable to have
them valued for insurance purposes to give us some idea of their
true worth. Furthermore, if, as these items appear, they are
worth considerably more than originally envisaged, the quickest
way of getting the best, or at least fair, price would be to
arrange auction of these particular items.

He has also handed to us your undated letter, the contents of
which we note and are dealing with accordingly.

Yours faithfully,

This is only one of many letters Joss received that clearly showed him as an active player in the world of collecting jewellery, paintings, and furniture. He was also the named beneficiary of a trust holding extremely valuable water-colours and oils. For example, on 17 November 1992 a Mr Mark Lea of Wilsons Solicitors' head office at Steynings House, Summerlock Approach, Salisbury, in Wiltshire sent Joss a signed fax stating that '500 paintings have been irrevocably ceded to the Jos de Wahl Trust. Only a small number have been authenticated and valued. The remainder are being seen

160

to and the lists will be sent to you as they come to hand.' The small number that had been authenticated consisted of the following:

Two watercolours by the Victorian English illustrator Myles Birkett-Foster (1825–1899) valued at £8000 and £12,000 respectively

Six watercolours by Eugène Boudin (1824–1898), who was one of the first French landscape painters to work outdoors, valued at a total of £300,000

One painting by the English Romantic painter John Constable (1776–1837) valued at £250,000

A watercolour by the English landscape painter David Cox (1783–1859) valued at £15,000

An English Romantic painting by John Crome (1768–1821) valued at £100,000

A watercolour valued at £10,000 by the British artist Peter de Wint (1784–1849)

Four watercolours by Sir Alfred James Munnings (1878–1959), two valued at £125,000 each and two at £100,000 each

A painting by the Scottish landscape artist Patrick Naismith (1787–1831) valued at £100,000

A painting by the Scottish Romantic painter Sir Henry Raeburn (1756–1823) valued at £200,000

Two painting by Joshua Reynolds (1723–1792) valued at £250,000 and £450,000

A George Romney (1734–1802) valued at £200,000

Two William Turner (1775–1851) paintings valued at £400,000 and £350,000 respectively

A John Varley (1778–1842) valued at £10,000

A Joseph Wright valued at £60,000.

Given that this fax pertains to only 25 out of a total of 500 paintings, and if one assumes that the rest of the paintings are of a similar value, the overall value of the paintings held in the trust must have been in the tens of millions. I have been careful to say that Joss was 'the custodian of' and again 'the named beneficiary of' – both expressions falling considerably short of the expressions 'the owner of' or 'the recipient of.' In the case of this fabulous hoard of paintings, Wilsons Solicitors were, presumably, the administrators of the trust. The company publicity proclaimed that 'Wilsons has built its reputation on a nationally recognised private client legal practice which deals in asset protection, trusts, succession [and] taxation.' The company also announced that 'Many of our clients have an international dimension to their interests and they benefit from our expertise in offshore work.' This was clearly an appropriate firm to look after the trust in question.

While the collection of paintings in the trust mentioned by Wilsons Solicitors was clearly out of Joss's immediate reach, nonetheless, judging from various documents I have examined pertaining to 1994 alone, Joss was the custodian of a large and valuable collection of paintings, furniture, jewellery, silver and porcelain. The paintings he had in his possession included original works by famous artists such as Charles LeBrun, Pieter Brueghel, Jan Vermeer, Diego Velásquez, van Rijn Rembrandt, Jan van Huysum, Thomas Gainsborough, George Romney, Sir Joshua Reynolds, Sir Thomas Lawrence, the miniaturist Samuel Cooper, Paul Sandby, Peter de Wint, Pierre Auguste Renoir, Pablo Picasso, Henri Toulouse-Lautrec, and Marc Chagall, among others. Joss was knowledgeable about and interested in art and furniture; in fact, he had a refined appreciation of all objects of beauty, especially man-made works of art.

If Joss was not a member of the royal family, one might ask, how on earth did he come to be associated with such incredibly valuable artworks? I certainly cannot imagine that his official father Joseph de Wahl Sr, an auditor (accountant) living in the agricultural town of Vryburg, would have had either the wherewithal to buy or the wish to acquire such

W. R. Harvey & Co (Antiques) Ltd.

FINE ANTIQUE FURNITURE & WORKS OF ART

5 Old Bond Street, London, W1X 3TA. Tel: 071-499 8385. Fax: 071-495 0209

J. De Wahl, Esq.,
14, Lourens Street,
Bredasdorp,
Cape Province,
South Africa.   10th. August 1994

Dear Mr. De Wahl,

We refer to our conversations of the past few months and are now delighted to
forward herewith the valuation of the paintings which were given to us by Mrs.
Pegram on May 15th. I apologise for the delay but as you are aware these matters
can sometimes be protracted. We would like to thank you for your promise to
reimburse us for all the expenses we have incurred upon your arrival and now look
forward to meeting you before too long.

Yours sincerely

A.D. HARVEY
Managing Director

Directors: W.R. Harvey, A.D. Harvey. Registered Office, RESTORATION & ADMINISTRATION
70 Chalk Farm Road, London NW1 8AN. Tel: 071-485 1504. Reg. No. 566633 England.
VAT Identification No. GB 233 4300 10

Evidence of Mrs Pegram's entanglement in Joss's affairs.

items, and so many of them. Certainly, from the few letters I
saw that he wrote to Joss, he did not sound like a loving father;
their tone was more one of exasperation than anything else,
and they concerned minor matters such as paying for medicines or intervening in a rental dispute between Joss and a
landlady. Why also, one wonders, was Joss being showered

with quite so many belongings? Were these gifts supposed to compensate for a loveless childhood? Or, alternatively, could he and Mrs Pegram have been engaged in some sort of racket? If not, what enabled her to become so intimately embroiled in Joss's financial affairs? Why, for example, does her name appear in so much of the correspondence pertaining to Joss's belongings? This seems to suggest that Joss had authorized her to act on his behalf and, if so, what exactly had he asked her to do? Were there other people behind her or was she acting alone? I suspect that Joss had taken her on board because he was too arrogant, lazy, and unskilled to do anything himself. Although he had several tutors over many years, he never emerged as what one might term a highly literate person. For example, he never developed an adult handwriting and when he did write something down, usually on the torn off inside of a pack of Gitanes cigarettes, it was always in block capitals.

He complained about having failed to keep proper records of his valuable possessions, and then excused himself by saying that 'my mother had this thing about having anything photographed' because she 'did not want articles written about the houses' in which she was living, so he, as he put it, 'sort of kept on the tradition.' He should, he conceded, have kept photographic records of his belongings, but was 'just so sort of lax about it.'

Significantly, I was unable to find a single bill of sale for the most valuable works of art among the documents I examined. (There were receipts and bills of sale for relatively trivial objects.) Joss, however, did have a friend who was concerned about his failure to keep proper records of his possessions and who offered to take photographs of his more precious paint-ings. This was a man called Shlovo Winnikow, who had some association with the World Diamond Bourse. As Joss explained, Shlovo photographed all the pictures, which he claimed included a Renoir, a Toulouse-Lautrec, and two Picassos,' but 'now the photographs have gone.' Where to?

One might ask, and why did Shlovo photograph them? Joss ascribed the loss of these photographs to the Duke and Duchess of Windsor's failure to provide him with a sound precedent. 'They had always had beautiful things' and, although they had cared *about* them, he did not think they cared *for* them. Joss was careless and, Joss felt sure that Shlovo Winnikow genuinely had his interests at heart.

Then, rather too late in the day because by then he had already lost everything, he started to hold forth about how each picture should be properly identified and 'photographed from various angles' and then a copy of the description kept in a different place because, as we shall see below, 'when a house burns down the photographs burn down with the pictures.' 'In Europe one had secretaries to do these things,' he lamented, but because the Windsors were so arrogant, he did not think that they 'listed or photographed' their possessions.[1]

In addition to the question of good record-keeping, acquiring so many precious pictures and valuables presented Joss with other practical problems. Given that he travelled extensively, he became dependent on finding safe and secure places of storage. In the days when Edward Winfield and his mother were alive, he used to leave them in Mrs Winfield's house for safekeeping. Some of his paintings hung on her walls and others he could leave in her cellar, which was 'a sort of strong-room' where they were quite safe. It is not unusual for wealthy South Africans to have a strongroom in their private homes – rather like a giant, walk-in safe in which the family might store its firearms or valuables too prized to be trusted to the gaze of the servants who were often, usually wrongly, assumed to be untrustworthy. In Joss's case the people who were dishonest were far closer to home.

The main culprit was Leonora Pegram. However, from Joss's behaviour at the time, it seems unlikely that he suspected her, for both his trust in her and their mutual friendship merely deepened. It was not until many years later and a lot more evidence of dishonesty that Joss began to recognize her true colours. Meanwhile, they became close friends and while Mrs Pegram was living at a farm called Firgrove in Constantia, Joss handed paintings to her for safekeeping. Joss admired her taste and felt that his possessions would be nicely offset against her own lovely paintings and furniture. Many years later, Joss realized that since 'all fortunes are made by means fair or foul,' her goal in life had been to become 'immensely rich' and that she probably 'amassed a better collection than anybody.' Not only did she have Joss's stuff, but she had 'really good stuff in her own house.'

However, he still failed to suspect her motives and felt uninhibited about entrusting his paintings, silver and porcelain to her for storage in a vault. She told him that she had placed his pictures and other *objets d'art* with a firm of financial advisers and trust managers in Cape Town and that they were secure in the firm's vault. (Though I know it well, I have omitted the name of this firm here.) Years later, she admitted to Joss that she had taken his possessions to England for safe keeping, but in the meanwhile he was under the illusion that they were safely in store in Cape Town, and he continued to trust Mrs Pegram.

Then Joss suffered another misfortune. On 23 March 1977, while he was out for dinner with his friend Henry Barrington, the house he occupied at Llandudno burned to the ground. South Africa is no stranger to bush and mountainside fires, and it is rare for the dry summer weather to pass without at least someone falling victim to this hazard. At the time, though devastated by the tragedy, Joss took it to have been a natural disaster. Later, however, he thought differently. As Joss's suspicions mounted, he subsequently came to believe that Leonora Pegram had removed the valuables before setting his house alight and then had let him assume that they had burned with the house. And these valuables, according to Joss, included six Gauguin paintings, which, Joss held, is reason enough to burn down a house.

Joss regretted very much that he had not kept proper records of the belongings he seemed to be losing at an increasingly rapid rate. As mentioned earlier, he recognized the value of keeping proper photographic records and Shlovo Winnikow, one of Wallis's friends and 'chairman of the World Association of Diamonds, or something terribly, terribly important like that,' had gone some way towards trying to help him protect himself better. Since I have no reason to believe otherwise, I am assuming that Shlovo Winnikow's motive was purely altruistic and that he wanted nothing other than to protect Joss. According to Joss, he was a wily man and had 'suspected that Mrs Pegram might want to steal the pictures,' which is why he went to the trouble of trying to ensure that they could be identified should the need arise. In fact, Joss claimed to have had a 'horrible suspicion' that Shlovo might have sent him the 'copies and descriptions' of all his pictures, but then, like everything else in his life, they had been mislaid, forgotten about, stolen or lost.

Unfortunately for Joss, by the time his Llandudno house burned down, Shlovo was already dead. He had been staying at the Palace Hotel in St Moritz in Switzerland when he broke his leg and complications had followed, probably a blood clot Joss thought, from which he never recovered. Joss described his death as 'a tragedy,' it is 'almost as if Mrs Pegram has got the luck of the devil.'

After her husband's death, Shlovo's wife, Sylvia, whom Joss claimed to know, albeit not very well, moved away and out of Joss's life. Joss said that she was an impressive woman in her own right. She had been with the United Metal Exchange in Cape Town and was 'the first woman to chair a company listed on the Johannesburg stock exchange and, I think, the first woman in history ever to ring the bell!' Shlovo had been her second husband. Her first was a member of the Smaller family and after Shlovo's death she moved her three Smaller children to Australia and continued to live between Israel, London, and Australia.[2]

Joss's trusts

At this stage of my investigation, the Jos de Wahl Trust administered by Wilsons was clearly the most munificently endowed. However, for the sake of completeness, I remind the reader that I recorded earlier in this book that throughout his childhood and until the mid-1960s Joss was the beneficiary of a trust, set up and administered by Graaffs Trust Ltd.[3] The existence of the Graaffs trust is perfectly explicable. Here was a young child in the care of a housekeeper, servants and his English tutor, Edward Winfield. All needed payment and the household needed to be maintained. Joss's claim that Mrs Billy Graaff was his foster mother is, indeed, reinforced by the existence of a trust administered by a well-established firm started by the Graaff family in 1905.

While it is reasonable to accept that Joss's finances and household expenses in South Africa were handled by a local family-linked trust, the picture gets murkier when we turn to his trusts located outside the country. Joss advanced several suggestions about why such trusts were created abroad, including at least one that was initiated without being completed. He was right in saying that the political situation in South Africa at the height of the apartheid period after the country declared itself a republic and left the Commonwealth discouraged many overseas investors and moneyed families from relying too heavily on depositing funds in, or sending valuable goods to, South Africa.

Where did the assets held by Joss's overseas trusts come from? Here, we are back straight into the core claim that Joss's parents were the Duke and Duchess of Windsor and they – more particularly Wallis – had gifted goods and money into trusts of which he was the beneficiary. Joss's account goes thus. Joss surmised that on the death of the Duke of Windsor in 1972, Wallis, who was to survive until 1986, began to think a little about Joss's circumstances. As I mentioned earlier, being lethargic and rather disdainful of money, in the later years of her life Wallis had entrusted her affairs to her lawyer, Maître Suzanne Blum (1898–1994), whom Joss trusted implicitly. In retrospect, Joss believed that Maître Blum should have looked after his money, but then she had not wanted to take responsibility for it because she herself was getting old and had suggested that the best idea would be to 'put it into a trust.'

At any event, Joss believed that Maître Blum had already set up a trust with him as the beneficiary, but that the trust deed had mysteriously disappeared and, despite reminders from Maître Blum for Joss to give his consent to the arrangement, he had never got round to it. Joss suspected a particular party (who to remain anonymous will be referred to here as Dirk) had stolen the trust deed – a servant had seen Dirk enter Joss's Bredasdorp cottage and rummage through his papers. However, Joss vented his anger not on Dirk, but on Mrs Pegram, who he claimed had encouraged the theft. He blamed Mrs Pegram for having brought Dirk into his life because, he said 'I am not really attracted to common people.' However, from what I can gather Joss could not bring himself to confront Dirk because he did 'not like scenes and it would have caused a scene, so I thought it easiest just to sit him out.' Did Joss's good manners and kind disposition prevent him from confronting Dirk even although he suspected that he had taken the trust deed and was convinced that he was working as Mrs Pegram's accomplice? Or was he not only a snob but also a coward?

Unhelpfully, Joss remembered little about the trust itself. He knew that it was going to be in one of the Channel Island banks but did not know which one. He also did not know whether it had been prepared by the London lawyer Mary Falk of Farrer & Company or by Coutts Bank. He also knew that it would not be on record anywhere because it was never signed. He knew that he had received a copy of it and that he had read through it, but because 'it looked terribly complicated,' he did not sign it. He then lost it, or Dirk 'must have pinched it.'

Joss then rather uncharitably began to speculate over whether the palace might have put pressure on Wallis to produce the trust deed because, he conjectured, it 'came just after Shirley Temple [Joss's nickname for Queen Elizabeth II] and company went to visit her.' Since Joss clearly enjoyed an occasional deviation into wild speculation, I shall make no further comment about that. Whatever the Duchess of Windsor's motivations or reasons, her assumed attempt to set up an off-shore trust for Joss never came to fruition because Joss failed to cooperate.

The 'American money': enter Bunny Mellon

Ignoring the Blum trust, which never materialized, Joss loosely described the source of the cornucopia of other trusts as 'the American money' to which his supposed mother had been heir. The enormous wealth that had lured the then Prince of Wales into his controversial marriage was firmly secured in the United States. This narrative centred on Bunny Mellon, who was married to the wealthy banker, Paul Mellon, but who was immensely wealthy in her own right (her father had been the proprietor of Gillette razors). Although Joss claimed to be on intimate terms with Bunny Mellon, he was muddled about her personal life and background, and seemed to presume that she was one of his mother's relatives on the Morgan side. On that front, Joss was quite wrong and, although Wallis and Bunny were clearly close friends and moved in the same moneyed circles in the United States, I can find no evidence of any genetic link between the two of them. Bunny (Rachel Lambert Mellon), who was born in August 1910, was in fact the daughter of Gerard Barnes Lambert and the former Rachel Lowe. When Bunny's marriage to her first husband Stacy Barcroft Lloyd ended in divorce in 1948, she married the banking heir Paul Mellon (1907–99) and together they became keen collectors of fine art. She, like Wallis, was a close friend of Jacqueline Kennedy and had helped her restore the house and gardens at the White House. Joss's vagueness about who fitted in with whom makes one wonder whether he was and had always been more of an outsider in Wallis's world than he wished to acknowledge.

However, be that as it may, according to Joss, the Duchess of Windsor turned to her American friend, who was clearly trustworthy, to take charge of her legacy. What Wallis failed to recognize at the time was that Joss was not necessarily going to want to cooperate with Bunny Mellon's plans for him. In any case, by the time it was evident that there would be a clash of personalities, Wallis had already handed her money to Bunny. Joss said that Maître Blum 'was horrified when she gave the money to Bunny.' However, given that Wallis felt unsure about what to do, Bunny's offer to handle the money came as a welcome relief. Joss found it easy to understand the motives behind Wallis's decision, for he too would have acted in exactly the same way.

The US money, Joss said, was not in a formal trust but given to Bunny Mellon for safekeeping for his benefit and she had discretionary rights over it. Although Bunny was willing to set up a trust for Joss and to let him live off its income, this took away his right to dispose of any of the capital as he saw fit. Bunny obviously was used to taking responsibility and had a strong sense of what was best for Joss. She wanted him to move to the United States and live in a fully staffed 30-roomed apartment in Park Avenue, New York. In exchange, he was to make over his entire fortune to the Morgan Trust or to the Windsor family. As he put it, Bunny 'feels that she wants me safely tucked away in the States out of harm's way, which is probably not a bad idea when one comes to think of it.' But Joss did not want to be tucked away out of harm's way and over this issue neither side seemed prepared to budge.

Joss felt that he could not appeal to Bunny because she was wary of sending him money in case it revealed his identity and whereabouts. Not surprisingly, she was also critical of how he had managed his affairs in the past. She disapproved of his South African lifestyle and friends and equated *her* guardianship of Wallis's money with *her* responsibility to ensure the secrecy of his identity. Although an American, she seemed to see her role as protecting the integrity of the British crown. Neither Joss nor Bunny was prepared to make any compromises, and this irritated them both, especially Bunny.

On one issue everybody, including Joss, agreed. This was that it would be unwise for Joss to have his entire fortune remitted directly to him in South Africa. He wanted Bunny to provide for him, but only on his terms. Bunny wanted to form a discretionary trust that went to all the heirs of George V, but Joss's objection to that was that it would strip him of his power to dispose of any assets after his death. As he explained, 'with *that* trust deed I would have had nothing to will, which is basically what I am resisting now. She is quite happy to implement *that* trust deed.'

Joss was determined to be the master of his own estate, and this was not only because he wanted to be able to show his gratitude to the people who had helped him during his life. He also needed access to his inheritance because, to put it crudely, he had developed a strategy whereby he secured the services and cooperation of people in exchange for either a valuable work of art, the guarantee of a percentage of the value of whatever they succeeded in retrieving on his behalf, or the promise of a substantial inheritance on his death. During his life, he made several such offers – the most enduring of which was his relationship with Leonora Pegram and her assortment of associates. To strip him of this weapon would deny him the only bargaining tool he possessed and, in any case, by the time all these discussions were going on, he was already deeply embroiled financially with Mrs Pegram, who had in effect assumed the role of his agent, guardian, protector and general factotum.

* * *

As he grew older, Joss sensed that plans were afoot to ensure that, at the time of his death, there would be no material proof that he had ever existed. It seemed unlikely that Joss would be allowed to die surrounded by an *embarras de richesses*. Instead, the possessions in his trusts would revert to the Windsors. Joss, however, did not want his estate to go to the Windsors. Somehow or other, partly because of his lazy privileged disposition, he had relinquished all responsibility for his affairs to Mrs Pegram and Bunny and he found it shocking that they were putting the interests of the British royal family before his own wishes and instructions. He then directed his vengeance towards Jean Tromp, who he believed should have protected him from Mrs Pegram when Wallis was still alive, and Bunny who 'is behaving in the most shocking fashion, and, to make it worse, she also believes that she is right.' Although Joss clearly found Bunny's recalcitrance infuriating and unreasonable, he had no doubts about her integrity because he knew that she would ultimately comply with his wishes. Poor Joss, he got that one wrong. Joss started to question Bunny's judgement and wondered whether it was being clouded by all the psychiatrists she was seeing, and towards whom Joss expressed a rather low view. Nonetheless, irrespective of Joss's view of psychiatrists and Bunny's reliance on them, he was in no mood to fall in with her or anyone else's plans for his inheritance. 'They are hoping that I will play ball, but I am not going to. I am not obliged to leave it to the Windsors. It is legally mine and I am not obliged to leave anybody anything,' and he continued, 'I cannot work with Bunny because she just dictates to me.'

With two such determined characters at loggerheads, both Joss and Bunny dug in their heels. Bunny then adopted a new strategy. Unless Joss agreed to things being organized *her* way, the money would remain right where it was, under her thumb in the United States. Joss was going to be made to experience poverty for the first time in his life. Predictably, he responded with equal recalcitrance. 'Money,' he said, 'is only important to the poor, the rich live very modestly.' He called worshipping money a sickness. 'Money,' he said, 'does not bring happiness or peace of mind.' 'All money brought me,' he said, 'was Mrs Pegram.' In other words, he was implying, but was too polite to say, 'keep your bloody money.'

Local dosh, local rogues

With the trust deed drawn up by Maître Blum in France down some rabbit hole, and Bunny Mellon holding on tight to his 'American money,' Joss was forced to resort to his local resources. In addition to furniture, some paintings and jewellery, these resources comprised gold bullion, British pound notes and US dollars, which he kept in a vault at the Trust Bank in Cape Town. The bullion had, he recalled, been a gift from his so-called 'foster father.' The notes, however, were acquired illegally through a private arrangement with one of Rab Cecil's banker friends who agreed to change South African money into British pounds and US dollars as they came into the country. In other words, Joss was committing quite a serious offence by illegally buying foreign exchange. This reflected the context of the times, when during the war in Angola in the 1970s, members of the rich white elite were very jittery about the stability of South Africa. On the advice of a friend who announced that assets in the banks in Angola were frozen when the country achieved independence from Portugal, Joss decided to take his bullion and money out of the bank's vault and, instead, place it in Mrs Pegram's strongroom. Although Joss's dollars and pound notes were in large denominations, he still needed four containers – two briefcases and a couple of tin trunks – to transport his cache from the bank in Cape Town to Mrs Pegram's house in Constantia. Although such arrangements now sound bizarre, the lengths to which some people were prepared to go to evade the South African Revenue Services may be illustrated by a personal experience. About to board an international flight from what was then called Jan Smuts Airport in Johannesburg, I observed an accountant of our acquaintance looking uncomfortable and sweating profusely. When my husband and I solicitously asked him if he was alright, he shushed us explaining that he was carrying several belts of Kruger rands (gold coins) under his clothing. Perhaps it was just as well that there were no beeping electronic wands in those days!

To return to the narrative, from 1992 onwards, Joss's financial world imploded when Mrs Pegram told Joss that the bullion and money he had left in her care had 'disappeared.' Nonetheless, she declared in writing that she owed him a debt of £1 million, but claimed to be unable to pay it to him immediately. Instead, she drew up a will leaving her entire estate to Joss and appointing him as her executor. Amazingly, perhaps because pursuing a legal claim against her would raise difficult questions about where he got the money from in the first place, Joss agreed to the arrangement.

The next misfortune in 1992 involved Joss becoming implicated in a criminal prosecution arising from Mrs Pegram having failed to return a Patek Philippe watch and a string of pearls that she had 'borrowed' on approval from Murdocks, a well-established jeweller in Adderley Street, Cape Town. Apparently, these items had once belonged to Joss. Although Mrs Pegram eventually returned the items to the jeweller and the criminal charges were dropped, she took the trouble to draw up an extraordinarily pompous affidavit to clear Joss's name. It read as follows:

Arising out of the retention by myself of the said items of jewellery apparently for a period in excess of the time frame expectations of the said jewellers they preferred criminal charges against me which implicated the said

175

Joseph de Wahl in the investigations which were carried out by the South African Police. I emphatically aver that since the said Joseph de Wahl bore no personal knowledge of my transaction with the said jewellers, he was unjustifiably implicated in the said criminal prosecution. In retrospect I realise that I was simply used by Murdocks Jewellers and persons unknown to me as a cat's paw and I deeply regret that the said Joseph de Wahl was implicated, more especially since he would not normally even come into contact with individuals of that class. The said Joseph de Wahl is a trusting person. In my view he is defenceless, and I consider that it is the duty of the community to protect him from unscrupulous, opportunistic and designing people.

Given that Mrs Pegram was the guilty party, it is perplexing in this context why she should feel the need to accuse the jewellers and their unnamed, apparently lower-class, allies of unscrupulous, opportunistic, and designing behaviour. Her defence of Joss was also indicative of their complicated relationship. They became so co-dependent on each other's finances, possessions, various business deals and finally, emotions, that it becomes well-nigh impossible to unravel the various strands of their complicated web of dealings.

In the early 1990s, Leonora Pegram brought another player onto the scene when she introduced Joss to a person who worked for one of Cape Town's many finance houses. To anonymise his identity, I shall merely refer to him as Joss's financial adviser. I have established that Mrs Pegram had a modest investment trust managed by the finance house concerned, so this was the basis of the introduction. Joss and his financial adviser formed a strong friendship, but in time it was to turn very sour. According to Joss, though the person in question came from a modest background, he had done well for himself and had married into a well-established and respectable Cape family, with quite a lot of money and a sub-stantial and incredibly beautiful Cape Dutch property in Cape Town.

So, where did it all go wrong? Well, to cut a long and rather sordid story short, the financial adviser, like Mrs Pegram, had offered Joss a safe home for his furniture, but went further in offering to lend him a small house on his property in which to live. Then, in May 1992, in a rather impulsive act of trust, Joss gave him his power of attorney. In September that year Joss told him that he wished to retrieve 20 pieces of jewellery from the Standard Bank in the Cape Town suburb of Kenilworth. He had deposited the items in two strongboxes on 16 October 1986 and had a receipt for them. Unfortunately, he confided in the wrong person. The financial adviser offered to accom-pany Joss on this mission and the two of them set out in the former's car on the short 15-minute journey to Kenilworth, where Joss retrieved the two strongboxes, for which he alone had the keys.

On their return journey, the two men started to quarrel. In retrospect, Joss believed that his financial adviser had manu-factured the row to get rid of him for a while. In any case, Joss got out of the car to find his own way back, while his adviser drove on with the strongboxes still in it. By the time Joss had calmed down and returned home, the adviser had got a lock-smith to open the boxes, which, he told Joss, had been empty. This jewellery was never retrieved, though both Joss and Leonora Pegram insisted that the adviser had kept it for himself. I have seen the bank receipt for the boxes and have a list, provided by Joss, of the 20 items of jewellery that had vanished (though that, of course, cannot be independently verified).

Joss also found himself in a protracted dispute with this financial adviser over some furniture that he had left in a store-room on an estate managed by the finance house. Most of these items were auctioned and Joss was paid out, but some were held back for private sale to the adviser. Again, Joss was paid, but he insisted that the adviser had not paid anything near the market value and had behaved in a deceitful way. The dispute eventually reached the head of the finance house in question, and I have seen a letter from him insisting that the adviser had behaved properly, and that the matter was closed. To provide some balance here, it must be remembered that Joss had been occupying a house at the adviser's invitation. It is possible that Joss had wrongly assumed that this was a rent-free arrange-ment and that his adviser had decided to appropriate payment in kind in lieu of rent.

Joss's wealth slips away

It is difficult to recall a riches to rags story that happened quite so quickly. One thinks perhaps of the Yorkshire woman, Viv Nicolson, who decided to 'spend, spend, spend' when her husband won the pools in 1961. She managed to dissipate their fortune in a few years. Except for some travel, Joss did not even have the satisfaction of living it up. Because both Leonora Pegram and the financial adviser were able to spin convincing stories, they successfully managed to retain their friendship with him for years while simultaneously denuding him of his possessions. It took Joss some time to realize exactly what had been happening, especially vis-à-vis Leonora Pegram and, because of his innate distaste for confrontation and professed lack of materialism, it took him even longer to want to strike back. Joss was neither a fighter nor a strategist, which were traits he perceived as beneath his dignity. Instead, he merely withdrew into increasingly severe bouts of depression. In the early days, Joss also had loyal and reliable protectors, most notably his tutor Edward Winfield, his friend Rab Cecil, and his claimed natural parents, the Duke and Duchess of Wind-sor. Now they were all gone.

At this point, I should perhaps stand back a little to ques-tion to what extent Joss himself may have been partially complicit in what was going on. Because of his laziness, carelessness, and perhaps misplaced trust, it was all too easy to separate him from his invaluable possessions and quite considerable wealth. The long and short of it all is that, in one way or another, between the mid-1980s and early 1990s just about all Joss's local resources – pictures, jewellery and money – had disappeared or found their way out of South Africa.

Why out of the country? In South Africa, it had by now became apparent that the days of white supremacy were numbered. While politicians were busy murmuring about the possible terms of Nelson Mandela's release from prison, asset-rich white South Africans huddled together to devise ways and means of protecting their wealth from what they had now come to fear as a calamitous shift to black-majority rule. Nobody could yet fathom quite how peaceful the transition would be, or quite how willingly the former white supremacists would shake the hands of their black compatriots, concede that apartheid had been a mistake and promise to open their hearts to the new rainbow nation. Joss shared the white elite's anxieties about the end of apartheid, and this provided an opening through which his so-called 'friends' and 'protectors' could manipulate his passivity and fears. Since he seemed incapable of doing anything for himself, his friends would protect his wealth on his behalf. Again, Joss's health was deteriorating, which increased his emotional dependence and prevented him from seeing the writing on the wall. Though disillusionment finally dawned, for a long time he retained an almost childlike belief in the basic goodness and integrity of those around him.

8

Creeping Doubts,
Old Patterns

A T THIS STAGE of my investigation, I had serious doubts about the veracity of several of Joss's claims, and at moments thought that he must surely be a serial liar. This was mainly because neither the story of Wallis's visit to South Africa in 1947, nor Joss's tale of his intimate association with the Rothschilds seemed at all credible. I was also feeling somewhat impatient with him and was trying to work out whether my negative assessment was influenced by my irritation rather than any objective judgement. Partly because my husband, Robin, and one or two close confidantes urged me to do so, on one visit to Bredasdorp I surreptitiously removed a few hairs from Joss's hairbrush in the bathroom for DNA analysis. I was uneasy about my deceit, but my mortification was complete when I found a forensic scientist in Cape Town willing to look at the hairs. He was openly scornful. 'There are no follicles here,' 'What am I supposed to compare the DNA with?' and 'Where is your reference sample?' were just three of his sneers. I humbly had to admit that my education in science was sadly deficient.

Feeling somewhat humiliated, I decided to stick to my own form of historical and literary investigation and look again at the questions I had set myself at the beginning of my quest. How plausible was his claim that he had the form of porphyria that ran in the royal family? Where did he acquire his very upper-class English accent and mannerisms and how did he know so much about the royal family? Also, why did Jean Tromp continue to validate his story so firmly and never seem to harbour any doubts about its authenticity? True, I knew a great deal more about his custodianship of items of jewellery, paintings, and furniture, but their provenance and current locations were still far from clear. And now I added Leonora Pegram to my list. I never in fact met her – she had already moved to the UK by the time I met Joss, so I was in no position to judge her myself, but I did listen to a lot of tape recordings of her phone calls to him. From these and from Joss's account, she seemed to come across as almost a pantomime villain who could reach her long fingers into his bags of valuables and then with one puff make them bafflingly disappear into thin air. Had I understood her behaviour and motivations? I come back to all these matters later, but in this chapter, I first consider two issues, the question mark around Joss's porphyria and another twist to the saga of Joss's overseas trusts, both of which led me to reconsider my tentative judgement that Joss was a liar. Then I update the story with yet another bout in the series of one-sided boxing matches between Joss and Leonora Pegram, this time involving the police.

Porphyria

Although Joss claimed that he was formally diagnosed with the disease in 1981, I had not seen any medical evidence of this diagnosis in black and white. This is important because the disease is quite rare (only about five in every 100,000 people ever develop it), but it is much more prevalent in the British royal family through its genetic connections to various European houses. The royal connection starts with a retrospective diagnosis centring on George III (1738–1820) and an assertion that his well-documented 'madness' was induced by porphyria. His 'madness' took the form, inter alia, of a non-stop 52-hour monologue, uttered before he collapsed and died. The word 'porphyria' itself is of Greek origin and denotes the colour purple, reputedly the colour of George III's urine and a key indicator of the disease. Some medical scientists doubt the validity of this retrospective diagnosis, but the theory was given considerable publicity by an Alan Bennett play, *The Madness of George III* (1991) and its subsequent adaptation into a film, *The Madness of King George* (1994).

Princess Charlotte Augusta of Wales, Queen Victoria's eldest daughter, her daughter (Princess Charlotte of Prussia), and Charlotte of Prussia's daughter Princess Feodora of Saxe-Meiningen were all said to have suffered from the disease. Other known royal sufferers included Frederick the Great of Prussia, Adelaide of Prussia and, notably, Prince William of Gloucester (1941–1972), the Queen's first cousin, who died so tragically while competing in the Goodyear International Air Trophy near Wolverhampton. Nor should we forget Anastasia Romanovna (1530–1560), wife of the Russian tsar Ivan the Terrible who, despite her ill health, nonetheless still managed to produce six children in her short thirty-year life. Joss said that he suffered from the same strain of porphyria as King George III, though he had not seen the film, which had been on general release some years earlier. Although I cannot find any published evidence of this, Joss also claimed that the Duke of Windsor's brother Henry, the Duke of Gloucester (1900–74) had also been a porphyria sufferer. Joss said that Henry 'did not try and fight the depression,' which is an inevitable side effect of the disease, 'but just locked himself up, which I suppose is one way of dealing with it.' Joss claimed that since he was only diagnosed with the disease after the Duke of Windsor's death, he did not know much about its incidence in the royal family, for it was not something he recalled discussing with him.

The symptoms of porphyria can be extensive and variable. They include severe stomach pain, painful urination, patches of numbness, tingling and burning, loss of strength in the muscles, an abnormally high heartbeat, high blood pressure, excessive sweating and sometimes even a tremor. The symptoms also affect the patient's psychological wellbeing in that anxiety, depression, nervousness, hallucinations, delirium and even seizures are not uncommon side effects of the illness.

On several of my visits, I nagged Joss to provide some proof of his diagnosis. He was characteristically vague, but on one occasion pointed me to an untidy assortment of notes, letters, papers, and memos where I might find something. Bingo! I turned up a faxed letter from his physician, Dr Daniel Milne of 43 Kerkstraat, Bredasdorp, dated 28 August 1997, describing the state of his health. Addressed 'To whom it may concern,' here it is in full:

> With this letter I confirm that I, Dr Daniel Milne, examined the 60-year-old Joss (Joseph) de Waal and found the following. He is obese (mass 129 kg); he suffers from chronic intermittent lumbago (backache) and nerve compression as a result of his backache in his left leg. He has a hereditary type of porphyria, namely Acute Intermittent Porphyria, which also gives him a high blood pressure from time to time. He uses Adalat 10 mg for that. He walks with great difficulty because of his back. He also suffers from insomnia (sleeplessness) and depression, which can fit in with his porphyria picture.

Given that porphyria is a rare inherited condition, this letter made me wonder what the chances were of randomly inheriting it. Could this concrete proof of his porphyria authenticate his royal connection? I previously had no idea there was such a profession as a porphyrinologist, but despite my lack of any formal medical training, I tried to grapple with several medical papers on the subject. I will not cite all of them (they are not exactly page-turners), but I think this is a fair summary of what I discovered.

Joss claimed that he suffered from the 'Swedish variety,' which was not much of a clue, as there are seven forms of the disease in Sweden, but the most common is indeed, the acute intermittent porphyria his doctor diagnosed. There is no evidence that the doctor took samples from Joss, so I assume that his diagnosis was based on manifest or reported symptoms. Non-South Africans might also question the verdict of a doctor in a small rural town, though I discount this possible concern. Medical education in South Africa is of the highest quality as many patients of South African-trained doctors in leading hospitals in London, Toronto and Houston will testify. Dr Milne probably got it right, but whether this indicated a royal connection is less certain.

The uncertainty arises on the other end. The retrospective finding on George III's illness at first identified acute intermittent porphyria (Joss's version), but the same, medically unqualified, writers subsequently asserted with equal vigour that George III was suffering from the milder form, variegate porphyria.[1] Again, Prince William of Gloucester, whose tragic death I mentioned, also had the variegate variety. As for the rest of the long list of members the European royalty, question marks remain – as the known aetiology, exact definition and conclusive tests did not exist at the time. There is one final and further complication. Without tests, it is possible that Dr Milne got it wrong. Joss certainly had porphyria, but whether it was securely diagnosed as the acute form is less certain. If he suffered from variegate porphyria it would also be more statistically likely in South Africa, where what is called a 'founder mutation' of variegate porphyria was introduced by a Dutch settler in 1688. There are between 30,000 and 40,000 South Africans with variegate porphyria, most of them of Dutch ancestry.[2]

Overseas trusts again: enter Patrick Guinness

While confirmation of Joss's porphyria does not conclusively demonstrate a royal connection, the coincidence is, to say the least, interesting. My doubts about Joss's story were challenged a second time when, while probing his paperwork, I came across the proposed creation in 1988 of yet another trust, this time of an eye-watering magnitude. The proceeds of the trust, excluding valuables, was to consist of the astronomical sum of £1000 million, to be paid in four instalments over a period of four years, namely £250 million a year. Supposing it is not a forgery, and large as this sum was, the arresting feature of the document is in its list of trustees. Mrs Leonora Pegram was there (surprise, surprise), but so too were Philip Sapsford (one of Britain's most reputable and distinguished QCs) and, even more remarkably, Patrick Guinness. Either Allen & Overy, or Farrer & Company, both highly regarded firms of London solicitors, were to draw up the agreement.

I need to linger on the name Patrick Guinness, as there are at least two Patricks with the Guinness surname. This one is Patrick Desmond Carl-Alexander Guinness, son of Desmond Guinness and grandson of Diana Mitford/Mosley. He is a well-published Irish historian, a financier and, of course, a prominent member of one of the most renowned Anglo-Irish families with all the elite connections that that entails. In a somewhat bizarre item on his Wiki page, someone has calculated that Patrick Guinness is 2259th in line of succession to the British throne. Though he has royal connections, I fear it would take a lot of people with porphyria to give him half a shot at the top job. Assuming the documents are authentic, the correspondence with Patrick Guinness commenced in mid-1988. Later that year Mrs Pegram, Patrick Guinness and Philip Anthony Sapsford provided the first draft of the trust document, an amended version of which was sent to Joss on 7 December 1988. At the same time, Patrick Guinness sent a telegram to Joss saying that he had introduced Philip Sapsford to Mrs Pegram and that the 'Assets should be in her control as settlor prior to control of trustees.' The cache of correspondence dried up for a while, then recommenced in mid-1990. I reproduce below just two of the many faxes going to and fro between Leonora Pegram and Patrick Guinness at that time.

Patrick Guinness Esq.
FAX NO. 242 - 742
DUBLIN
IRELAND

Dear Patrick

This is the Trust Deed that is wanted. The American connection also wants this and do not want it changed in any way either, otherwise the money and assets will not be forthcoming. I am sorry this is what they want. They do not want a lot of legal jargon and they made this quite clear. The sum is very substantial coming from that source. We all want to be able to read and understand the Trust without having to have a solicitor present - Jos's American cousin says an English Judge told her a Trust Deed need only be one page long and contain no legal phrases - Jos says he told you this the one time you two met in London and you confirmed this.
Nothing in the Trust Deed must contradict or interfere with Clause 5 and 6 as the family is reluctant to lose control of the money and it is only being put in trust because Jos de Wahl is a South African citizen - there will be no problem that he can forsee. We are all civilised people and on his death he can instruct trustees to use their own discretion, if he feels the beneficiary is not capable of instructing (he can cancel Clause 5 and 6 out if necessary at any time or change it to a more normal trust clause by simply writing a letter) but at this stage it is the condition of the American settlement.

I have to make it a condition of our agreement that the Trust Deed is drawn up by All n & Overy or Farrer & Co or Maxwell Batley or Farriers (all solicitors in London) - it is also a condition that you and Philip Sapsford be co-trustees - the Bank to be other trustee - and receive 50% of trustees remuneration - I would deem it a great favour if you could get one of the above solicitors to fax me a copy of trust deed as soon as it is completed (if it is satisfactory). I would then be prepared to give the bank my power of attorney which can be faxed out here to collect various valuables lodged in London as well as £ 1,000,000,000 (One thousand million pounds) which is to be paid to me in 4 instalments over 4 years - the first instalment of £250,000,000 (Twohundred and fifty million pounds) is already available and is being kept for me by my cousin in Yorkshire. I have already had some negotiation with Coutts and Miss Mary Falk of Farriers, who I tentatively asked to draw up the Trust Deed so you better cut them out, but as Jos wants you to do the trust you had better renegotiate and pick a solicitor.
I have to insist on a bank and the above solicitors as this is a condition of both my settlement (which I had to get out of a Trust) and the American settlement - which will come at a later stage, but is intended to go into this Trust - you will still be able to protect Jos's interests and ½% of a thousand million is not to be sneezed at - Jos feels that you and Sapsford should be entitled to the full remuneration, but this is not possible as the bank will want their 50%.
The agreement is also subject to the trust being made and being fully operative within 30 days hereof. By fully operative I mean, signed, sealed and delivered and registered with no inee account fully operative.

Fax sent from Leonora Pegram to Patrick Guinness
on 5 July 1990.

PICKERING FOREST, CELBRIDGE. CO. KILDARE.
TEL. 01 · 627 2568

MRS. L.L.PEGRAM
c/o P.O. BOX 6
CALEDON

Fax No. 0251 41136   7 July 1990

Dear Leonore

Thank you for your fax of 5 July concerning the proposed
trust for Jos de Wahl. I have spoken with several large
institutions who can assist in line with the requirements.

At this stage I will need the last two certified accounts
for the trusts in the U.S.A. and Yorkshire, along with
letters from the trustees confirming that you and Jos are
beneficiaries. Also, their bankers must confirm that the
funds are "clean and clear" (unencumbered). In view of
the requirement to close by 5 August these details must be
faxed to me as well as posted.

Some further thoughts at this stage:

1. The proposed trust powers and objects can be met by an
English trust with a letter of instruction alongside. May
I suggest that it be drafted by Travers Smith Braithwaite,
a respected City firm? I will need a modest sum to cover
the costs involved.

2. The Surety Bond is unusual in that all banks in the U.K.
are closely supervised by the Bank of England. It will be
based on the trustee bank's undertaking to keep the funds on
deposit. The risks are internal fraud and collapse; the
former would be met from reserves and the latter by a life-
boat fund. Failing these, Lloyds would then be obliged to
pay the amount covered.

3. Currently a life interest trust as proposed would suffer
inheritance tax in the U.K. However, we can restructure the
trust after five years once Jos has his U.K. passport.

The procedure should now be:
    --Details to me from the current trustees
    - The trust drafted to your approval
    - Appointment of the trustee bank
    - Purchase of the Surety Bond
    - Signing and sealing the trust Deed

My 'phone line is down but I can be reached on 01.628 8205
next door. I will be in London later this week and it will
help if the trustees' faxes have arrived by then.

Kind regards to you both.

Patrick Guinness

PATRICK GUINNESS

Patrick Guinness's reply to Leonora Pegram's fax about
setting up a trust for Joss.

187

That Mrs Pegram had inveigled her way into the very heart of Joss's financial arrangements, was to benefit financially from the arrangement, was now on first-name terms with none other than Patrick Guinness and was holding forth about the terms and conditions of the trust as if she were an authority on the matter, could not have happened without Joss's knowledge, say so, and blessing. In addition, how and under what provisions were they planning to get Joss a British passport?

However, after a period of initial optimism on Joss's part, the whole structure started to crumble. Yet another castle in the sand! Joss grew increasingly resentful and wrote to Leonora Pegram in some exasperation. He said that her presence aggravated his illness and that she was 'a confused, bitter woman' who could not speak the truth, or at least distorted the truth for her own ends. 'Your one aim in life,' he wrote, 'is to keep me in bondage and you have turned me from a positive person … into a snarling incoherent animal.' He then went on to admit that he had lost the blueprints that he had asked her to read to Patrick over the telephone and wondered if he had taped them. Could she also sound him out on what the 'baubles' are worth, and this time, 'perhaps you will tell him the truth,' he concluded.

Joss was growing increasingly distressed and clearly not thinking straight. In some desperation, he decided that the only way to deal with Leonora Pegram was to offer her a massive inducement to get the trust established. On 19 July 1992, while still staying at the Cape Town property provided by his financial adviser (whom we met in my last chapter), Joss signed a declaration to the effect that 'I, Joss de Wahl undertake to cede 10 per cent of my income to Mrs Leonora Legge Pegram on condition that she creates a trust fund for me (the value of said trust to exceed £5,000,000 (five million pounds British sterling).' He then went on to say that the gift, which he called 'an *ex-gratia* payment' was subject to her setting up the trust within 21 days.

According to the documentation I scrutinized, there was no doubt that Leonora Pegram was trying hard to get the trust established and had secured the full cooperation of both Patrick Guinness and Philip Sapsford. However, any trust needs capital to commence operation and, apparently, Bunny Mellon quite sensibly refused to release the US funds so long as Mrs Pegram was involved. Leonora and Bunny had taken an instant dislike to one another, presumably, Joss thought, because Mrs Pegram was too transparent in her wish 'to get hold of the Morgan money,' and, Joss went on, 'Bunny has consistently refused everybody access to it.'

With such fabulous sums of money being bandied about it is little wonder that the failure of the trust to materialize was a bitter disappointment to Mrs Pegram. That this trust, like at least two others before it, turned out to be chimerical was no surprise to me. What I wondered was why Patrick Guinness (and an eminent barrister whom he had recommended) went along with the plan for so long. Was Leonora Pegram unusually persuasive? Or did his involvement derive solely from him diligently carrying out his role as Sotheby's representative in Ireland?

Joss vs Leonora: next round

I now need to wind the clock back to 1989 when, with an atypical display of energy, Joss decided to travel to London to track down those of his possessions that Mrs Pegram had claimed she had placed in 'safe-keeping' there. Leonora Pegram had managed to convince Joss of her goodwill and was going to help him in his quest to retrieve the items. This time they brought a third party with them, a former neighbour in Bredasdorp whom they both knew well, but with whom Mrs Pegram had a particularly close personal and business relationship. This is the person I referred to earlier as Dirk, the person a servant had spotted rifling through Joss's papers and whom he suspected of stealing the trust deed that Maître

Blum had drafted. Why, one might ask, did Joss agree to go to London with someone he distrusted? I can understand why Mrs Pegram came along because she had shipped Joss's valuables to the UK in the first place, but why Dirk? What possible use was he going to be?

In any case, the odd trio travelled together on the 13-hour flight from Cape Town to London's Heathrow airport. Fortunately for Joss, these were the days before smoking on aeroplanes was outlawed, for Joss was a chain smoker and would never have lasted that long without a cigarette. On their arrival, however, Joss derived a certain smug satisfaction from being able to demonstrate to his companions that he had some standing in British society, that even with his South African passport, he could command certain privileges. He said that he had been standing dutifully in the queue with Dirk when a man approached him and, without asking any questions or checking his documents, merely escorted him through customs and into a chauffeur driven car. Dirk had apparently had a difficult time. Joss said that 'he had to lie his way into England,' though I suspect that was an exaggeration, and even 'Mrs Pegram with her British passport took hours to get in.'

Having been escorted through customs, Joss continued to be the recipient of some unseen hand of privilege. 'Bells had started ringing because things were made easier, and I was sent in the courtesy car to a flat in Ovington Square.'[3] Joss claimed to have no idea how he had 'landed up in that nice flat' or who might have organized it for him. Dirk and Mrs Pegram, for their part, had to find a taxi to take them there, along with some 'wretched picture' that had been 'hidden somewhere at the airport in a locker or something.' That phrase struck an odd note. Whose picture, what picture? And apparently more pictures mysteriously arrived in the flat in Ovington Square. So too – in a characteristically extravagant flourish by Joss – did Diana, the late Princess of Wales, in the form of a Santa cigarette girl. Joss said that Diana used to bring him cigarettes when he was in London in 1989, and sometimes she would also bring a friend of hers called Canary. Once when they were there – Diana, wearing blue denim jeans, was sitting cross-legged on the floor with Canary and Joss – Dirk, who had a key to the flat, burst in, so Joss 'duly introduced him to them and then he ran away.' To burst in unexpectedly on Princess Diana sitting on the floor in blue jeans would be a challenging social experience for just about anyone, but for a rather unsophisticated South African from the hinterland, it must have been daunting and highly embarrassing. No wonder he made a hasty retreat!

The assorted members of the ménage seemed to be hanging around a flat in London surrounded by several valuable paintings and not quite knowing what to do next. Joss suggested that it would be a good idea to take the pictures to Coutts for safe-keeping and asked Dirk and Leonora to do just that. Unfortunately for Joss, the manager of the trust department at Coutts, Joss's contact from previous encounters, was decidedly unimpressed by his unusual visitors, particularly since they indicated that they wanted to borrow £100,000 on the strength of the pictures being deposited with him. This ridiculous scheme had clearly been cooked up in the taxi. The first Joss knew about it was when 'the trust manager rang me up and said, "Why on earth did you send those two awful people to me? They wanted to borrow £100,000 and I said no."' No wonder he said 'no,' for at that time Coutts was very particular about the credentials of its clients. It catered exclusively to the rich, famous, and royal members of British society, so would immediately have been suspicious of two strangers off the street asking for a large loan, even if they had come with a cache of pictures and a recommendation from Joss. Joss surmised that he should have undertaken the transaction himself, but, as he explained yet again, 'I am no good at doing things because I have always had people to do things. I have made decisions and things have been done.' Joss hotly denied Dirk's story that the only reason that Coutts refused to take the pictures was 'because Coutts is not a storage place':

> That is not true. They would have sent them to Christie's warehouse where all their stuff is stored. It was because of the £100,000 that he said 'no.' Then Mrs Pegram saw the gap and next thing, the pictures disappeared. Actually, Patrick Guinness and his new wife Louise saw them going out.[4]

Exactly what was removed was unclear, but I have seen a written receipt from a removal company, T. Rogers & Son, that Impressionist pictures and other possessions of Joss's were taken from Lady Carrington's flat in Ovington Square to where Mrs Pegram was staying. For the first time in this sorry saga Joss now involved the police, who turned up further documentation from Rogers & Son saying that they had once transported the goods, but that Mrs Pegram had later removed them. A woman who lived near the Ovington Square flat also reported having seen the men in the Rogers van taking pictures out of the flat. Joss said that they had gone to Rogers, but that Mrs Pegram then admitted that she gave them to somebody she knew, though not someone Joss knew, but that he and a friend of his had left the country and that 'the police know all about it.' Joss could not imagine why Mrs Pegram did that when they were safely stored at Rogers. In fact, the documentation shows that she had removed the pictures from Rogers before and then sent them back under her own name.

As far as Joss was concerned, his belongings had been moved to an unknown destination and this time he felt a strong urge to hit back. Continuing enquiries were initiated by the police. Though many of the leads looked promising and even lasted for a few years, every avenue merely led to a dead end, every enquiry went cold, and every lead petered out. Joss returned to South Africa virtually penniless and in despair.

Mrs Pegram had responded to the accusations made against her with a barrage of contradictions. At one point she claimed that the belongings were hers, at another that she was a penniless widow reliant on the social services. However, on 18 March 1995 she signed an affidavit at Kensington police station in London to the effect that she owed Joss £1 million. A South African named Charles William Newton both witnessed the affidavit and produced a list of paintings that Joss had asked Sotheby's to value. In addition, Mrs Pegram had signed a letter at Belgravia police station, which established Joss as the rightful owner of the paintings taken from the London flat. Joss had been convinced that, with these two documents, he would be able to retrieve both his belongings and the £1 million that Mrs Pegram had agreed she owed him.[5] However, neither the debt nor the missing belongings ever materialized.

In June 1993, when Joss was living at 27 Mount Street in London, his hopes were temporarily buoyed when it seemed as if the police were beginning to take his complaints seriously. A man from Scotland Yard apparently turned up out of the blue. He said that he had been asked to try to locate the missing valuables but did not say by whom. He then asked Joss if he was sure that his belongings had come to England. He replied that he was not sure because he had not seen any of them since they were in South Africa. All he had seen in England, he claimed, were 'the four or five Impressionists' that Dirk brought over. So now we have not one, but four or five Impressionist paintings, plus others that might or might not have been shipped from South Africa. In addition to the involvement by the police, Joss had instructed a firm of London solicitors called Carter Lemon to attempt to recover his possessions. Seamus Smyth, a lawyer with the firm, confirmed in a letter to Joss of 17 February 1997 that he had an affidavit from Mrs Pegram acknowledging Joss's ownership of certain items but, he added, he would refuse to release it to anyone, not even to Joss, unless or until his firm's invoice was settled. Since the invoice was never settled – by then Joss had lost any means with which to do so – the firm withdrew from the case. The prospect of a dramatic Perry Mason-style court case that had gripped Joss's imagination, slowly receded. He thought that Leonora Pegram must have hidden his belongings somewhere safe several years earlier but remained convinced that she still had them and would either return them or make a substantial settlement before the case came before the court.

As time passed nothing materialized. The matter never reached the court and Joss's belongings never came to light. As promises of their recovery appeared on the horizon and then faded as inevitably as night follows day, Joss reluctantly began to accept that he would be the ultimate loser. With the help of his inborn arrogance and crackpot religion he could take a lot, but a fresh claim by Leonora that the property was not legally his (she changed her story frequently) outraged his sense of dignity. 'Now she is making me out to be a liar,' he fumed, 'that stuff does belong to me and has always belonged to me. I did not sell it to, and I did not give it to Mrs Pegram.' By now Joss was becoming increasingly weary from fighting his cause, but he continued to live in hope that he would eventually retrieve his missing belongings and the £1 million that Mrs Pegram admitted she owed him.

Old patterns

In the event, nothing was retrieved. Mrs Pegram remained in London and Joss returned to South Africa. In innumerable telephone calls to him, which were taped as evidence, she continually promised to honour her £1 million debt to him. She even went so far on several occasions as to say that she had already sent it by courier, but something always went wrong.

Joss finally decided to turn to the local police, and, on 20 October 1994, he made a statement to the South African Police in the presence of Commissioner of Oaths Lieutenant-Colonel Peter Lister. In his statement, he accused Mrs Pegram of appropriating paintings, jewellery worth approximately £8.8 million, one hundred eighteenth-century miniature paintings, as well as silver and chinaware, and of refusing to return any of the items to him. He said that Mrs Pegram had told him that the paintings and jewellery were stored with a cousin of hers in Yorkshire, but that during the six months he spent in England in 1989 she claimed that she could not retrieve them because her cousin was away on a world tour. Despite a hopeful start and many promises over what was clearly a criminal matter, this lead also went cold. Having been extremely interested in the case and promising to follow all sorts of leads – 'they were going to go to Interpol and God knows what else' – Lieutenant-Colonel Lister suddenly announced that he was retiring from the police force, that the matter was 'civil, not criminal, and that was the end of that.' Was Lister warned off in some way? Why did he suddenly say that it was a civil rather than a criminal matter? I do not know the answer to those questions, but it is apparent from the paperwork that the South African police were suddenly no longer interested, Lister disappeared from the picture and the case was dropped.

* * *

It is extraordinary that, despite the help of reputable lawyers, two police forces, and ample evidence of their existence, so much money and so many valuable works of art can just evaporate into thin air. Surely there must be more to moving artworks from one country to another than simply packing them up and sending them off, perhaps adding a fake declaration or two? Perhaps not. With the sheer volume of people and goods transported around the world each day being so great that not even a deadly pandemic seems capable of stopping the flow, it was probably easy for Mrs Pegram to do so, especially given that Joss was too blinded by his privileged class background and sense of importance even to recognize avarice and greed when it was staring him straight in the face. Even in the face of all the evidence that Mrs Pegram had defrauded him, Joss continued to interpret her actions as an assault on his sensitive, noble identity rather than those of a criminal. For instance, she should not, he thought, have taken things that were close to his heart and that he had really loved, which included an emerald necklace carved in India along with the other jewellery that was of so much sentimental value to him, mainly because of its provenance, which he felt had been the last remaining evidence that, although unacknowledged and probably unloved, he was nonetheless terribly important. He felt particularly aggrieved about a 'self-portrait of Picasso and his wife. The strange thing is that it was completely abstract, but really did look like them.'

It took some time before Joss gave up hope completely. Although it clearly looked as if he had reached the end of the line, he still clung to the naïve expectation that one day he would regain the precious reminders of his unique place in the world. He thought that if he concentrated for long enough, he might will the stuff to come back, but eventually had to concede that 'nobody ever got the better of Mrs Pegram.' I seem to recall that Bunny Mellon was one exception to that rule. However, he rather charitably concluded that 'if the stuff does not come back, I do not want anybody destroyed by the fact that it does not come back.' To cope with his misfortune, Joss turned to his 'crackpot religion,' his pride, his non-materialist values, and his disdain for greed. Without money and denuded of nearly all his material possessions, he was quietly slipping into a state of resigned desolation.

In this chapter, I have documented and discussed the issue of Joss's porphyria and suggested that while having the disease is not conclusive it at least points to a possible royal connection. It is also, frankly, puzzling that so eminent a person as

Patrick Guinness was interacting with Joss and interceding on his behalf. Why, one might ask, was he giving the likes of someone like Mrs Pegram the time of day?

Disillusionment finally dawned. Joss in pensive mood.

9

Letting Go

DESPITE NUMEROUS ATTEMPTS by the police and several lawyers in both the UK and South Africa to track down Joss's missing possessions and retrieve his £1 million debt from Mrs Pegram, it had become clear that no amount of believing was going to bring them back. Forces far stronger than the law, far stronger than any due legal process, had clearly contrived to separate Joss from his purportedly fabulous inheritances, from the proceeds of his trusts and from all his worldly goods. The affidavits he claimed the Duke and Duchess of Windsor had signed to authenticate his identity had mysteriously disappeared, along with most of his papers. Sequestration orders, acknowledgements of debt, written promises to return the objects, threats of court proceedings, the involvement of the South African Police and of Scotland Yard had all failed to yield a single farthing, a single jewel, a single painting, a single keepsake, or a single viable lead.

The cottages in Bredasdorp

In 1984, Joss opted for the quiet life and decided to move his base out of Cape Town. He bought a pair of simple, though distinctive, and attractive cottages in the small town of Bredasdorp, a few miles north of Arniston, which lies on the Indian Ocean a couple of hundred miles northeast of Cape Town. This is where my cousin Georgina first met him, and where I got to know him so well. Jean Tromp, Joss's admirer and someone who never wavered in her conviction that he was indeed the royal son he claimed to be, visited him frequently. And guess what? Mrs Pegram moved into the second of the two cottages with a female servant. Later, Joss regretted having had her so close at hand and felt angry with Jean Tromp for having failed to protect him from her. In defending the accusation against her, Jean had said that one had to give Mrs Pegram her due insofar as she did look after Joss. Joss retorted, 'well, I do not know how she works that out. In what way did she look after me?' I asked if Mrs Pegram perhaps helped him with everyday housework, but this too he denied, saying that 'the household did not function ... and was so dirty you could not get into it.' Joss seemed resentful that Mrs Pegram never instructed her maid to clean his cottage. He said that 'she used to pinch my cigarettes and Coca-Cola ... and I had no means of getting anybody to shop for me.' She also, he claimed, 'in fits of anger used to flush my medicine down the loo and never said a polite word to me in 20 years.' And oddly, yet again, he seemed to be holding poor defenceless Jean Tromp responsible for the wrongs that Mrs Pegram had inflicted on him. His rant about Jean was clearly fake because, although often irritated by her, there is no doubt in my mind that they were dependent on one another and, at heart, very fond of each other.

His rage about Leonora Pegram, by contrast, continued unabated. Early in 1987, a while before Joss became incandescent about Mrs Pegram's behaviour, Joss decided to leave Bredasdorp for a while and take a holiday at McGregor, a small, rather isolated yet attractive rural village in a mountainous area about an hour's drive north of Bredasdorp. He took some jewellery with him in a large bag, which seems an odd thing to do. However, given that Joss lived with the constant inconvenience of having to accommodate his 'stuff,' perhaps it was not so odd after all. In a country like South Africa, where inequalities are so marked, there is a high level of crime and an awful lot of petty theft. If Joss valued his jewellery, it probably was a good idea to keep a close eye on it.

On the road from Bredasdorp to McGregor.

Cottage with vintage car in McGregor
where Joss spent his holiday.

Anyway, while he was on this holiday in McGregor, Mrs Pegram visited him there regularly. Why, might one wonder, did she come when he was ostensibly trying to get away from her? Nonetheless, on one of these visits, she managed to persuade him that it was too risky to keep his jewellery next to him in a big bag. So, on returning from her visit and, with his agreement, she took the bag of jewellery with her to deposit in a bank in Bredasdorp. Joss should probably have done that himself before going on holiday, but he did not think that way – he did not do things; other people did things for him.

During 1987 Joss started to notice thefts from his Bredasdorp cottage, including the discovery that some paintings he had stored in some cardboard boxes had disappeared. He thereupon checked the three metal containers in which he kept the one hundred eighteenth-century miniature paintings mentioned earlier and found that they too were empty. He reported the theft to the local police, but when Mrs Pegram heard that the police were investigating, she admitted that she had retrieved the paintings and sent them to England for safekeeping. It was only years later that Mrs Pegram admitted to Joss that she had failed to deposit his jewels in the bank but had also sent them to England.

Why and under whose authority was she doing this? Was it because she genuinely wanted to protect Joss and his art? It certainly does not look like it. Why, for instance, did she act in such an underhand way? Was she acting on behalf of someone else, and if so, who? Jean believed that the decision had come from 'higher up' and that if Joss were to die while still in possession of these things it would raise questions about his parentage, which as far as Jean was concerned was royal, and having royal connections was important to her self-esteem and something by which she set great store. Be that as it may, Joss interpreted the requisitioning of his belongings as a personal affront to him and one that he desperately wanted to resist.

Leonora Pegram moves to London

Having spirited away the last of Joss's possessions, Leonora decided to decamp to London. Before her departure, on 6 June 1995, when Joss was still living at Lourens Street in Bredasdorp, Leonora handed him her power of attorney to enable him to manage her affairs in South Africa. This would seem to suggest that they were on good terms at the time and that there was a level of trust between the two of them. However, it was an empty gesture because Leonora had already cashed in all her chips in South Africa and, as far as I could ascertain, there were no affairs left for him to manage, not that he would have been capable of managing them if there had been.

Whatever residual goodwill existed between Joss and Leonora Pegram eroded when, in November 1995, Joss recruited my cousin Georgina to try to recover certain items of jewellery, paintings and *objets d'art*, including about twenty pieces of Fabergé. Georgina is a competent person with a lot of contacts in the auction houses in both London and South Africa, so she was a force to reckon with. The knives were out. Georgina turned to a Mr John Sykes of Charles Russell, 8–10 New Fetter Lane, London, to act on Joss's behalf and they put a lot of effort into the task at hand. Then, a couple of months later, in January 1996, Mrs Pegram hired a London firm of solicitors called Straiton & Company to defend her.

Now, with lawyers on board on both sides, there were no holds barred. Straiton & Company made the first move by writing to John Sykes to say that Mrs Pegram was a widow on state benefits and that they should drop the case, an assertion that John Sykes firmly contradicted in a letter dated 8 February 1996. As we are all aware, the mills of justice, like those of the gods, grind exceedingly slowly. We also know that justice is expensive and that some people have more influence and power than others – even before the law. So, as much as one might like to believe in the notion of a level playing field, we all know that it does not really exist in real life. And so, predictably, time went by with neither side really getting any-where. Then, in 1998, Mrs Pegram consulted another London solicitor called Karina Leapman and there was another flurry of correspondence between lawyers, but nothing ever came out of any of it and Joss eventually had to give up because he had no funds left with which to pay his lawyers' fees.

At this point, it might be worth mentioning that my cousin Georgina, who was very good at her job and is, I can vouch, capable, persuasive and charming, had gone to considerable lengths to secure legal representation on Joss's behalf, and that Phillips, her employers at the time, had agreed to lend some financial support. However, they could not do so indefinitely and, although the lawyers tried valiantly to follow up on all the leads, they kept hitting brick walls, so once it became apparent that nobody remained who was either willing or able to meet their not insubstantial fees, they ultimately withdrew their support and Joss lost any further form of legal represen-tation.

Meanwhile, Mrs Pegram would phone Joss regularly, for she seemed eager to keep in touch and was still promising to repay her debt to him. By the late 1990s, however, he was getting increasingly impatient with her and, as witnessed from the following extracts of taped telephone calls from her, with her string of lies and broken promises. Early on in one such phone call, on 4 March 1998, Joss implored Mrs Pegram to be straight with him. He said, 'I cannot be encouraged that everything is going to come right and then have it dashed immediately again. I am trying to put this to you nicely, but if you have not got it, you must tell me.' 'No, no,' she insisted, 'I have got it and you are going to get it. ... I have got the full million pounds. It cost £30 to send.' Joss then asked her if it had really been sent, to which she responded: 'Yes, but it has been given to *them* to send,' whoever them might be, 'and they said although the cheque was guaranteed they still had to clear it, but they did start sending the money ... well three days ago.' To Joss's question of whether she was sure of that, she replied 'Yes,' but then went on to say that 'I personally do not think they did anything on Friday. You know how bad they are on Friday afternoon? And I think it only started at …,' at which point Joss interrupts her to say, 'I do not want to start an argument because I am too ill to argue. I just want to make it clear to you that if you have not got it, I must accept it and understand it, but then I must make some other arrangements.'

Mrs Pegram then thanks him for his generosity and says, 'It makes me love you more, darling. … And I have been praying the whole night for you, you know, on my knees.' Joss asks her again if she has got the money, and she answers, 'I have got it.' He asks her if she is 100 per cent sure of that, to which she replies, 'I am sure, a million per cent sure.' At this point, somewhat reassured, Joss ends the call by saying, 'All right, then I'll speak to you again this evening.'

In a subsequent taped phone call, Joss and Mrs Pegram wander a little off the point and on to the subject of Joss's health, about which she seemed confused. When, in response to her, 'Oh, how are you today?' Joss said that he was losing a lot of blood, she immediately launched into, 'You know, I went to this lunch, and I met a Dr Burman, and he is an expert on blood, and he just mentioned something that clicked in my head. You have not got haemophilia, have you?' Joss then explained that he had porphyria, but that haemophilia was one of its side effects. Mrs Pegram then volunteered that she had been 'introduced to other people – real specialists in haemo-philia, real specialists in porphyria … and they will be able to help you.' At this point Joss began to grow irritated with her and, after a diatribe of complaints about having nothing to live on and being starved to death, he repeated, 'Now, tell me, these million pounds you have sent me, is it the million pounds you owe me or is it your *ex-gratia* gift?'

'Well, my dear,' says Mrs Pegram, 'it will have to be the money I owe you because I do not know how I am going to pay the people I borrowed it from.' Who, one wonders, would have lent her a million pounds so that she could refund the million pounds she stole? Surely, no one in their right mind would do a thing like that! 'Never mind,' she continued, 'You know God will help me,' to which Joss replied, 'Yes and Bunny Mellon probably will. The money will come from Bunny Mellon.' 'What?' says Mrs Pegram, 'I cannot hear' and Joss reassures her that it will be all right. She then tries to change the subject by saying, 'What I was shocked about yesterday. There were posters all over the town that Charles has Camilla in St James's Palace, and she is sleeping there with him.' This annoyed Joss who concluded, 'I am not really interested in all this petty gossip. I could not care who slept with whom.'

And so, these kinds of telephone conversations continued, with Mrs Pegram assuring Joss that the money had been dispatched and yet it never arriving and Joss moaning about his illness and threatening to die of starvation and of exasperation. Mrs Pegram occasionally complained that Joss's phone had been engaged when she had tried to ring or that she had to spend every Thursday morning having her 'damned dandruff' treated. Joss would then ask her again about the money and she would always say that it was coming, and she would give her word of honour that it had been dispatched and he would then question what her word of honour meant. The phone calls came regularly and resolved nothing. Joss could not have made his point any more forcibly.

Then, on the night of 15 December 1996, Mrs Pegram made a telephone call from London to my cousin Georgina in South Africa to try to ascertain Joss's whereabouts. Georgina said that she would get a message through to him to phone her back and when he did later that night, she said that she had sent the DHL during the preceding week, but that it had been returned to London because Joss had not been there at the time to receive it. Joss had indeed been away during that week, so there is no way of knowing whether Mrs Pegram was telling the truth about the dispatch. At this time Joss was considering flying to London but was refusing to do so until he had confirmation of the whereabouts of his goods and Mrs Pegram had returned his missing million pounds, which she now promised to do in the week of 16 December. None of this of course happened.

* * *

Since at least August 1994, Mrs Pegram had been living at Flat 25, 7 Runcorn Place, London W11, but she later moved to 46 William Dromey Court, Dyne Road, London NW6, where she was living when the High Court of Justice granted her a petition of bankruptcy on 21 July 1998. Until then, Joss still felt that he had a chance of getting at least something back from her, but now all his hopes were dashed. It is difficult to surmise quite what was happening at this juncture or why she was declared bankrupt if five Impressionists were being, or had been, stored in her name.

Could Mrs Pegram's declared bankruptcy have been a convenient ploy that her lawyers, acting on instructions from higher up in the British establishment, devised to invalidate Joss's claims against her? Alternatively, as Joss and Jean surmised, could Bunny Mellon's refusal to release the funds necessary to implement the trust that Patrick Guinness, Philip Sapsford, and Mrs Pegram were preparing to set up on Joss's behalf have been a factor? As mentioned earlier, Bunny Mellon had wanted Joss to move to the United States and she seemed to be the kind of person who was used to getting her own way, especially given that she clearly disapproved of Joss's friends and lifestyle in South Africa. Whatever the explanation, what transpired was that, despite all the efforts of the various parties concerned, Joss was reduced to penury and any hope of retrieving even a minute fraction of his fortune was fading fast. As Joss put it during one of Mrs Pegram's innumerable phone calls to him from London: 'I am living in the most abysmal conditions. And I am not used to them, you know.'

Jean Tromp in Bredasdorp: the odd couple

With Mrs Pegram now firmly ensconced in London and locked into a running battle with Joss, now back in Bredasdorp and still living in his cottage in Lourens Street, Jean Tromp was comfortably ensconced in a retirement flat at Butler Court in Somerset West. She used to visit Joss regularly and took a motherly interest in his welfare. However, after having witnessed him suffering from a severe attack of internal bleeding at the end of July 1997, which lasted for approximately three days, she felt sufficiently alarmed at the state of his health to think that he should not risk living on his own and offered to move into his second cottage in Lourens Street, which Mrs Pegram had vacated when she moved to London.

Joss, however, saw the situation in terms of him doing Jean a favour rather than the other way around. As her 'heir' and 'only living relative in this country,' he said, he felt duty bound to keep an eye on her. He thus decided to put her in the second cottage for a year, after which he had planned to sell the cottages, by which time Jean, he said, 'will have had her fill of Bredasdorp.' I cannot imagine why Joss should suddenly claim to be Jean's relative. Although Jean was related to the Queen Mother, Joss was not, irrespective of who his birth parents were, so perhaps his notion of family was rather loose. Joss may well have been Jean's heir, but I know that by the time Jean died – and Joss phoned me with the news that she had – no fortune seemed to be falling into his lap. Her assets seemed to be tied up in Scotland and, with the passage of time, her failure to act fast enough when she received an inheritance, as well as her increasing age and infirmity, meant that at the end of the day Jean did not really have much to hand on to anybody, and she was certainly living very modestly when I knew her, for by then she was already in her eighties and not in very good health.

Well, maybe these two ageing aristocrats (or assumed aristocrat in Joss's case) needed each other because, despite their noble origins, they had both washed up in a relatively remote corner of Africa without any of the trappings that had once placed them so far above the rest of us. Joss's main protectors were all long gone and the one who remained, Bunny Mellon, was insisting on terms he refused to accept. He was prepared to live unacknowledged, but he did not want to die without being able to give even a nod of gratitude to the various kindly people in South Africa who had extended a hand of friendship to him in his hours of need, the ordinary people who fed him when he was hungry, who talked to him when he was lonely, and who gave him shelter when he was destitute. And he was now clearly destitute.

Jean, like Joss, had been born into a privileged family of which she felt proud. As a young debutante, she had her season in Scotland and was presented at court to King George VI in 1936 shortly after his coronation. The season had culminated in her getting engaged to a rich and successful young man who died shortly afterwards when he overturned his Bentley because the sun blinded his view. She then came back to South Africa and, after getting engaged first to 'a Churchill with syphilis,' as Joss described him, and later to a Mr Richard Bawden (nicknamed 'Den') Stuttaford, who went off with someone else, she finally married Baron Tromp and went to live with him at a place called Dover Farm in what was then Rhodesia, now Zimbabwe. Joss referred to Tromp as the 'booby prize' and went on to say that she had been extremely unhappy with him because he was impatient and expected too much of her. He expected her to cater for 150 people when, as Joss put it, 'she cannot even cater for one person.' Tromp had apparently embarrassed her acutely (not to mention committed a heinous crime) when 'he shot and killed a black man for stealing cabbages or something and they had to pull all sorts of strings' and after that 'she was too embarrassed to show her face' again and so stopped visiting her family in Scotland.

Poor Jean's life had not always been easy, but she had a kind heart and clearly cared deeply for Joss. In fact, both Jean and Joss had been reduced to living in abysmal surroundings and, by this stage, Jean was in no position to improve them. In any case, she was not used to running a house. In addition, Joss's health was deteriorating. By the time I met Jean she was already beginning to find it difficult to move around. Although Joss was still in his early sixties, his poor health did not help alleviate the squalor in which they were living. Neither of them had ever mastered simple skills such as rinsing a cup or wiping down a work surface. In fact, it would have been difficult to imagine a more unconventional couple – so dishevelled they both were, yet so sublimely assured in their bearing. Joss's fall had been spectacular, but, as he explained: 'Well, if Jean Tromp can live on R2300 [approximately £168] a month then why can't I? You know, that is her argument.'

And so that is just what happened. Once Joss had sold his cottages in Lourens Street, Bredasdorp, which he needed to do to keep going, he agreed to move into a modest ground-floor flat with Jean in nearby Viljoen Street, which Jean first rented, then later bought, and where they lived together until Jean grew too old, frail, and infirm to manage without full-time care. She eventually moved into a care home in Somerset West where she remained for several months until her death in 2005.

The flat in Viljoen Street, Bredasdorp, which I first visited with my cousin Georgina, was rather depressing. It had one bedroom, off which there was a Spartan bathroom on one side and a living room cum kitchenette on the other. Jean occupied the bedroom and Joss slept on a mattress on the floor wedged between a filthy cooker and a cream-coloured leatherette sofa. There were a couple of photographs on the walls. One of these was of Jean being presented at court and the other, which hung

Exterior of Jean Tromp's flat, which she shared with Joss in Viljoen Street, Bredasdorp. They occupied the ground-floor one on the right of the photograph.

above Jean's bed, was of her mother as a young woman. Jean told us that Cecil Beaton had taken both photographs. The flat contained virtually no books other than a few paperback detective novels strewn around Joss's mattress on which there was a rather grimy crumpled sheet. Lined up on the two windowsills in the kitchen were numerous empty Ouma Rusk packages arranged almost as if they bore the status of a sculpture. Empty packs of Gitanes cigarettes, which Joss smoked incessantly, were piled up next to his mattress. There were no mod cons – no washing machine, dishwasher, or microwave oven. The premises were always filthy, even although a maid was supposed to come and clean twice a week.

It was just as well that Joss had never possessed more than two outfits, for there would have been nowhere to put them. His two outfits were identical and consisted of shorts, which looked rather like sleeping trunks, and white short-sleeved shirts. On his feet he always wore a pair of sheepskin-lined slippers, and he had a brown jacket for when the weather was cold. There was no iron in sight and no evidence that anything was ever ironed. Jean did, however, have a wardrobe in her bedroom and she clearly did have more than two outfits, but not many more. There was invariably a piece of dirty clothing soaking in a washing-up bowl in the bathroom adjoining her bedroom. There was a television and a telephone, though the only telephone book there was the 1984 *Yellow Pages* – and this was in 2002! There were two sofas placed at right angles around a small occasional table and a smallish table wedged against the work surface in the kitchen. The floor and all the surfaces were caked in dust, grime, and cigarette ash. There was also a chair in the living room on which Jean invariably sat, next to which was a small round occasional table that housed her ashtray. The one nice thing about the flat was that it was light, yet not too hot. Here Jean and Joss sat and talked, smoked, and bickered.

Joss and Jean's health deteriorates

Jean's health was deteriorating and there were occasional spells in hospital, but never for long. Her ankles and feet were badly swollen, and she had difficulty walking. As the sufferer of a hereditary type of porphyria, Joss was also in shocking health. Among the side effects of his illness were intermittent bleeding (as in haemophilia), high blood pressure, insomnia, and depression. He claimed that his haemophilia got worse when he felt stressed and was especially acute during the period before he had given up hope of ever retrieving anything from Mrs Pegram. In 1996, at the peak of his drama, he had said that he did not expect to live for very much longer given that at the time of his diagnosis he had been told to expect to live for another five years and that was 15 years earlier, so as he said, 'I am now ten years overdue.' He said that his illness caused his blood pressure to fluctuate wildly, which is destructive to the kidneys and induces extreme tiredness and depression. It also had a disastrous effect on Joss's teeth, virtu-ally all of which he eventually lost, probably mainly because of the bleeding, which he said they could only stop by cauterizing his mouth after freezing it. He found the whole procedure 'quite traumatic' and now 'cannot have another anaesthetic.'

*　*　*

Anyway, despite their numerous ailments, Mrs Pegram eventually stopped telephoning and Joss eventually accepted defeat, so he and Jean began to make plans about how they were to carry on. Jean, who still had supportive, well-heeled relatives in the UK and USA who telephoned her regularly and expressed willingness to help in any way they could, as well as a few resources of her own, threw her loyalties behind Joss. In effect, Joss became the son she never had. However, being more frugal than most people, she was reluctant to spend money and seemed happy to descend into the kind of squalor in which they lived. In any case, her eyesight was failing; she was growing older and more infirm and, to Joss's chagrin, was becoming increasingly dependent on and possessive of him.

In contrast to her cautious approach to spending money on everyday items, Jean was quite willing to buy them a nice house in which to live together. However, it never materialized because Joss could never make up his mind about what he would like her to buy. They toyed with a house in Greyton for years, but procrastinated for so long that it was eventually sold to someone else, at which point they both expressed tremendous disappointment because they were so sure that it had been the right house for them. In fact, they were so distressed by this news that Joss summoned me to come and see him and Jean on 31 January 2002 and to bring some food with me. I arrived to find Jean sitting in her usual chair and she greeted me warmly in her regular polite manner. Joss was lying on his mattress, but on my arrival, stirred himself and came and joined us on the sofa. He said that he was feeling very, very depressed at the news they had received the day before about the Greyton house having gone. Jean was also bitterly disappointed about it because it meant having to put off the visit of her cousins Adèle Coates and Charles Churchill. Anyway, since the house had been on the market for four years and was going for next to nothing, it seemed odd that they had failed to anticipate that the vendors might eventually find another buyer. While I was there someone came in with a sofa catalogue, which Joss showed me. He was already choosing furniture for the house before they had even made an offer!

He went on to describe how his despair and emptiness reminded him of how he had felt after two other devastating experiences in his life. The first was when his neighbour poisoned his beloved ridgeback called Zark while he was living in the cottages in Bredasdorp. The second was when he discovered that the Colonna pearls had been stolen from the safe box in which they had been placed in the bank.

His sorrowful mood then reminded him of a suicide attempt he had made on a farm in the Northern Cape. On that occasion, he had just come back from England after having had a fallout with his purported mother, which upset him greatly. He failed to give any details about or reason for the fallout but said that he felt as if he no longer wanted to go on living. However, he explained, 'the problem was to find somewhere to die, for if you did it in your bed someone was bound to come in and find you and you would end up alive with a stomach pump.'

He reckoned that he had enough sleeping tablets to do the job and his opportunity arose when he was invited to stay on a farm in the Northern Cape that belonged to some friends of his called the Jacksons. At that time the main building was being renovated and the family had temporarily moved into accommodation on another part of the farm. Workmen were on site from 8.00 a.m. until 6.00 p.m., after which they would lock up and vacate the premises for the night. He arranged his entry by wandering onto the site during the day and ensuring that a window through which he could gain entry was left unlatched. At 6.00 p.m. when the builders had gone, he gained entry as planned, took his bottle of sleeping pills and very quickly passed out.

The next thing he knew was that he saw some green walls and thought 'hang on; surely they do not have Afrikaans taste in heaven or hell!' All South African hospital wards tend to be painted in the same shade of green and he had woken up in the Beaufort West Hospital with a policeman at his side and a drip in his arm. Apparently, a workman had come back to fetch a bottle of wine he had left in the house and found Joss unconscious on the kitchen floor. As a result, he lived to see another day and quite a few more years.

While relating this story, Joss was dabbing Preparation H (haemorrhoid cream) onto an open sore on Jean's shin, which she had acquired from falling on the grass while starting to run for the telephone. A neighbour had seen her and brought her in, then phoned the doctor, but the graze had subsequently become infected, and she was on a course of antibiotics, for which I had brought her some yoghurt. Joss said that although Preparation H was meant for haemorrhoids, it was excellent for everything, which was news to me. Joss talked a bit about the alternatives to Greyton. He really felt like going back to London, he said, but with Bunny Mellon in control of his remaining assets, he felt that that option was no longer available to him.

When I was about to leave, I asked Joss if he had heard from Mrs Pegram. 'Just a Christmas card,' he said, but 'Jean, tell Selina your theory about that stuff.' 'What was my theory?' she asked. 'You know, about the Windsors!' Jean's theory was that the Windsors had recruited Mrs Pegram to separate Joss from all his valuable belongings. Joss had always been perplexed about the thefts because he knew that the works of art were too distinctive and too well known ever to be sold on the open market. 'When a Vermeer comes onto the market, it is world news,' he said, and 'how do you conceal silver turkey platters with four handles that are so heavy that four people are needed to carry them into the dining room?' Joss seemed to suspect that Jean's theory might well have had some validity, but what he refused to accept was that the powers controlling his purse strings would deny him the right to make any bequests in his will. However, during the three or so years when I was spending quite a lot of time with Joss and Jean, most of their energy was being put into dealing with the day-to-day difficulties of just surviving. The reversal of his fortunes was something that Joss found difficult to comprehend.

The psychological mechanisms Joss constructed to deal with what he saw as the willingness of those closest to him to deny all knowledge of his existence had left him strangely detached from the world around him. He and Jean were merely muddling along and making little headway in trying to handle their lot in life.

* * *

With the Greyton house off the agenda, Joss and Jean began to think about a house overlooking the sea at Arniston. When visiting Joss and Jean, I sometimes took them to the Arniston Hotel for lunch, which Joss always enjoyed. He loved the subtle green colour of the sea against the white sands and blue sky, and rather liked the idea of living there. Consequently, we went to look at a vacant house for sale, which was pleasantly huddled up on some rocks alongside a few other houses. The subsequent negotiations began, but when they were almost concluded they too petered out. Then, a couple of weeks later, a beautiful historic house came onto the market in the picturesque farming town of Tulbach, which the Rupert family owned but now wanted to sell because of a family tragedy. Curiously, the Ruperts had moved to Parel Vallei in Somerset West, which was where Joss had lived as a boy with Ouma

Wessels. They had even arranged for Joss and Jean to look after their cat, which had miraculously found its way back to Tulbach from Somerset West (though 109 kilometres, nearly 68 miles, seems a long way for a cat to travel on its own). Again, Joss and Jean prevaricated and eventually let the lovely historic property go on the grounds that the winters in Tulbach were too cold, the summers too hot and the town in an earthquake-prone area.

Joss, Jean Tromp and author, about to embark on an
excursion to Arniston, 1999.

I visited Joss and Jean again on 1 March 2002. I had put the visit off for a week because we had been having trouble with our car, but when I eventually arrived at about 11.45 in the morning, I found them waiting expectantly for me. Joss had been sent details of an old and very pretty Cape Dutch house on the main road in Montagu and I suddenly found myself thrust into the role of chauffeuse, for neither Joss nor Jean was in a fit state to drive. So, after eating the lunch I had brought for us, we set off to see the house. The drive was much longer than any of us had anticipated – it took us about an hour to get there, with Joss giving directions, which he did with great skill. I was a little thrown by his attire – shabby slippers, grubby shorts, and crushed shirt. He said they were his pyjamas and asked me if they looked like pyjamas. I said that I did not think that pyjamas had turn-ups, to which he replied that they only turned up because they were so crushed and slept in. He brought his trainers with him but did not put them on when we arrived at our destination.

The owner of the house, who introduced herself as Barbara, looked quite alarmed by the apparitions confronting her, but kindly helped me and Joss drag Jean out of the car, which took some doing. Barbara then apologized profusely about her own appearance, which was odd because she was immaculately turned out in a fresh cotton blouse and skirt. She then escorted Jean into a darkened front room in which a Chopin CD was being played at full volume. I walked around the garden a bit before joining them for a beautifully presented cold drink and grapes that were so enormous that I at first thought were plums. Joss shuffled around in his slippers making comments about the authenticity of the house, but quickly retired to the back patio for a cigarette, which he fished out of a plastic bag. At this juncture Mrs Cooper, the estate agent, arrived heavily made up and all a glitter with chains, necklaces and various baubles in tight-fitting pinstriped trousers and a hugging top. It was all smiles and syrup. Barbara was clearly eager to sell the house to anyone who would buy it. Barbara was able to speak some English, but Joss conversed with them in Afrikaans. He quite liked the house but hated its garage doors, the absence of a view and the mean flatlet adjoining the garage. Jean found the house dark and gloomy. Thus, yet another opportunity to move had been deferred. Once back in Bredasdorp we each had a cup of coffee and Jean talked a bit about herself and her life.

She was fretting about an inheritance she seemed to have lost. Her uncle Patrick had left her a house in Perth. A firm called William, Dickie & Sons in Dundee was supposed to be administering his estate, but it no longer seemed to exist, and

Jean had lost track of the house. Also, the jewellery that Kate Playfair had left for Jean and her sister Olive Melrose also seemed to have been mislaid. Poor Jean, she was obviously wondering how she was going to pay for Joss's dream house. Joss, for his part, thought that Jean's anxieties were ill-founded because, as he saw it, she was just mean, not poor. He said that Margaret, the char who cleaned for Jean once a month 'because it is too expensive to have her every week, but who does not really work because she talks the whole time,' had decided that Jean was wealthy because, as she put it, 'if the Madam did not have plenty of money, she would have bought new curtains!' So, there we have it. Poor people spend their money and rich people squirrel it away, or allow other people to squirrel it from them, which is exactly what seems to have happened to both Joss and Jean.

* * *

Tensions had been mounting between Joss and Jean and, on Tuesday 5 March 2002, Joss phoned to say that he and Jean had had a terrible row. In fact, it had been so bad that the neighbours had called the police, who helpfully suggested that he walk out and leave Jean alone. He obviously could not do that, and they eventually calmed down.

On 18 May 2002, my husband Robin and I visited Joss and Jean. The visit was memorable because it was when Joss, as ever eager to impress with a good tale, told us that Lucky Lucan was living within a ten-kilometre radius of Bredasdorp and that he had seen him in South Africa since his spectacular escape and disappearance after murdering his children's nanny, Sandra Rivett, in London in 1974. Lucky Lucan, Richard John Bingham, the 7th Earl of Lucan, hit the headlines when his escape from Britain following the murder led to a worldwide police hunt. His whereabouts were never located, and he was eventually declared dead. No reports of his sightings were ever substantiated, and his disappearance remains a mystery. Joss told us that before his most recent move, Lord Lucan had lived first in Clanwilliam, a small town in the Western Cape about 230 kilometres north of Cape Town (with a population of about 6000), and later in the much larger (about 80,000 people) seaside town of Hermanus, approximately 95 kilometres southeast of Cape Town. During this time, a manservant and a relative of his mother's, whom Joss described as 'a Bingham and a genuinely nice woman called Lucy Alexander,' had been looking after him.

Joss said that he had known Lucky all his life and that they were about the same age (in fact Lucan was a little older than Joss). Joss said that Lucan had come to see him with two of his children and the nanny in question when he was living in Waverton Street in London. It is common knowledge that Lord Lucan's marriage to Veronica Duncan had failed in late 1972 and that the couple had been locked in a bitter dispute, which Lord Lucan lost, over the custody of their three young children. By the time of the murder, Lord Lucan had moved out of the marital home and was living in a nearby flat. The consensus at the time was that Lucan had intended to murder his former wife but had mistakenly killed Sandra Rivett instead. Joss said that he had never spoken to Lucky about the murder or about how he managed to come to South Africa incognito, but says that Lucy Alexander returned to Hermanus to look after him but was incredibly old so may have died and now another woman takes care of him. Lucky was living as a recluse and Joss found him depressing. It has been difficult for him, Joss said, because he was a gregarious chap who loved the Clermont Club and the bright lights of London. He says he never had cosmetic surgery and looks the same as he always did, though a lot older than before. Journalists have been hovering, but Joss thinks that the British police were put off the scent and that the South African police are not interested in solving a crime that took place in Britain so long ago. Joss remembered that he was living in Llandudno when Lord Lucan arrived in the country shortly after the murder, for he came to see him there.[1] Anyway, that said, Lord Lucan had got away with murder, but then quite a few other people had got away with reducing Joss to a pitiful state of penury.

Jean and Joss fade away

Eventually, the owners of the Bredasdorp flat wanted to sell and, rather than have people coming round to see the place, Jean decided to buy it and there she and Joss remained for as long as they could. Meanwhile, Joss dreamed on; Jean acquired a Zimmer-frame and the highlights of their lives revolved around such things as Jean's bed collapsing, or Joss having a fall while trying to retrieve Jean's credit card from the crevices of the leatherette sofa and, consequently, losing his two good eye teeth – the ones between had already gone and the remaining one is capped in gold. Then there was the incident of Jean getting stuck in the bath and paramedics having to rescue her. Nonetheless, despite his frequent complaints about and rather low opinion of Jean's taste, capabilities and intelligence, Joss loyally stood by her as they muddled along together, forever complaining, bickering, and gossiping about all the interesting people who had touched their lives. Though Joss was looking decidedly scruffy and unkempt, he had still not lost the unshakeable arrogance he claimed to have acquired from the woman he insisted was his mother. 'Well, she was a princess of a new and better royalty, the royalty of money,' he said. He thought that 'people who belong to the blood,' (ouch!) whose families are worth in excess of £1000 million, are set apart. It makes no difference if you take it away from them, 'if you reduce them to living in a little cottage in Bredasdorp without enough to live on, as I have been. It is still there.' It had by then become clear to Joss that Jean's days as his constant companion and carer would soon be ending.

Once when I came to visit Joss in 2002, I was surprised to find that he and Jean were not alone. Sitting quietly with them was a man who was simply introduced to me as Kobus. He was probably in his mid- to late forties, but his quiet demeanour, innocent expression and slim build made him look younger. He worked in a local garage, though I never established in what capacity and, as an Afrikaans-speaker from Bredasdorp, seemed slightly uneasy conversing in English, though, like most South Africans, was able to do so. Was Joss, I thought uncharitably, lining up his next carer? And what incentives, I thought even more uncharitably, were going to be put on the table?

Anyway, lunch time was approaching and there was clearly nothing in the flat to ingest apart from instant coffee, the remnants of some slightly sour milk and various scattered packs of Gitanes cigarettes, so we decided to take the 35-minute drive to the hotel on the beach at Arniston, where we could at least rely on bountiful supplies of fresh fish and they could rely on me, as usual, and this included Kobus I noted, to foot the bill. The four of us spent a pleasant day together, though I never established whether Joss had deliberately arranged for Kobus to be there when I came, or whether he had just turned up for want of a bit of company and a chat, an informality that is characteristic of life in South Africa.

Kobus was not there on subsequent occasions and some months later Joss told me that he had gone to the United States to earn some 'forex' (foreign exchange). On one occasion Joss asked me to write to Kobus in the United States, enquiring about his welfare and keeping him up to date with Joss's news, which I did – though I never quite understood why Joss did not write to him himself.

Eventually, my long sojourn in South Africa was coming to its close and my husband reluctantly accompanied me to Bredasdorp to say our goodbyes. At the end of my husband's contract with the University of Cape Town, we returned to our normal lives in the UK. Joss would phone about once every two or three weeks, so he kept me abreast with what was happening in his life, and we were never out of touch for long.

His health deteriorated further when he suffered several minor strokes and he had a few stints in the local hospital in Bredasdorp, where they rather kindly accommodated his eccentric wish to sleep on a mattress on the floor.

Jean's health also deteriorated and when it became untenable for her to remain in the flat, she sold it and moved into a frail-care centre in Bredasdorp where she died in 2005. Joss phoned me to tell me the news. He said that they 'had a little service in Somerset West.' He said that her Scottish relatives had felt awful about the end of her life but did not want to step on any toes. He said that 'Janet (a tricky person from Rhodesia) came with her husband' and that Jean's ashes were to be scattered at Arniston. I find some comfort in that because I had many happy meals at the Arniston Hotel with Joss and Jean.

Georgina and Jean Tromp outside the
Arniston Hotel, 1999.

Joss, on his part, moved into a house at 8 van der Byl Street in Bredasdorp where Kobus Fenwick's wife and family were living with Kobus's father-in-law, whom everyone called 'Oupa,' Afrikaans for Grandad (Kobus was still earning forex in the United States). I visited Joss there on several occasions over the next few years when I made shorter holiday trips to South Africa. On the first of these occasions, I went there with my cousin Georgina and Oupa ushered us around to the quarters in which Joss was staying. We were slightly taken aback by the family's two snarling, rather menacing looking Rottweilers, especially given that there were children running around, but Oupa dismissed my concerns on the grounds that the Rottweilers were necessary because 'this is a dangerous country.'

We found Joss in the most appalling squalor on a mattress on the floor of what had clearly once served as the servants' quarters at the rear of a modest bungalow, surrounded by piled up furniture. The lavatory in the adjoining passage was filthy, but Joss seemed in good spirits and suggested we walk to a nearby café for a cup of tea and cake. His fortunes had improved marginally because, although the large trust had never materialized, he told us that an arrangement had been made whereby his bank account now covered any expenses he incurred. He suspected, though he was not sure, that Bunny Mellon was behind the arrangement. He seemed more relaxed than I had seen him in a long while and he even paid for the tea and cakes.

Kobus eventually returned from the United States shortly before his wife died of cancer. He then decided to move to Swellendam, a beautiful historic town nestled at the foot of the Langeberg Mountains, which after Cape Town and Stellenbosch, is the third oldest town in South Africa. Joss stayed on with Oupa for a while and I visited him there on several more occasions. Joss spoke of wanting to move to Swellendam to join Kobus there and Kobus, in turn, would be expecting some nice pickings from his will. Again, Joss was in good spirits. His room was now being kept clean and there was always a bowl of fresh fruit at his side. However, he had suffered from further strokes and attacks of porphyria, and I noticed that a wheelchair was now added to the clutter around his mattress on the floor. At least it gave one a place to sit!

It was there in that room that I last saw Joss. However, he continued to phone me in England, and he would chat about his new life in Swellendam where he seemed settled and relatively happy. He was in a wing of Kobus's house, which had eight bedrooms, several bathrooms, a living room, which Joss always spoke of as a sitkamer (sitting room), and which he said had a special charm of its own. Kobus, who seemed to be managing a car hire business in Swellendam, had recovered from his wife's untimely death and had started a new relationship with an estate agent. According to Joss, Kobus ran a relaxed household in which various people came and went. The last time I spoke to Joss he said, 'I have got these dicky kidneys, so I have not got much time.'

Then, in late June 2010, I received a phone call from my cousin Georgina to say that Joss had died on 26 June. He had been, according to Kobus, tired and depressed but otherwise much as usual. He was never in any pain and was smoking and eating bananas until the end! He asked that his death be kept quiet, that there be no announcements of any kind, and that his body be cremated. There was no funeral – nobody to weep for him or even to acknowledge that he had ever existed. Those of us who mourned him had to do so alone. Among the various papers that came my way after his death was an attempt by Joss to write a poem. Perhaps it tells us something about how he saw his life. He called it 'Futility.'

Futility

Bare, chapped, calloused feet hug a dirty pavement as a
small insignificant lost soul wanders the cruel world in
search of a soul. Not his own but another one in this black
box of life. His father an alley and mother a cardboard box
bear testament to the unjust hand he has been dealt by a
poverty breathing society.

Knees exposed to the world, covered in blood, scabs, and
dirt place him in his slot machine of society. The lever was

pulled many years ago, but not by him. He lights candles in the wind. Futile!

Transparent and fathomless his eyes stare at all and nothing. Society's not done with him yet. Conform or die.

An explosion breaks the noisy silence of his life. Blood spews forth into a dirty pool draining his existence and letting his life ebb away, leaving blood-stained skin witness to its final voyage. Ship of the lost souls?

Stuffing and cramming all his own into a suitcase of a tear he leaves his corpse to thrive for one second on happiness in his futile life; his futile death, the tear falls, only to smash into a million crystal pieces on a hard, cold concrete floor.

Life washes the pieces into a pool only to join others who have passed the way. This way being the way of the world to come, but not to form pools, but seas and oceans of futility.

10

Conclusion

M Y COUSIN GEORGINA had known Joss for 15 years before his death and I, Selina, had known him for 13 years. As the reader can easily imagine, she and I have had long discussions about the extraordinary man we knew and his astonishing account of himself. We perhaps need to say again that neither of us is gullible. We have drunk deep at the well of life and lived long and varied lives in several different countries and have got to know a wide range of people from different backgrounds. In our time, we have come across more than our fair share of honest sorts, rascals, con-men, thieves, and liars, not to mention people who are psychologically insecure or more seriously mentally disturbed. Yet, our experience and extended knowledge of Joss often left us uncertain as to how to understand him and evaluate his claims.

Three hypotheses

In concluding my account, I worked initially on three hypotheses. First, Joss was a fraudster, who consciously deceived the people around him, including us, for his personal or material advantage. Second, he was who he said he was – the son of the Duke and Duchess of Windsor. He was hidden from history because he was an embarrassment and, possibly, a threat to the royal family. Third, Joss was in the grip of an extended delusion that had been with him for many years and had consumed him to such a degree that he was no longer able to tell the difference between fact or fiction, invention or reality.

I have decisively rejected the first proposition. Joss was not a fake or a fraudster in the conventional understanding of those terms. He was not like a second-hand car salesman who rolled back the odometer to trap an unwary customer into thinking that a car was newer than it was. He was not selling snake oil or doing the three-card Monte trick. Such activities suggest planning, intention to deceive and a clear material benefit from executing the scam. None of these applied. Joss was extraordinarily passive and even inept. He was reluctant to tell his story for many years; he dragged out the details and constantly professed nervousness that I would not honour our agreement to keep it to myself until after his death. Georgina and I passed him no money and gave him no gifts of any value. It is true that we would treat him to a modest meal from time to time and to a '*melktert*' (a sort of custard tart) from the local bakery. On one occasion, Georgina provided him with temporary accommodation. Yet, in no sense could these paltry acts of friendship be seen as material remuneration for him sharing his story. In short, there was insufficient volition, intent, or reward for the conman hypothesis to hold up.

I have spent much of the book enunciating, sometimes in Joss's words, the second hypothesis – namely, that he was for real. The story is so bizarre that instinctively a sceptical inner voice baulks at the whole notion. Yet, although like most people, Joss was not beyond occasionally exaggerating or embellishing a point for effect, he certainly never gave the impression that he was deliberately lying or rehearsing a well-worn narrative. I hope this comes across but would emphasize that to secure a logical narrative I had to elide some of the meanderings that would have served to lose the plot. However, in a sense, these digressions gave the flavour of a real conversation about real events and experiences. Over the years, I sometimes planted a deliberate 'misunderstanding' of what he had earlier said – only to find he corrected me with a similar account to the original one. He was open about saying when he did not know something or when he had forgotten a name or date. In short, he 'sounded' as if he believed what he was saying and rarely struck a false note. His manner was that of a confident, arrogant, albeit gentle and often amusing man who spoke in a posh voice about the preoccupations (good furniture, art, family scandals, royal gossip, money, and power) of the class from which he claimed to have come.

Another important plus point to Joss's story is that, with some important exceptions, much of the detail proved to be correct. This is remarkable, bearing in mind that Joss was not a particularly literate man. He had a few books, but very few. He read slowly and ponderously, usually struggling with a thriller (Robert Ludlum was a favourite). He wrote appallingly, in childish block capitals, usually on the back of discarded Gitanes cigarette packets.

For much of his life, including the period when he was telling his story, he lived in rural Afrikaans-speaking small towns in the Cape. There were no significant sources for him to consult and no libraries of note. Needless to say – but perhaps this requires spelling out to a younger generation – he had no idea of how to use a computer, never accessed the internet and would have had no notion of how to use a search engine like Google.

One of the technical difficulties in checking Joss's story was that the tapes were indistinct and transcribed literally (with many misspellings) by someone who had no historical knowledge. They had to be laboriously checked by consulting histories and reference books of the time. The task was speeded up considerably when internet searches became common – searches that revealed time and again that Joss knew his stuff! There was a Pauline Rothschild, Glamis Castle came alive, Jean's family was exactly as described, as were Marie Louise, Princess Mary and various other members of the royal circle and the people they considered their friends.

PLEASE BIC PLEASE PUT ALL MY PAPERS IN A BOX BY THEM SELVES (I HAVE GIVEN YOU ALL THE ORIGIONALS) AT LEAST THEY ARE SAFE WITH YOU.

CHRIS HAS SOME PAPERS RE HARVEY + JOHN FRANKS (THE ORIGIONALS) ASK HIM FOR COPIES I HAVE NEVER PARTED WITH THE ORIGIONAL ACKNOW LEDGMENT OF DEBT OR ANY OF THESE ORIGIONALS.

PAGE 2
THERE IS MORE TO THIS THAN MEETS THE EYE (SOMETHING QUITE BIG)(JEAN THINKS) -(DISCUSS IT WITH HER)(IT HAS COME TO HER)(SUPPOSITION ON HER PART SHE SAYS)(WHEN THINGS COME TO JEAN IT IS USUALLY TRUE)
SAY HI TO JULIAN + ANABELLE + DON'T FIGHT WITH POOR OLLIE + PLEASE SAY HI TO HIM BLESS YOU + YOURS
P T. O

OF COURSE I AM VERY DEPRESSED (MORE SO THAN IS OBVIOUS)(GOOD AT HIDING MY FEELINGS)(MY FATHER'S BLOOD)(COULD BE DANGEROUS).

Joss's musings were invariably written on the backs of his empty Gitanes cigarette packs.

Some of the properties to which he referred, long before we all had access to the internet, turned out to be just as he portrayed them. I visited quite a few and was impressed by the accuracy of his recollections.

I was still reluctant to accept his account and came to a cautious conclusion. I took the view that important aspects of Joss's account were highly suspect, but that some of his claims *could* be true. To be more specific, the close association with the Rothschilds seemed far-fetched. It is implausible that the Duchess of Windsor travelled to South Africa on board HMS *Vanguard*. I seriously doubt that Princess Diana visited his flat in London (but have no proof one way or another). The 'American money' disappeared as fast as it appeared. However, many of his depictions of people and places were accurate and there was a good deal of documentation to authenticate his possession of valuable paintings, jewellery, and furniture. He clearly knew some of the people he said he knew. Much of the narrative of his life and associations had the ring of authenticity in what was said and unsaid, what was remembered and forgotten.

My doubts drew me to consider the third hypothesis, namely that Joss was a self-deluding fantasist. Clearly, there were and are such people. According to a common trope, mental asylums are full of patients who think they are Napoleon, Marie Antoinette, God, or Jesus Christ, though apparently these delusions are rarer than is commonly thought. Joss claimed to have consulted a psychiatrist in his middle years to treat the depression he suffered because of his porphyria. However, as far as Georgina and I know, he was never institutionalized. Over the long years of our acquaintance Joss lived a functional life. It would be an exaggeration to say it was a normal life, but he rubbed along in a satisfactory, if unconventional, way. So, to use highly unscientific and politically incorrect language, he was not a raving lunatic. Assuming he was a fantasist, he was so in a more complex sense.

A psychological explanation

Just as I had to read a few medical papers on porphyria (see Chapter 8), I now had to embark on a crash course in psychology and its related disciplines. First, how common is the incidence of grandiose delusions? There is ample early testimony describing people with such an affliction. For example, an historian of medieval Italy painstakingly documented the case of a Sienese merchant named Giannino di Guccio, who, in 1354, during the Hundred Years' War, became convinced that he was Jean I, the king of France. He went from country to country with forged documents, royal robes and a pocket-sized mercenary army pleading his case. While many rulers, including the Pope, denounced di Guccio as a fake, there were some who egged him on, less perhaps because they believed his fantasy than because his mischief-making was useful in effecting tactical advantages in the complex kaleidoscope of European medieval politics.[1]

Contemporary discussions of the incidence of delusions of grandeur yield a mixed picture, with some cross-cultural studies showing a low incidence among mental-health patients with 'ordinary' diagnoses such as anxiety and depression, the latter of which affected Joss. Grandiose delusions are found more commonly in more serious conditions – including two-thirds of those with bipolar disorder, one-half of schizophrenics and a 'substantial proportion' of those engaging in substance abuse.[2] As far as I could judge, Joss never suffered from any of these three afflictions (apart from the fact of course that he was a heavy smoker) and he never touched alcohol.

In addition to the literature on 'grandiose delusions,' there is a closely related set of studies on the 'imposter syndrome.' Here I must carefully distinguish two divergent uses of the idea of an imposter syndrome. The first, which is the one with which psychologists are more familiar, is the subjective experience of phoniness in people who believe they are unworthy of the success they achieve and who, despite being highly motivated to succeed, live in perpetual fear of being found insufficiently intelligent, capable or creative to deserve the recognition they receive. They thus feel themselves to be 'imposters' wrongly playing prestigious and responsible roles.

The second, more technical, use of the expression 'imposter syndrome' is closer to the literature on grandiose delusions, but now mostly obsolete in psychology and confined to the literature of psychoanalysis, although rare even there. Here are a few examples. K. Abraham described an army conscript who seemed to have an uncanny ability to gain the confidence of others and who had invented his non-existent rich parents.[3] On more speculative Freudian territory, H. Deutsch[4] and Phyllis Greenacre,[5] suggest that those who manifest an imposter syndrome have malformed superegos, have displaced their father through a cross-generational Oedipal coup and have invented, at an early age, a maternal phallus. I have no idea whether Joss invented a phallus for his mother, thereby striving (according to classical Freudian theory) to protect himself from castration anxiety. Somehow, such notions did not come up in our conversations.[6] It is worth noting that the web-based *International Dictionary of Psychoanalysis* is doubtful about the whole idea of an imposter syndrome, saying that,

> in truth none of the descriptions given in the literature goes much further than … relatively superficial findings. The attempt to create a composite picture of the imposter has failed because of the inaccuracy of the term itself, which is not conceptual, and the diverse personalities included under this term.[7]

However, there is one strain of psychological research that seems to echo Joss's life. This is the notion of 'the family romance' – a fantasy, Freud surmised, that a child's actual parents are adoptive parents and that a child's birth parents are of noble origin, or at least are socially elevated, the so-called Mignon delusion.[8] What is much more unusual is to sustain the family romance throughout one's life. It is possible that that is exactly what Joss did. If this hypothesis is valid, it could be that Joss's biological father was Joseph de Wahl Sr (whom he recognized as his foster father). Using the interpretive framework of 'the family romance' allows us to understand children's fantasies in general, but there is a particular variant gripping adopted children that is worth mentioning. As Elinor B. Rosenberg and Thomas M. Horner[9] explain.

> When a child living with biological parents fantasizes another set of parents, the groundless nature of the fantasies in relation to reality defines its character as romance. … For adopted children, the birthparent romance fantasy … is lifelong. For them there is an additional romance process which involves gathering facts about their biological origins. These facts shifted and embellished over the years, constitute the foundation of identity formation and identity conflicts. Having no autobiographical data to call up from their adoptive parents, they must construct their own stories about their genetic roots, conception, prenatal life and birth.

Although Joss was probably not adopted in the manner he suggested, of the psychological literature I have read, this passage comes closest to describing Joss's persona and explaining some of the anomalies in his account. There are undoubtedly shards of reality and great chunks of irrefutable fact, but they are held together by a latticework of an enduring 'family romance' – one that was so imbricated in his lifestyle and way of being that there is no telling where reality ended, and the imagination began.

I add that Joss's fantasies may well have been generated by his broken and unconventional childhood. This is the view of

Mimi Kester, a senior accredited psychodynamic counsellor whom I consulted. She hypothesized that Joss rejected Ouma Wessels and Wallis because they betrayed him, and that this had left him feeling hurt and angry. She also felt that because his mother could not be bothered, he too could not be bothered to look after himself, and that this shaped his whole life, especially his passivity, low level of literacy and inability to take responsibility. Something else that she noticed in his personality – and he was good at post-rationalizing – was that he always sought to blame someone else. 'Poor me,' 'the victim' are defences against the pain of being abandoned by his parents or not cared for as other children are cared for. He was neglected and, in consequence, is neglectful in terms of his self-care, finances and everything else. His fantasy may well have been a way of coping with the fact that he did not really belong, had had a very unstable childhood with many carers, and had lived a chaotic life in different locations and countries.[10]

Who was Joss?

Other than accepting Joss's own claims, it is possible that he was the biological son of Joseph de Wahl Sr, but that he was born 'out of wedlock,' to use an old-fashioned expression wholly in keeping with the narrow, Calvinist outlook of white Cape, particularly Afrikaner, society at the time. Whereas in French, Spanish, or Portuguese colonial settings, 'outside' children were often openly acknowledged, this was not the case in white South Africa. Its social constraints were such that Joss either had to be given away at birth to another family or raised in secrecy. This latter choice may have everything to do with Mrs Billy Graaff, who Joss acknowledged as his foster mother, but may have been his biological mother. She is a powerful persona in Joss's account precisely because she is a non-person, an absent presence – whom he does not even dignify with a name separate from her former husband's name. The only mother who appears in Joss's account as 'real' is his 'invented' mother, Wallis, whom he describes affectionately and fully, warts and all.

Assuming that Joseph Sr and Mrs Billy Graaff are Joss's biological parents and that they decided to hide him away at birth solves a few puzzles. This could be why he was raised by housekeepers and educated by private tutors recruited (and this clearly is salient) from far-off places, so less likely to spread gossip. When that arrangement was compromised by a neighbour complaining about the housekeeper's childrearing practices (something we would now call child abuse), it is perfectly explicable that Ouma Wessels, Mrs Billy Graaff's mother, should come to the rescue. Incidentally, Joss's descriptions of his life with Ouma Wessels and his playmate Sophie (later the Queen of Spain) are wholly convincing. He could easily have been her playmate without necessarily having royal credentials.

So, the shadowy figure of Mrs Billy Graaff slowly comes into focus as much more significant a player than I thought she was. I was blindsided by Joss's studied indifference to her, which could be the negative part of his fantasy. However, despite being marginalized and effectively anonymized by Joss, she was powerful enough to elicit the support of her husband's family company, Graaffs Trust Ltd, which looked after Joss's welfare until he was eighteen. She was able to persuade her mother to take over Joss's care, perhaps reluctantly given Ouma Wessels's position in Cape society. Again, I do not think it is too much of a leap to suppose that it was Mrs Billy Graaff, not her lover Joseph Sr, who insisted on going ahead with the birth and secret upbringing of her love child. The nature of her relationship to her husband, Mr Bill Graaff, is lost in the mists of time. Readers might remember he committed suicide and it is impossible not at least to speculate on the reasons for this act of desperation. Had he given his wife a hard time over a long period, prompting her infidelity? Was he mentally unstable in clinical terms? Was he impotent? Was the relationship in trouble? Did his wife's affair with Joseph de Wahl Sr and the birth of Joss push him over the edge?

If Joseph Sr was Joss's biological father, there is a tenuous provenance for Joss's porphyria. I refer to a possible ancestral link to 1688 when a 'founder mutation' of variegate porphyria was introduced to South Africa by an early Dutch settler. However, this squares with neither Joss's diagnosis of acute intermittent porphyria, nor with the claim that Joseph de Wahl Sr's father was the eminent administrator, Nicolaas Frederic de Waal, who only came to South Africa in 1880. Joss could just have been very unlucky (the incidence of porphyria in most European populations is 0.13 cases per million per year). At any event, however it arose, Joss's porphyria was all too real. Even if it were not inherited from his royal provenance, it provided in abundance the necessary grist to his fantasizing mill. He was of royal blood, therefore was prone to porphyria. That he had porphyria was proof of his royal descent. This is a good example of what logicians call 'confirmation bias,' or 'a self-confirming hypothesis.'

While Mrs Billy Graaff (Joss's conceivable mother) disappears into the background, Joss alludes to Joseph de Wahl Sr (his conceivable father) more often. Nonetheless, one cannot escape the sense of Joseph's disapproval of his son, whether biological, fostered or adopted. He helps, but only occasionally and with a mean spirit. Some rent is paid for Joss, some small bills at the pharmacy are met. He sells property that Joss believes is rightfully his. In addition, Joss has a hostile relationship towards his stepbrother, Joseph Sr's acknowledged natural son.

What is the source of Joseph Sr's disapproval? I think that this turned primarily on Joss's homosexuality. Despite describing himself to me on several occasions as asexual, I have strong grounds to believe that he was probably a practising gay for much of his life. At one level this is neither here nor there – like many people, I am relaxed about people's sexual preferences. However, it must be remembered that being gay in apartheid South Africa was not fun – the sodomy law dating from 1872 prohibiting anal or oral intercourse between men carried harsh penalties and was brutally enforced. In Joss's case, there was a secret bond shared with other gay people that on the one hand opened significant sources of information to Joss among (particularly) upper-class men and, on the other, led to the need for a cloak of discretion, which may have prolonged his adherence to the family romance.

Having crafted these feasible building blocks of Joss's identity, or assumed identity, I am able to answer the questions I posed at the beginning of my enquiry. First, as I established, Joss did indeed suffer from porphyria. While it plausibly could have been inherited from the royal family, it could also have been randomly contracted or perhaps derived from a known South African variant. However, his porphyria was crucially important at the psychological level, feeding his delusions and imagination.

Second, Joss's unusually secretive private education could be explained by Joseph Sr and Mrs Graaff wanting to conceal his illegitimate birth, if indeed they were his parents. Certainly, neither Georgina nor I know of any white South African of a similar class position who had so eccentric an education. Private tuition over a long period in South Africa is rare, yet we were able to verify most of Joss's description of his educational experience. He must have developed his unerring English accent and manners from his English tutor, from periods of residence in the UK and from long friendships, perhaps gay relationships, with members of the English aristocracy. Although, as I have maintained before, it is difficult for South Africans to lose all trace of their native accent, there are of course occasional exceptions. Joss, who was certainly an anglophile, could have acquired both upper-class English manners and perfect pronunciation.

Third, why did Baroness Jean Tromp (née Jean Playfair, cousin of the Queen Mother) unequivocally validate Joss's claims? This remains difficult to explain. I can testify that, when he was not describing totally off-the-wall events, Joss could be very convincing. He completely and utterly persuaded several people in whom he confided that he was exactly who he said he was. Jean was totally unwavering in her acceptance of Joss's story. I do not want to sound derogatory about Jean (I liked her a lot), but it is true she had a little of the ingenue about her all her life. Though older than me, she seems to have spent little time doing anything other than being waited on and chatting about the old countries (more Scotland than England). Although her living standards, like Joss's, eventually collapsed in a heap, she never lost her genteel innocence. Insofar as she had a reason for living after her divorce, it was to protect the reputation of the royal family and as she saw it that, in turn, meant protecting Joss. Jean Tromp believed in Joss because she wanted to believe in him.

Fourth, how could I account for the valuable art and furniture of which Joss was indisputably the custodian? Time after time the 'big stuff' seemed to be so near yet so far. Trusts are formed, then fail to materialize. Jewellery, furniture, paintings, currency, and bullion cascade into sight, then vanish into thin air. Their disappearance towards the end of Joss's life is consistent with the idea that 'the Palace' (to use a vague term) needed to separate Joss from his possessions, lest they lend force to any claimed links to the royal family. Leonora Pegram could have been acting in support of this plan. Alternatively, attentive readers might have noticed that more than a whiff of criminality is detectable in several transactions. A yacht brings paintings to and from South Africa. Rab Cecil ships art out of the country in apparent defiance of export regulations. Joss admits that, at one time, he had a bag full of foreign currency and bullion, which, if undeclared, was certainly illegal. At least one painting is retrieved from a locker at Heathrow Airport, and then four more suddenly materialize. Leonora Pegram is charged with theft when she failed to return some items to a Cape Town jeweller, with Joss being implicated in her wake. (And something I have not mentioned before is that I was able to establish that one of Leonora's minor associates was convicted of passing a dud cheque.)

Need I go on? All these admissions, large and small, might indicate that there is another intriguing story lurking beneath Joss's account. Was he part of a gigantic criminal network set up to service rich South Africans who were buying and selling art and furniture on a massive scale? Incoming purchases could be intended to protect wealth against a falling rand (adopted in 1961, the rand rapidly fell in value against the British pound) while having some beautiful objects to show for it. Outgoing sales could be a means of bypassing exchange controls and holding objects or cash abroad for a rainy day. Having articulated this theory, I must immediately insist, as it were in capital letters, that all the lawyers, auctioneers, valuers, jewellers, banks, and well-wishers mentioned in this account who were drawn into Joss's world (and the various schemes set up by Leonora Pegram) were reputable people and firms acting with the utmost integrity and professionalism. Can I underline that point once again? It is possible that entirely innocent people were drawn into a criminal conspiracy and that this could have applied to Joss himself. It is possible that his mysterious origin could have been used to conceal the provenance of *objets d'art*. Given the fantasy that might have gripped him, he could have been made to believe he was a true owner of such objects, thereby providing additional cover.

An even bolder hypothesis is that Joss was a criminal mastermind, overseeing a gigantic fraud with me as the naïve bearer of the veracity of his brilliant cover story. This hypothesis fell apart immediately. Joss believed his own account before and long after rich South Africans needed to fiddle their exchequer. He was far too incompetent to have organized a bun fight in a bakery, let alone a fraud on the scale described. He called in police forces in South Africa and the UK to investigate 'his' missing goods, not a good move for a criminal. Finally, he asked me to convey his account, not the best way of covering his tracks.

So, by a circuitous route, I am back to two thoughts. Much of what Joss said was plausible and/or Joss was in the grip of an extended 'family romance' in which he believed he was Wallis Simpson and Edward VIII's son. The bonding experience of his two big secrets – that he was royal and gay – drew certain people into his close circle. I can now answer one of the questions I posed when embarking on this book – how did Joss know so much about the royal family and its wider circle? He was a compelling conversationalist and his amusing manner invited reciprocal confidences. So, paradoxically, although Joss might have elevated his parentage, a lot of the gossip he recounted about the royal family could have been completely reliable information from his companions. Because certain people in high places believed Joss's narrative, or perhaps they were just humouring him, they shared salacious and probably trustworthy chats about the world they inhabited. So, even if Joss's account of himself is not fully credible, the stories told to him and recounted by him may be entirely accurate. For all these reasons it is impossible to draw a rigid line between reality and fantasy.

Much of this must remain speculative. While the principal argument hinges on the duality of 'truth' or 'fantasy,' there are some subtle positions between the two. We all deny and imagine things. Perhaps in our minds we all walk that fine line between being a 'somebody' and being a 'nobody.' But Joss's story was sufficiently poignant, compelling, and plausible for him to make sense of his own life, and for others to trust, support and love him. Joss might have liked the German philosopher, Schopenhauer, who proclaimed that 'the world is my idea.' The world, Schopenhauer continued, is conditioned by the subject, and only exists in the subject's eyes and brain. In this sense, my task here has mainly been to render Joss's account faithfully in his own terms rather than pass a final judgement on its veracity.

Chapter Notes

1. Introduction

1. Princess Mary of Teck (1867–1953), wife of George V and mother of Edward VIII and George VI.
2. Little did Joss know that our families were connected in a more unfortunate way. My aunt's husband, the psychiatrist, Bernard Armitage (1890–1976), had written to the British prime minister, Stanley Baldwin, that Edward VIII had suffered from 'social and sexual inadequacy' as a young man and that he had 'over-compensated' in his singular and persistent attachment to Wallis Simpson. 'The stage was set for disaster,' he rather pompously concluded (Robert Beaken, *Cosmo Lang: Archbishop in War and Crisis*, London: I.B.Tauris, 2012, p. 171).
3. Anastasia Romanov (1901–1918), the youngest daughter of Tsar Nicholas II of Russia, died aged 17 along with the rest of her family at the hands of the Bolshevik secret police. A woman called Anna Anderson claimed that she had survived and that she was Anastasia, but subsequent DNA tests proved that her claims were false.
4. Information from the late Dr C. J. Molteno, my father quoting a member of the club.
5. Edward VIII abdicated on 10 December in South Africa, on 12 December in the Irish Free State and on 11 December in the king's other realms.
6. Quoted by Robert Rhodes James in *Sunday Express*, 1 December 1996.
7. The Colonnas were nobles who played a prominent role in Rome during the medieval and Renaissance period.
8. Mary Raffray later married Wallis's former husband, Ernest Simpson.

9. Bryanston Court, George Street, London, W1, was where Wallis and Ernest Simpson were living at that time.
10. Charles Higham, *The Duchess of Windsor: The Secret Life* (New York: Charter Books, 1989) pp. 180–1.
11 Ibid., p. 188.

2. The Motherless Child

1. Eric Hobsbawm, *Interesting Times: A Twentieth-Century Life* (London: Allen Lane, 2002) p. 87.
2. Ibid., p. 88.
3. Susan Williams, *The People's King: The True Story of the Abdication* (London: Penguin Books, 2003) pp. 8–11.
4. HRH the Duke of Windsor, *A King's Story: The Memoirs of HRH the Duke of Windsor KG* (London: Cassell & Company Ltd, 1951) p. 136.
5. Ibid., p. 332.
6. Susan Williams, *The People's King: The True Story of the Abdication* (London: Penguin Books, 2003) pp. 197–81, 198–9.
7. Lord Beaverbrook, edited by A. J. P. Taylor, *The Abdication of King Edward VIII* (London: Hamish Hamilton, 1966) p. 68; Lewis Broad, *The Abdication* (London: Frederick Muller Ltd, 1961) p. 188; Susan Williams, *The People's King: The True Story of the Abdication* (London: Penguin Books, 2003) pp. 138–44.
8. Philip Ziegler, *King Edward VIII: The Official Biography* (New York: Alfred A. Knopf, 1991) p. 308.
9. George Ladbrook was Edward VIII's chauffeur.
10. Peregrine Cust, 6th Baron Brownlow (1899–1978), was Edward VIII's Lord in Waiting.
11. Presumably, this was the La Pyramide at Vienne, just south of Lyon, where they stopped on their way to Cannes and where Wallis jumped through the window to escape being photographed by the press.
12. Villa Lou Viei was the name of the Rogers's house in France where Joss was, supposedly, born.
13. The Duke and Duchess of Windsor rented the Chateau de la Cröe in the Cap d'Antibes between Cannes and Nice, which Wallis renovated before purchasing it in 1938. They sold the villa to a Greek shipping magnate in 1952.
14. Joss thought that Joseph de Wahl's father was Frederic de Waal (1853–1932), who went to South Africa from the Netherlands in the 1870s. He entered Parliament in 1898 and subsequently became a prominent administrator of the Cape Province. The

spelling 'de Wahl' and 'de Waal' is used inconsistently in South Africa, so this is possible.

15. Joss's newly-constructed South African birth certificate was dated 16 December 1937, namely one year after he claimed to have actually been born.

16. Simon van der Stel was born in Mauritius, the son of a woman whose mother had been a slave, Monica da Costa van Goa. His father was the Dutch governor of Mauritius. See Patric Tariq Mellet, *The Lie of 1652: A Decolonised History of Land* (Cape Town: Tafelberg, 2020).

17. Funnily enough, on seeing the main Parel Vallei house in the late 1990s, I immediately recognized having been there as a child. My maternal grandmother had been a friend of Mrs Wessels and was sometimes invited to have tea with her, though we children were never allowed into the house and had to amuse ourselves outdoors.

18. Westbrook, which was built in the early eighteenth century, became the official residence of the governor-general of South Africa in the early twentieth century. In 1995 it was renamed Genadendal and now serves as the official residence of the president of South Africa when in office at Tuynhuys, Cape Town.

19. A poem by Oscar Wilde, which he wrote in May 1897 after having served two years' hard labour in Reading prison for homosexuality. In 1896, while serving his sentence, a 30-year-old man was hanged for killing his wife. This had a deep effect on Wilde and inspired him to write the poem. This interest in Wilde may provide a clue to Joss's emerging sexuality.

20. It is highly unlikely that Ouma Wessels was 'restructuring Anglo-American,' a massive mining house based in Johannesburg. There were to be other occasions when Joss wildly exaggerated the power of those around him.

21. Dolly Roussouw was a member of Ouma Wessels's household staff.

22. Thomas Milton was a furniture shop in Somerset West, Cape.

23. The vicarage in Somerset West. It is now a B&B and restaurant, but in those days, it was a private house.

24. The seaside resort closest to Somerset West.

25. Le Corbusier, alias Charles-Édouard Jeanneret-Gris (1887–1965), was a Swiss-French architect and pioneer of modern architecture and the international style. His style may have inspired the architect of Sonnekus, but I could find no evidence that Le Corbusier was directly involved.

26. Sir De Villiers Graaff (1913–1999), former leader of the United Party, which for many years was South Africa's main opposition party.

27. After the F. Scott Fitzgerald novel, *The Great Gatsby* (1925), set on the north shore of Long Island, New York, during the summer of 1922.
28. The fashion and portrait photographer Cecil Beaton (1904–1980) photographed just about all the rich, famous, and stylish people of his time.
29. Milnerton is a suburb of Cape Town on the coast of Table Bay north of the city.
30. A luxury car taken over by Aston Martin in 2010.
31. I also remember that my grandmother, the one who used to have tea with Mrs Wessels at Parel Vallei, had been invited to meet the royal family at a garden party at Government House and that for the occasion my mother made her a beautiful dress to wear in sage green broderie anglaise.
32. Genetic testing subsequently showed that it was improbable that George Rex (1765–1839) had been of royal descent.

3. Wallis: Princess of Elegance

1. Greg King, *The Duchess of Windsor: The Uncommon Life of Wallis Simpson* (London: Aurum Press, 2000) pp. 11, 13; and Charles Higham, *Mrs Simpson* (London: Pan Books, 2005) p. 4.
2. Georgina and I knew Henry Petersen (Viscount Barrington), who had been a schoolfriend of my older brother, but he was guarded in his responses to our questions about Joss.
3. Grace Kelly, aged 52, died in a car accident in which she was the driver in September 1982, perhaps after having suffered a stroke.
4. Peter Carl Fabergé (1846–1920) was a Russian-born French jeweller.
5. Ron Chernow, *The House of Morgan: An American Banking Dynasty and the Rise of Modern Finance* (New York: Simon & Schuster, 1990) p. 171.
6. Charles Higham, *The Duchess of Windsor: The Secret Life* (New York: Charter Books, 1989) p. 9.
7. Ibid., p. 9.
8. Michael Bloch, *The Duchess of Windsor* (London: Weidenfeld & Nicolson, 1996).
9. Wikipedia quoting Patrick Howard, *George VI* (London: Hutchinson, 1987) p. 61.
10. HRH the Duke of Windsor, *A King's Story: The Memoirs of HRH the Duke of Windsor KG* (London: Cassell & Company Ltd, 1951) p. 338.

11. Elsie de Wolfe (1865–1950), also known as Lady Mendl, was an interior designer who referred to herself as a 'rebel in an ugly world.' She was author of *The House in Good Taste* (New York, 1913).

12. Lilly Daché (1898–1989) was a French milliner and fashion designer who purportedly said 'Glamour is what makes a man ask for your telephone number. But it also is what makes a woman ask for the name of your dressmaker.'

13. Unfortunately, I have been unable to ascertain who Anna Henry was or is.

4. The King and I and Other Royals

1. Elgin is a fruit-farming area near Cape Town in which the little town of Grabouw hosts an annual rose show.

2. Jacob Rothschild, 4th Baron Rothschild (born 1936) is the eldest son of Victor Rothschild.

3. Christopher Warwick, *Abdication* (London: Guild Publishing, 1986) p. 52.

4. Frances Donaldson, *Edward VIII* (London: Weidenfeld & Nicholson, 1974) p. 63.

5. Marlborough House is a mansion in Pall Mall, London.

6. Frances Donaldson, *Edward VIII* (London: Weidenfeld & Nicholson, 1974) p. 184. Fort Belvedere, a country house on the border between Berkshire and Surrey, was Edward VIII's home and was a royal residence between 1750 and 1976. The Crown still owns the property, but it is no longer a royal residence.

7. Aga Khan, *The Memoirs of Aga Khan: World Enough and Time* (London: Cassell & Company Ltd, 1954) pp. 249–50.

8. Prince Charles, however, subsequently moved into Clarence House, the home of the late Queen Mother, in 2003.

9. The Bahamas, of which Nassau is the capital, are made up of a group of 29 islands, plus numerous cays and islets, in the Atlantic Ocean north of Cuba. The islands gained their independence from the United Kingdom in 1964.

10. Michael Pye, *The Windsors in Exile: The Untold Story of a Sensational Wartime Scandal* (Feltham: Hamlyn Publishing Group, 1982) p. 10.

11. Ibid., pp. 9–10.

12. Grosvenor Chapel is an Anglican church in South Audley Street, Mayfair, London.

13. Farm Street is a Jesuit church in Mount Street, Mayfair.

14. Queen Elizabeth II was born on 21 April 1926 and crowned queen on 2 June 1953.

15. Greg King, *The Duchess of Windsor: The Uncommon Life of Wallis Simpson* (London: Aurum Press Ltd, 2000) p. 196.
16. George VI died on 6 February 1952 and Queen Mary on 24 March 1953.
17. Alexander, Prince of Teck (1874–1957) was one-time governor-general of South Africa and, Joss said, helped to conceal his identity and to organize his upbringing in South Africa. Although he only died in 1957, he was governor-general of South Africa from 1924 until 1931, so Joss could not have come across him. His wife Princess Alice, however, made frequent trips to South Africa and Joss claimed to have got to know her well.
18. The Duke of Windsor travelled from New York on 6 March 1953 on hearing of his mother's impending death.
19. Marie Louise (1872–1957) was the youngest daughter of Helena (Lenchen) (1846–1923) and Christian, Prince of Schleswig-Holstein (1853–1920).
20. Edward Winfield was Joss's tutor who later moved to South Africa where he spent the rest of his life.
21. First Earl Louis Mountbatten of Burma (1900–1979) and uncle of Prince Philip, Queen Elizabeth II's husband.
22. His wife Edwina Mountbatten (1901–1960) née Edwina Ashley was a wealthy heiress and socialite in her youth, but during and after the Second World War she devoted her time to good works.
23. He was assassinated in Ireland in 1979 while fishing near his country home Classiebawn Castle in County Sligo.
24. India Hicks (born 1967) is the daughter of Louis Mountbatten's daughter Pamela (born 1929) and the late designer David Nightingale Hicks (1929–1998).
25. She died suddenly in 1960, at the age of 59, while on an official tour of Borneo for the St John Ambulance Brigade.
26. Edwina Hicks was born in 1961.
27. Glamis Castle in Angus, Scotland, belongs to the Earl and Countess of Strathmore and was where the late Queen Mother, née Elizabeth Bowes-Lyon, spent her childhood.
28. Jack the Ripper was an unidentified serial killer in the Whitechapel area of London in 1888.
29. Air Marshal Patrick Henry Lyon Playfair (1889–1974).
30. Charles Higham, *The Duchess of Windsor: The Secret Life* (New York: Charter Books, 1989) p. 358.
31. Ibid., p. 117.
32. Ibid.
33. Ibid., p. 347.

34. John W. Wheeler-Bennett, *King George VI: His Life and Reign* (London: Macmillan & Co Ltd, 1958) pp. 546–7.
35. Charles Higham, *The Duchess of Windsor: The Secret Life* (New York: Charter Books, 1989) pp. 115–16.
36. Noel Coward (1899–1973) the actor, composer, singer, playwright, and director.
37. Princess Marina of Greece and Denmark (1906–1968) married the Duke of Kent in November 1934.
38. Sandringham House in north Norfolk has been a royal retreat since Queen Victoria bought it in 1862.
39. Gloria Vanderbilt (1904–1965) is best known for being the mother of fashion designer and artist Gloria Vanderbilt (born 1924) and for her role in the sensational trial over the custody of her child.
40. Prince Michael of Kent was born in 1942.
41. Kaiser William II (1859–1941).
42. Princess Victoria (1840–1901) who married Kaiser Frederick III (1831–1988).
43. Charles Higham, *The Duchess of Windsor: The Secret Life* (New York: Charter Books, 1989) pp. 165–6
44. Diana Mosley née Mitford (1910–2003).
45. Shirley Temple (born 1928) was a famous child star and started appearing in films from the age of three.
46. He is presumably implying that his father would have been able to retain the British Empire and thus prevent the decolonization of Africa.
47. Maxims is a fashionable restaurant in the rue Royale in Paris.
48. Nickname for King George VI.
49. From Rudyard Kipling's poem, 'You'll be a Man my Son.'
50. Argyle House is where the socialite and interior decorator Lady Sibyl Colefax (1874–1950) lived and entertained.
51. Charles Higham, *The Duchess of Windsor: The Secret Life* (New York: Charter Books, 1989) p. 148.
52. Greg King, *The Duchess of Windsor: The Uncommon Life of Wallis Simpson* (London: Aurum Press Ltd, 2000) p. 394.
53. Ibid., p. 456.
54. There is a royal burial ground at Frogmore, which is not open to the public.
55. Rita Hayworth (1918–1987) American film actress and dancer of the 1940s. Her marriage to Prince Aly Khan, the third of her five marriages, lasted from 1949 to 1953 and resulted in the birth of one daughter, Princess Yasmin Aga Khan, in Switzerland in December 1949.

56. Presumably, he is referring to Margaret Trudeau, wife of the late Canadian prime minister Pierre Trudeau. I do not remember any such scandal, though they were apparently friends and Margaret had a crush on one of the Rolling Stones.

5. Rothschilds and Ashrams

1. Louis Nathaniel de Rothschild was born in Vienna on 5 March 1882 and died of heart failure while swimming in Montego Bay, Jamaica on 15 January 1955. He was the son of Albert Salomon von Rothschild who owned a spectacular palace in Vienna. After the Anschluss with Austria he found himself in Nazi Germany in March 1938, where he was arrested and taken into custody because he was a Jew. He was imprisoned at least until the end of July 1938. Finally allowed to leave Austria, Louis survived the Holocaust and Second World War, but all his possessions were confiscated. In 1946 he married the countess Hildegard Johanna von Auersperg (1895–1981) and lived in Vermont and England. (This information is derived from a Wikipedia entry.)
2. Niall Ferguson, *The World's Banker: The History of the House of Rothschild* (London: Weidenfeld & Nicolson, 1998) p. 771.
3. She died on 20 January 2005.
4. I have been unable to trace Parker.
5. Vera K. Fast, *Children's Exodus: A History of the Kindertransport* (London: I.B.Tauris, 2011) p. 13.
6. Fast, *Children's Exodus*, p. 172, citing Hartley Library, Brodetsky, Ms 119 (AJ3/1–150, part 1), de Rothschild to Brodetsky, 16 December 1940.
7. Frederick Morton, *The Rothschilds: A Family Portrait* (London: Secker & Warburg, 1962) pp. 81–3.
8. The Prince of Wales (1841–1910) succeeded his mother Queen Victoria as Edward VII in 1901.
9. Morton, *The Rothschilds*, p. 185
10. Ivor Edwards was quite a character. He had a background in the Coldstream Guards and had a second salon at White's Club. Many of his clients were rich and titled. He died in 2012, after which, presumably, his salons were closed.
11. Lord Richard Cecil (1948–1978) who, as we shall see later, became an important person in Joss's life, probably the closest friend he ever had.
12. Cipolin is a green and white streaked Italian marble.
13. Strictly, for psychologists the term 'paternity uncertainty' refers to the fact that, given the possibility of secret sexual liaisons, one can

never know with absolute certainty who one's father is. In Joss's case, this uncertainty was even more marked. In such situations, the caregiving and protective role of grandparents, uncles and aunts is enhanced. See, for example, S. J. C. Gaulin et al. 'Matri-lateral biases in the investment of aunts and uncles,' *Human Nature*, 8, 1997, pp. 139–51.

6. The Uncertain Years

1. Margery Perham, *The Colonial Reckoning: The Reith Lectures* (London: Collins, 1961) p. 144.
2. John Reader, *Africa: A Biography of the Continent* (Harmonds-worth: Penguin, 1997) p. 657, quoting Crowder, 1993, in Unesco, vol. 8, p. 94.
3. The Nationalists, or Nats as they were commonly referred to, were members of the right-wing National Party, which governed South Africa between 1948 and 1994. The party's main support came from the white, Afrikaans-speaking members of the population. The party was best known for its policy of 'apartheid' under which only white people were allowed to vote and the different races were kept strictly apart. Cinemas, beaches, schools, residential areas, restaurants, public transport and even park benches were all segregated.
4. I am not sure when Joseph de Wahl Sr died, but there is evidence that he was still alive in 1982.
5. A small orange citrus fruit with a distinctive tangy taste, which originally came from China.
6. Since Joss was not yet fourteen when Smuts died in September 1950, it somehow seems unlikely that they would ever have discussed Cape architecture together.
7. Quoted in S. B. Spies and G. Natrass (eds) *Jan Smuts: Memoirs of the Boer War* (Johannesburg: Jonathan Bell, 1994) p. 19.
8. Pauline de Rothschild (1908–1976) and Wallis Simpson were close friends, so presumably Joss had a dinner engagement with her that evening.
9. Pauline's second husband was Philippe de Rothschild who owned the French winery at Chateau Mouton Rothschild in Pauillac, near Bordeaux. The nearby Lafite Rothschild produces the most col-lectable Bordeaux on the market.
10. Mick Jagger, British singer, musician, and actor (born 1943) who formed the Rolling Stones rock band with his friend Keith Richards.
11. Tessa Meltzer was a landscape gardener in Cape Town.

12. Lyon Playfair, 1st Baron Playfair (1818–1898) was a scientist and Liberal politician.

13. He might have been referring to James Scott and Sons, Dundee, who were jute merchants, or alternatively, given that Eastwood, which lies on the border between the English counties of Nottinghamshire and Derbyshire and is mentioned in the Domesday Book, was a former coal-mining town, they could have made their money in coal.

14. I am unsure who Oliver is, but presume he is a relative of hers.

15. The Anglo-Boer War, which lasted from 11 October 1899 to 31 May 1902, was fought in South Africa between Britain and the white, Afrikaans-speaking inhabitants of two independent Boer republics, the Transvaal, and the Orange Free State. The British ultimately won the war, but at the cost of a legacy of extreme bitterness. Thenceforth, until 1961, South Africa became the Union of South Africa, a part of the British Empire and a member of the Commonwealth.

16. This was Hugh Grosvenor (known as 'Bendor') (1879–1953), 2nd Duke of Westminster, who sold a farm to Jean's father on the Westminster estates in the Orange Free State, South Africa.

17. Sir Herbert Baker (1862–1946) was a British architect who made a substantial contribution to South African architecture in the period between 1892 and 1912. His building and designs, in this case for the gardens on the Westminster Estate, are highly valued.

18. Ian Smith (1919–2007) served as prime minister of the British colony of Southern Rhodesia from 1964 until 1965 when he unilaterally declared independence from Britain. He was prime minister and leader of the Rhodesian Front until white rule ended in 1979.

19. Lady Rose Alice Elizabeth Cecil (born 1956) was the second youngest of Rab's six siblings and the only girl among them.

7. Riches and Rogues

1. Joss's suggestion that the Windsors were careless about documenting their possessions seems at odds with the issue of a 1200-page sale catalogue of their goods offered by Sotheby's in 1997, which included thousands of items, down to a slice of wedding cake. Of course, this was most likely compiled by others after their deaths.

2. Whatever the veracity of Joss's account regarding the missing photographs, I have been able to verify that the late Sylvia Smaller-

Winnikow moved from South Africa to Australia and had made various gifts to charities in Israel. She seems to have been every bit as impressive as Joss suggested.

3. The history of this company is described on its website http://www.graaffs.co.za/. It administered the affairs of the Graaff family and 'selected private clients.'

8. Creeping Doubts, Old Patterns

1. Timothy Peters 'Royal maladies: inherited diseases in the ruling house of Europe' https://www.ncbi.nlm.nih.gov/pmc/articles/PMC4952518/
2. http://www.porphyria-patients.uct.ac.za/ppa/types/variegate
3. The flat at 32A Ovington Square belonged to the distinguished Conservative politician Lord Carrington of Upton, who died in July 2018, and his wife Lady Iona Carrington, who died in June 2009.
4. Louise Arundel and Patrick Guinness married in March 1990, so they were not yet legally married at the time. I have no proof of Guinness having visited Joss in London.
5. This was the £1 million in bullion and notes that Joss had transferred from the Trust Bank in Cape Town to Mrs Pegram's strongbox at her house in Constantia.

9. Letting Go

1. Lucan certainly escaped from the UK but reports of his location were many and varied. South Africa was rarely mentioned as a possible bolthole, though it is relatively easy to 'disappear' there and his brother, Hugh Bingham, had lived in the country until his death in 2018, aged 78.

10. Conclusion

1. Tommaso di Carpegna Falconieri, *The Man Who Believed He Was King of France: A True Medieval Tale* (Chicago: Chicago University Press, 2008).
2. R. Knowles et al. 'Grandiose delusions: a review and theoretical integration of cognitive and affective perspectives,' *Clin Psychol Rev.* 31 (4), 2011, 684–96.
3. K. Abraham, 'The history of an imposter in the light of psycho-analytic knowledge,' in Karl Abraham, *Clinical Papers and Essays on Psychoanalysis*, New York: Basic Books, 1955.
4. H. Deutsch, 'The impostor: contribution to the ego psychology of a type of psychopath,' *Psychoanalytic Quarterly*, 24 (483) 1955.

5. Phyllis Greenacre, 'The impostor,' *Psychoanalytic Quarterly*, 27 (3) 1958, 359–82.
6. Though perhaps it is interesting that he insisted that both he and the Duchess of Windsor were asexual.
7. https://www.encyclopedia.com/psychology/dictionaries-thesauruses-pictures-and-press-releases/imposter
8. The Mignon delusion, the belief that the parents who brought one up are not one's natural parents and that one really belongs to a more distinguished family, alludes to a character of mysterious origins in Goethe's novel *Wilhelm Meisters Lehrjahre*, and the heroine of the opera *Mignon* based on it, who pines away and dies without her longings for her imagined family being fulfilled. For Freud, 'the child's imagination becomes engaged in the task of getting free from the parents of whom he now has such a low opinion and of replacing them by others, occupying, as a rule, a higher social station.' Sigmund Freud, *Collected Papers volume 5*, ed. James Strachey (New York: Basic Books, 1959), 74–8.
9. Elinor B. Rosenberg and Thomas M. Homer, 'Birthparent romances and identity formation in adopted children,' *Amer. J. Orthopyschiat*, 61 (1), January 1991, pp. 71, 77.
10. A professor of psychology at Leicester University, Andrew M. Colman believes that 'the delusions of people with this syndrome are generally far vaguer and more ethereal than Joss's,' and claims never to have 'heard of cases in which they have so much grounding in reality. They're usually more dreamlike' (personal email, November 2021).

Dramatis Personae

Aga Khan III (1877–1957), head of Ismaili Muslims.

Aga Khan IV, Sultan Karim, present Aga Khan (b.1936). Son of Aly Khan and Joan Yarde-Buller.

Aitken, Max (1879–1964), 1st Baron Beaverbrook, also known as the 'First Baron of Fleet Street.'

Albert, Prince of Saxe-Coburg (1819–61), husband of Queen Victoria.

Alexander, Lucy, relative of Lord Lucan.

Alexandra (1844–1925), Queen and wife of Edward VII, formerly Princess Alexandra of Denmark.

Alexandra (b.1936) daughter of George, Duke of Kent and Princess Marina, sister of Prince Michael of Kent.

Alice, Princess, Countess of Athlone (1883–1981), Queen Victoria's granddaughter and wife of Earl of Athlone.

Argyll, Margaret Duchess of (1912–1993), Wallis's friend and notorious socialite.

Asquith, Margot (1864–1945), Countess of Oxford and Asquith, wife of Herbert Henry Asquith, prime minister of the United Kingdom from 1908 to 1916.

Athlone, Alexander Earl of (1874–1957), governor-general of the Union of South Africa (1923–31), also Queen Mary's brother.

Attlee, Clement (1883–1967), leader of the opposition at the time of the abdication.

Baker, Sir Herbert (1862–1946), British architect who designed numerous public and private buildings in South Africa.

Baldwin, Billy (1903–1983), 'Charming Billy,' interior designer.

Baldwin, Stanley (1867–1947), Conservative prime minister of Britain.

255

Barrington, Viscount Henry (b.1938), longstanding friend of Joss's in Cape Town and Knysna. Formerly Henry Petersen, he changed his name on inheriting a title.

Beaton, Cecil (1904–1980), society photographer.

Beaverbrook, Lord; *see under* Aitkin, Max.

Bingham, Hugh, brother of Lord Lucan (1939–2018) who lived and died in South Africa.

Blum, Maître Suzanne (1898–1994), French lawyer who looked after Wallis Simpson's affairs.

Breytenbach, Breyten (b.1939), South African writer and painter who lived in Paris and was a staunch opponent of apartheid.

Brownlow, Lord Perry, Peregrine Francis Adelbert Cust, 6th Baron Brownlow (1899–1978), Edward VIII's Lord in Waiting, who accompanied the Windsors to France in 1936.

Cadogan, Primrose, Wallis's friend; *see under* Yarde-Buller, Primrose.

Camilla, Duchess of Cornwall (b.1947), second wife of Prince Charles.

Camrose, 2nd Viscount, John Seymour Berry (1909–1995), politician, newspaper proprietor and Joan Yarde-Buller's third husband.

Catania, Prince, the man who Victoria Colonna's father made her marry. I have been unable to establish who he could possibly have been.

Catherine the Great of Russia (1729–1796) Empress of Russia following the deposition of her husband Peter III.

Cavendish, Deborah ('Debo') (1920–2014), Duchess of Devonshire, née Mitford.

Cecil, Rab (Lord Richard Valentine Gascoyne-Cecil, 1948–1978), Joss's close friend who was killed while observing the Second Chimurenga in Zimbabwe.

Cecil, Lady Rose, Alice Elizabeth (b.1956) sister of Rab Cecil.

Charles, Prince of Wales (b.1948), heir apparent to the British throne.

Churchill, Charles, Jean Tromp's cousin.

Churchill, Winston (1874–1965) British politician and statesman who took Britain through the Second World War.

Coates, Adèle, Jean Tromp's cousin.

Colonna, Victoria (Tia), Italian aristocrat and Wallis's purported natural mother.

Daché, Lilly (1898–1989) French-born milliner and fashion designer.

Dalai Lama (b.1935) who became more political than spiritual in his attempts to resist the encroachment of communist China into his territory.

de Waal, Nicolaas Frederic (1853–1932), Dutch-born parliamentarian and administrator of the Cape Province. Perhaps the father of Joseph de Wahl (Sr).

de Wahl, Joseph (Sr), Joss's purported foster father.

de Wolfe, Elsie (1865–1950) American interior decorator who apparently decorated one of the Duchess of Windsor's rooms at Boulevard Suchet.

Diana, Princess of Wales (1961–1997), first wife of Prince Charles and mother of Princes William and Harry, who died in a car accident in Paris.

Dirk, pseudonym for person in Bredasdorp whom Joss suspected of having stolen a trust deed and who travelled to London with him and Mrs Pegram in 1999.

Duff Cooper, Diana (1892–1986), Paris hostess and close friend of the Duchess of Windsor.

Duke, Doris (1912–1993) American heiress, horticulturalist, art collector and philanthropist who organized Joss's visit to Trappist monastery.

Eddy, Prince (Albert, Victor, later the Duke of Clarence, eldest son of Edward VII (officially 1864–1892, but presumed to have been kept prisoner at Glamis Castle, and for a while suspected to have been associated with Jack the Ripper.

Edinburgh, Philip Duke of (1921–2021), husband of Queen Elizabeth II.

Edward VII (1841–1910), became king on Queen Victoria's death in 1901.

Edward VIII (1894–1972), after his abdication in 1936 he became the Duke of Windsor, allegedly Joss's natural father.

Elizabeth, Queen Mother (1900–2002), known by Joss as 'Cookie.'

Elizabeth II, Queen (b.1926), present queen of the UK and 15 Commonwealth realms.

Esteva, Princess, untraceable cousin of Victoria Colonna.

Eugénie, Empress (1826–1920), wife of Napoleon III, q.v.

Fabergé, Peter Carl (1846–1920), Russian born French jeweller.

Fenwick, Mr Kobie ('Kobus'), friend with whom Joss lived at the end of his life.

Furness, Thelma (1904–1970), twin sister of Gloria Vanderbilt (q.v.) and purported to have been the Duke of Windsor's former mistress.

George, Duke of Kent (1901–1942), younger brother of Edward VIII and George VI.

George III, King (1738–1820), rumoured to be the father of George Rex (q.v.).

George V (1865–1936), father of Edward VIII and George VI; husband of Queen Mary.

George VI (1895–1952), King of England before the reign of Queen Elizabeth II.

George Rex (1765–1839) – widely believed to be the illegitimate son of King George III who was shipwrecked in Knysna in 1804 and started a settlement there, but subsequent genetic testing showed that royal descent was improbable.

Givenchy, Hubert de (1927–2018), clothes designer.

Graaff, Bill, Joss's foster mother's former husband.

Graaff, Mrs Billy, Joss's purported foster mother.

Graaff, De Villiers (1913–1999), leader of the opposition United Party in South Africa.

Grew, Jane Norton (Jessie) (c.1870–1925), Jack Morgan's wife.

Grimaldi, Princess Charlotte Louise Juliette (1898–1977), Duchess of Valentinois, Countess of Polignac and mother of Prince Rainier III, q.v.

Guinness, Desmond (1931–2020), son of Diana Mitford (Mosley) and father of Patrick Desmond.

Guinness, Loel (1906–1988), Joan Yarde-Buller's first husband.

Guinness, Patrick Benjamin (1931–1965), son of Loel Guinness and Joan Yarde-Buller.

Guinness, Patrick Desmond Carl Alexander (b.1956), son of Desmond Guinness, grandson of Diana Mitford/Moseley.

Harlow, Jean (1911–1937), film actress.

Harmsworth, Harold (1868–1940), 1st Viscount Rothermere, British newspaper proprietor.

Hicks, David (1920–1998), husband of Pamela Hicks (née Mountbatten).

Hicks, Edwina (b.1961), Louis Mountbatten's granddaughter.

Hicks, India (b.1967), Louis Mountbatten's granddaughter.

Hicks, Lady Pamela (b.1929), Louis Mountbatten's daughter.

Hitler, Adolf (1889–1945), German dictator.

Hussein, King of Jordan (1935–1999).

Jackson family, friends of Joss's who owned a farm in the Northern Cape.

Jagger, Mick (b.1943), British singer, musician and actor who formed the Rolling Stones rock band with his friend Keith Richards.

Julius Caesar (100 BC–44 BC), Roman general and statesman.

Kelly, Grace (1929–1982), late film star wife of Prince Rainier III of Monaco.

Kemsley, Lord (1883–1968), newspaper publisher.

Kennedy Onassis, Jacqueline Lee Bouvier (1929–1994), first lady of the United States when married to Jack Kennedy.

Khan, Prince Aly (1911–1960), son of Aga Khan III who married Joan Yarde-Buller.

Khan, Amyn Mohammed (b.1937), son of Aly Khan and Joan Yarde-Buller.

Khan, Princess Yasmin Aga (b.1949), daughter of Aly Khan and Rita Hayworth.

Knatchbull, Patricia ('Pat') (1924–2017), 2nd Countess Mountbatten of Burma, daughter of Louis Mountbatten.

Kynoch, George (1834–1891), munitions manufacturer in Birmingham, who emigrated to South Africa in 1888. Mrs Pegram's (q.v.) grandmother had been a Kynoch.

Lacroix, Roger Vandercruse (1728–1799), a great Parisian cabinet-maker.

Ladbrook, George Stanley (1893–1967), Edward VIII's chauffeur.

Lascelles, George (1923–2011), son of Viscount Henry Lascelles and Princess Mary.

Lascelles, Gerald (1924–1998), younger brother of George.

Lascelles, Viscount Henry (1882–1947), 6th Earl of Harewood, husband of Mary, the Princess Royal.

Lascelles, Miss Joan, companion, and lady-in-waiting to Princess Alice.

Leapman, Karina, London solicitor whom Mrs Pegram hired.

Le Corbusier (1887–1965), Swiss-French architect, designer, urban planner.

Leopold, Prince, Duke of Albany (1853–1884), youngest son of Queen Victoria and Prince Albert.

Lloyd George, David (1863–1945), Prime Minister of the United Kingdom between 1908 and 1915 and leader of the Liberal Party between 1926 and 1931.

Louis II, Duke of Valentinois (1870–1949), who ruled the principality of Monaco between 1922 and 1949.

Lucan, Lord ('Lucky'), Richard John Bingham, 7th Earl of Lucan (b.1934), who disappeared mysteriously in 1974 after having purportedly murdered his children's nanny, Sandra Rivett.

Macmillan, Harold (1894–1986), Conservative British Prime Minister who made the famous 'winds of change' speech in the Cape Town parliament in February 1960 that ushered in the decolonization of Africa.

Mainbocher, clothes label founded by US couturier Main Rousseau Bocher (1890–1976).

Marie Antoinette (1755–1793), wife of King Louis XVI of France.

Marie Louise, Princess of Schleswig-Holstein (1872–1956), Queen Victoria's granddaughter.

Marie Louise (1791–1847), Empress and second wife of Napoleon Bonaparte.

Marina, Princess of Greece and Denmark (1906–1968), married George, Duke of Kent, q.v. in November 1934.

Mary (1897–1965), Princess Royal, daughter of George V and Queen Mary.

Mary, Queen (1867–1953), wife of George V and mother of Edward VIII and George VI.

Mellon, Bunny (1910–2014), American heiress, widow of Paul Mellon and close friend of Wallis who, Joss claimed, was entrusted with the management of her financial assets.

Melrose, Olive, Jean Tromp's sister.

Merryman, Aunt Bessie (1864–1964), lived with Wallis in Baltimore when she was a girl.

Michael, Prince of Kent (b.1942), son of Duke of Kent and Princess Marina, whom Joss believed was the unacknowledged natural son of the Duke of Windsor.

Michelangelo (1475–1564) Italian sculptor, painter, architect, and poet.

Milne, Dr Daniel, Joss's doctor in Bredasdorp.

Mitford, 'Debo'; *see under* Cavendish, Deborah.

Mitford, Diana; *see under* Mosley. Her first marriage was to a Guinness.

Mitford, Nancy (1904–1973), author.

Mitford, Unity (1914–1948), one of the Mitford sisters who became a fascist and supported Hitler.

Morgan, J. P., Sr (1837–1913), US railroad, steel, and banking baron.

Morgan, J. P. ('Jack') (1867–1943) Wallis's purported natural father.

Mosley, Diana (1910–2003), née Mitford who married the fascist leader Oswald Mosley.

Mosley, Oswald (1896–1980), fascist leader who married Diana Mitford.

Mountbatten, Edwina (1901–1960), née Edwina Ashley, wife of Louis Mountbatten.

Mountbatten, Lord Louis (1900–1979), uncle of the Duke of Edinburgh (Prince Philip).

Murray, Kathleen (1891–1984) relative of the author who was a close friend of Princess Alice.

Mussolini, Benito (1883–1945), fascist leader of Italy during the Second World War.

Napoleon I, Napoleon Bonaparte (1769–1821), Emperor of the French.

Napoleon III, Emperor (1808–1873), last monarch of France who married Princess Eugénie, q.v.

Napoleon, Louis (1856–1879), Prince Imperial, Napoleon III's son who was killed in Zulu war.

Paul I, King of Greece who spent the war years in South Africa.

Pegram, Leonora Legge, née Schofield (1918–2011), who managed Joss's affairs and eventually appropriated most of his valuables. (Her first name is sometimes rendered as Leonore, or Leonara, but she was known as Leonora and she signed most documents in this fashion.)

Playfair, Kate, relative of Jean Tromp's, who bequeathed some jewellery to her in her will.

Playfair, Lyon, 1st Baron Playfair (1818–1898), scientist and Liberal politician who tutored King Edward VII as a child.

Playfair, Pip (Air Marshal Patrick Henry Lyon Playfair) (1889–1974), head of the Royal Air Force during the Second World War and uncle of Jean Tromp.

Ponsonby, Sir Frederick (1867–1935), keeper of the privy purse under George V.

Pringle, Mrs, housekeeper from the Eastern Cape who looked after Joss after Mr Smithers was killed.

Raffray, Mary (1896–1941), married Wallis's former husband Ernest Simpson.

Rainier III (1923–2005), Prince of Monaco from the Grimaldi family who married Grace Kelly, q.v.

Ribbentrop, Joachim von (1893–1946), Hitler's special adviser and ambassador to the court of St James.

Rogers, Katherine and Herman, close friends of the Duke and Duchess of Windsor and at whose house Joss was supposedly born.

Romanov, Anastasia (1901–1918), youngest daughter of Nicholas II of Russia.

Roosevelt, President Franklin Delano (1882–1945), US president and godfather to Prince Michael of Kent.

Rosebery, Earl of (1847–1929), prime minister of the United Kingdom from 1894 to 1895, married Hannah de Rothschild.

Rothermere, Lord; *see under* Harmondsworth, Harold.

Rothschild, Anthony Gustav de (1887–1961), owner of Ascott.

Rothschild, Baron Eugene (1884–1976), who with his wife Kitty received King Edward VIII at their Schloss Enzesfeld residence shortly before his abdication.

Rothschild, Ferdinand de (1839–1898), Lady Rosebery's cousin, Liberal MP and art collector.

Rothschild, Hannah de (1851–1890), wife of Earl of Rosebery.

Rothschild, Jacob, 4th Baron Rothschild (b.1936), eldest son of Victor Rothschild.

Rothschild, Lionel de (1868–1937), active with the *Kindertransport* during the build-up to the Second World War.

Rothschild, Dame Miriam Louisa (1908–2005), entomologist, zoologist, and author.

Rothschild, 'Nathan,' exact identity unknown but perhaps a member of the wider Rothschild family living at Ascott during Joss's sojourn there.

Rothschild, Pauline (1908–1976), Wallis's friend and house decorator from Baltimore whose second husband was Philippe de Rothschild, owner of the French winery at Chateau Mouton Rothschild in Pauillac, near Bordeaux.

Rupert family, prominent South African family in the Cape.

Russell, John (Ian) (1917–2002), 13th Duke of Bedford who renovated Woburn Abbey.

Santostefano, Fulco, Duke of Verdura (1898–1978), Italian jeweller.

Sapsford, Philip, prominent London QC.

Simpson, Ernest Aldrich (1895–1958), Wallis's second husband.

Simpson, Wallis, later known as Duchess of Windsor (1896–1986).

Sinclair, Sir Archibald (1890–1970) leader of the Liberal Party at the time of the abdication.

Smith, Ian (1919–2007), Prime Minister of Rhodesia who declared UDI in an attempt to stave off black majority rule.

Smuts, General Jan Christian (1870–1950) an important South African and Commonwealth statesman.

Sophia of Greece, Princess (Queen of Spain 1975–2014) (b.1938), Joss's alleged playmate Sophie.

Spencer, Earl (b.1964), brother of Princess Diana.

Spencer, Lieutenant Earl Winfield (Win) (1888–1950), Wallis's first husband.

Stuttaford, Richard Bawden (nicknamed 'Den'), former fiancé of Baroness Jean Tromp.

Stuttaford, Georgina (b.1940), author's cousin who introduced her to Joss.

Sykes, John, senior litigator for Charles Russell, 8–10 New Fetter Lane, London.

Thatcher, Margaret (1925–2013), British Conservative Party politician and prime minister (1979–1990).

Thatcher, Mark (b.1953), son of Margaret Thatcher.

Torbitt, Bill, friend of Joss's, who taught at the School of Information at the Polytechnic of Namibia.

Tromp, Baroness Jean, née Playfair, cousin of Queen Mother and companion of Joss de Wahl (died 2005).

Tromp, Baron Bob, Jean's former husband who was a farmer in Rhodesia, now Zimbabwe.

Vanderbilt, Gloria (1904–1965), mother of Gloria Vanderbilt, q.v.

Vanderbilt Gloria (1924–2019), fashion designer, artist and twin sister of Thelma Furness, q.v.

van der Stel, François, descendant of Simon van der Stel.

van der Stel, Simon (1639–1712), first governor of the Cape Colony.

Victoria, Queen (1819–1901) Queen of the United Kingdom from 1838 until her death.

Warfield, Alice (née Montague) (1869–1929), Wallis's 'official' mother.

Warfield, Solomon Davies (1859–1927), US railroad executive and banker, official paternal uncle of Wallis Simpson.

Warfield, Teakle Wallis (1869–1896), official father of Wallis Simpson.

Wessels, Danie, Ouma Wessels's late husband.

Wessels, Ouma (Granny), the mother of Mrs Billy Graaf, q.v.

Westminster, 2nd Duke of, Hugh Grosvenor (known as 'Bendor') (1879–1953), who sold a farm to Jean Tromp's father on the Westminster estates in the Orange Free State, South Africa.

Winfield, Edward Pennington, Joss's tutor who remained with him until he died in 1969.

Yarde-Buller, Joan (1908–1997), first married Loel Guinness with whom she had Patrick Benjamin Guinness (b.1931) and then married Aly Khan with whom she had two children – Sultan Karim Khan IV, the present Aga Khan, and Amyn Mohammed Khan.

Yarde-Buller, Lydia (1917–2006), married Duke of Bedford who inherited Woburn Abbey.

Yarde-Buller, Primrose (1918–1970), sister of Joan (q.v.) and Lydia (q.v.), who married the 7th Earl of Cadogan.

Index

B

Bahamas, 81–2, 100, 247n.9
Baker, Sir Herbert, 153, 252n.17
Baldwin, Billy, 50
Baldwin, Stanley, 18–19, 243n.2
Baltimore, 8, 42, 48, 50, 59–61, 64
Bank of England, 128
Barberini, Don Augusto, 54
Barrington, Frances, 55–6
Barrington, Viscount Henry, 55–6, 166, 246n.2
Barrow-in-Furness, 146
Beaton, Cecil, 38, 61, 210, 246n.27
Beaufort West Hospital, 214
Beaverbrook, Baron, 12, 20
Beaverbrook, Jane, 156
Bedford, Duke of, 77, 107
Belgrave, 107
Belgravia, 193
Bennett, Alan, 182
Berkeley Square, 106
Berkshire, 114, 247n.6
Berlin, 11, 80, 92
Bingham, Hugh, 253n.1
Birkett-Foster, Myles, 161
Birmingham, 153
Bloch, Michael, 62
Blum, Maître Suzanne, 62, 73–4, 169–71, 174, 189
Board of Deputies, 115
Boer War, 23, 40, 153, 252n.15
Boleyn, Anne, 79
Bond Street, 126
Bophuthatswana, 149
Boudin, Eugène, 161

Boulevard Suchet, 69, 108
Bourbon, 27
Bourbon-Condé family, 27
Bowes-Lyon family, 153
Bredasdorp, 1–2, 6, 82–3, 147, 169, 180, 183, 189, 198–202, 207, 209–10, 213, 217–18, 220–2
Bredenkamp, Mrs, 29
Brendal, Mrs, 33–4, 47
Breytenbach, Breyten, 38
Brinton, Mrs, 30–1, 35–7
Britain, 10, 17–18, 20, 25, 50, 58, 76, 78, 98, 114, 118, 120–1, 131, 134, 185, 218–19, 252n.15, n.18
British Empire, 76, 80, 131, 249n.46, 252n.15
British Legion, 102
British Union of Fascists, 96
Brotherfield, Arthur, 87
Brownlow, Perry, 10, 21, 46, 244n.10
Bryanston Court, 11, 48, 244n.9
Buckingham Palace, 49, 68, 78–9, 90, 102–4, 126
Buddhism, 125, 130; Buddhist, 122, 124
Bureau of State Security (BOSS), 137
Burger, Ben, 38
Burman, Dr, 204
Butler Court, 207
Buzenval, 27, 33, 37

C

Cadogan, Earl of, 107
Cadogan, Primrose née Yarde-Buller, 49, 107, 112

GW00569909

PLYMOUTH TRANSPORT

THROUGH TIME

Derek Tait

AMBERLEY PUBLISHING

Acknowledgements

Photograph credits: Derek Tait, Maurice Dart, Steve Johnson, Keith Parker, Alison Hanson and Marshall Ware.

Thanks also to Tina Cole and Tilly Barker.

I have tried to track down the copyright owners of all photographs used and apologise to anyone who hasn't been mentioned.

Please check out my website at www.derektait.co.uk

Bibliography

Books
Plymouth From Old Photographs
Plymouth at War From Old Photographs
Plymouth Through Time
Plymouth at War Through Time
River Tamar Through Time

Websites
Cyberheritage at: www.cyber-heritage.co.uk
Derek Tait's Plymouth Local History Blog at: plymouthlocalhistory.blogspot.com

Newspapers
The Evening Herald
The Western Morning News

First published 2012

Amberley Publishing
The Hill, Stroud
Gloucestershire, GL5 4EP

www.amberley-books.com

Copyright © Derek Tait, 2012

The right of Derek Tait to be identified as the Author of this work has been asserted in accordance with the Copyrights, Designs and Patents Act 1988.

ISBN 978 1 4456 0725 2

British Library Cataloguing in Publication Data.
A catalogue record for this book is available from the British Library.

Typeset in 9.5pt on 12pt Celeste.
Typesetting by Amberley Publishing.
Printed in the UK.

Introduction

It's hard to imagine a time when the streets of Plymouth were empty and devoid of traffic. Approximately 120 years ago, the only vehicles on the road would have all been horse-drawn. The railway was well established by the late eighteenth century and allowed people to travel – many for the first time – cheaply and further afield.

The first tramway was opened in 1872 by the Plymouth, Stonehouse and Devonport Tramways Ltd. Their line ran from Derry's Clock, along Union Street and ended at Cumberland Gardens in Devonport. By 1874, the tramway also included Fore Street. A plan to run steam trams from West Hoe to Compton Lane came to an abrupt end ten days after intervention from the Board of Trade and the Devonport Corporation. The Plymouth Corporation Tramways Department opened its first electric service in 1899 and the tramway eventually covered much of Plymouth, Devonport and Stonehouse until its demise in 1945. By the time the last tram ran, motor cars and buses were well established in the city.

A Dr Pearse owned the first car in Plymouth, a German Benz, and William Mumford built the first car body in the West Country in the early nineteenth century. Using the chassis of a Model T Ford, he also constructed the first motor taxi in Plymouth and ran the first motor bus service in the town in 1908 which travelled from the heart of Plymouth to Crownhill. Mumford also tried to construct his own flying machine in 1912.

For a while, cars, trams, buses and lorries all ran alongside each other. By the time the Second World War started, much of the main part of Plymouth was congested with heavy traffic and policemen had to guide large amounts of vehicles safely to their destination. In little over forty years, Plymouth had gone from a place of quiet streets, where the only traffic was the odd horse and cart or tram, to a city congested with motor vehicles.

The Blitz of 1941 devastated Plymouth. When the city was rebuilt after the war, much was cleared away and later replaced with roads more readily able to cope with the ever growing volume of modern traffic.

Today, it's impossible to travel anywhere without seeing some form of traffic. People are unable to live without their cars and the demand for fuel is great. It's all so different to the Plymouth of 150 years ago and a great deal has changed within that time.

Within the pages of this book, I've tried to show the many different forms of transport that have travelled along the roads of Plymouth over the years as well as showing their effect on the surrounding area.

Two Buses Pass Near to the Tamar and Royal Albert Bridges

Elephants in Bedford Street

The circus arrives in town in the older photograph showing Bedford Street in the early 1900s. There are several elephants and a young boy on the left of the picture is busily feeding one of them. The Globe Hotel can be seen in the background. The whole area was destroyed in the Blitz of 1941 and the later photograph shows the route that Bedford Street would have once taken.

Horses and Carts in Union Street

Union Street has changed greatly over the years and many of the buildings seen in the older photograph have now long gone. On the right of the first picture is Walter's Farley Hotel which stood at 46 Union Street. In the days before motor vehicles, there is still much traffic but all of it consists of horses and carts.

Millbay Station

The earlier photograph shows Millbay Station with the Duke of Cornwall Hotel in the background. The station has long since disappeared and the Pavilions entertainment complex now stands on the original site. The Duke of Cornwall Hotel, originally built in the 1800s to accommodate rail passengers, still stands and is much the same in appearance.

Fred Cole and Shire Horse at St Budeaux
The older photograph shows Fred Cole near to the railway station at St Budeaux. In the background is Yeoman's Terrace which today forms part of St Budeaux Square. The horse and cart belonged to James Ware who owned and operated Ware's Coal Merchants from nearby Saltash Passage. Lidl's stands near to the spot where Fred once stood and the later photograph shows the buildings in Yeoman's Terrace today.

A Gathering at Guildhall Square

There are many horses and buggies in the earlier photograph. Westwell Street and St Andrew's Hall can be seen in the background. St Andrew's Hall was one of the original meeting places for the Salvation Army in the late eighteenth century. Heavy bombing in 1941 obliterated the scene and today, Armada Way stands in its place.

A Horse-Drawn Tram in Tavistock Road

Two horse-drawn trams carry their passengers up the steep hill at Tavistock Road in the older picture. On the right is Sherwell Church and this area is instantly recognisable today, forming part of North Hill. An advert for 'James' Starch Blue' appears on the front of the closest tram which is being pulled by three horses.

Tamerton Foliot Railway Station

The railway station at Tamerton Foliot has long since disappeared although the building still exists. Today, it's a private dwelling found at the beginning of Warleigh Point Nature Reserve. The view in the later photograph is taken from the bridge that can be seen in the background of the older photograph. The neat and tidy platforms, including the Pampas Grass, have long-since disappeared beneath the undergrowth.

Horses and Carts Crossing Stonehouse Bridge
Harry Houdini once jumped off the Stonehouse Bridge in chains while appearing at the Palace Theatre of Varieties in Union Street in 1909. The bridge has seen much transport over the years and was the main tram route from Stonehouse to Devonport. The bridge seen in the older photograph was severely damaged in the Second World War but was later rebuilt. Today, it carries an endless stream of traffic to and from the city centre.

Staff at St Budeaux Station
St Budeaux station still exists but isn't as popular as it once was in its heyday. Gone are the waiting rooms and shelters, together with the staff. Two porters and the station master can be seen in the older photograph waiting for the next train to arrive. The later photograph shows the line as it is today with Pemros Road and Wolseley Road in the background.

Much Activity on the Barbican

Horses and carts wait by the cobbled harbour in the earlier photograph. Many of the buildings still exist and the area is instantly recognisable. In the background are the premises of the French Transatlantic Mail Steamship Company belonging to Luscombe, Bellamy & Co. The later photograph shows an ice cream seller near to the same area.

The Reverend Green at Higher St Budeaux Church

The Revd W. L. Green was appointed to the church in 1886 and lived at the new vicarage which is now the Cornwall Gate Inn. The old vicarage had by then fallen into a state of disrepair. He travelled everywhere in a buggy pulled by a Shetland pony. The later photograph shows the church as it is today and little appears to have changed over the years.

The Station Master at St Budeaux Station
Edmund Tolley, shown, was the first station master at St Budeaux station in 1890. He was well liked and was remembered for holding up the trains for latecomers. The station was originally known as St Budeaux Platform and opened on the 1 June 1904. In 1906, because of its popularity, the platforms were widened and a new ticket office and waiting room were built.

Many People Gathered at Bank of England Place

The earlier photograph shows a very busy scene close to Derry's Clock. In the background is a wagon belonging to T. Easterbrook who was a fruit and potato merchant who supplied the market at Devonport. The shop behind belonged to Limpenny who were well-known for manufacturing umbrellas. The building on the right is now the Bank Public House.

A Funfair Ride at West Hoe

At one time, the only cars that people would have travelled in were the ones on rides at the funfair. The fair was a very popular attraction at West Hoe in the early 1900s and included a helter skelter, a coconut shie, a rifle range and swing boats. The fair was run on the main part of the Hoe by Whiteleggs for many years and today it's still a popular attraction.

A Horse-Drawn Tram in Ebrington Street

Several people watch as the number 7 tram passes by in Ebrington Street. It's busy with passengers and one has an umbrella, possibly from Limpenny's. An advert stretches along the side advertising 'Fry's Cocoa'. Nearby is a gas lamp and from the clock on the building in the background, it appears to be 4.55 pm.

Horses and Cabs Wait for Passengers at Millbay Station

Millbay Station was once very popular and would carry passengers from the many liners that stopped at Plymouth onto their next destination. These included celebrities of the day such as Charlie Chaplin, George Raft and Gloria Swanson. The Duke of Cornwall and Continental Hotels were built nearby to cater for the many passengers who alighted at the station.

Home-Made Entertainment

At one time, children made their own transport from a couple of old pram wheels, a wooden packing crate and any spare wood that they could find. Home-made go-karts were very popular for many years and included a piece of rope to aid steering. Today, it would be very unusual to see anyone with a self-made go-kart, and skateboards and bikes are far more popular.

A Carnival at Mutley

The carnival, with its many highly decorated wagons, can be seen proceeding through Mutley in the older photograph. The cart at the front belongs to Voddon & Johns who were coal and salt merchants who operated from 30 Old Town Street. Many people have turned out to watch the procession. Nowadays, it would be rare to see a horse in Mutley and today the area is regularly congested with buses, cars and taxis.

A Steam Train at Plymouth Station

A Victorian boy peers through the railings to see the passing steam train and carriages at Plymouth station in the early 1900s. Nearby, a man pulls a heavy handcart uphill while another man watches from a horse and buggy. Newer buildings have been built in the passing years and much has changed, although the area and streets are still instantly recognisable.

Laying Tracks at the Royal Albert Bridge

Railway workers are busy laying tracks leading towards the Royal Albert Bridge in the older photograph. The bridge was opened in 1859 and allowed people to travel easily and more cheaply between Devon and Cornwall. Many people commuted from Saltash to work in the dockyard at Plymouth and sixpenny day trips became very popular.

A Tram Climbing Tavistock Road

A horse-drawn tram laden with passengers makes the steep ascent up Tavistock Road. Sherwell Church can be seen in the background. There are many pedestrians; most are heading back from the main part of Plymouth. Today, many of the buildings shown in the older photograph still survive and the later photograph shows the scene from the other direction.

The Ferry at Saltash Passage

The ferry ran between Saltash Passage in Plymouth and Saltash in Cornwall, for hundreds of years. It ceased in 1961 when the Tamar road bridge was opened. The earlier photograph shows the ferry, complete with gas lamps, returning to Plymouth. In the background are the many old buildings that once stood on the waterfront at Saltash. Many were cleared away in the 1950s.

The Ferry Leaving Saltash Passage

Another early scene of the ferry shows it pulling away from Saltash Passage. A young boy sits on the railings and watches as it leaves. More children can be seen sitting on the wall nearby. In the foreground of the picture are the tramlines that led right into the heart of Saltash Passage and terminated near to the Royal Albert Bridge Inn.

A Tram at Old Town Street

The number 3 tram travels along Old Town Street in the older photograph. The only car to be seen is parked nearby. A huge sign on the building in the background advertises Bovril. This was replaced by equally as large letters advertising Guinness. The Guinness Clock was installed on the building in 1937 by the Electric Sign Company. Beneath it was the slogan 'Guinness is good for you'.

Trams Waiting by the Theatre Royal

There is much activity in the older photograph which shows the trams' terminus near to Derry's Clock. On the right is the grand old Theatre Royal building which was demolished in 1937, in preparation of the building of the Royal Cinema. The tram nearest the theatre is on its way to Peverell and the conductor can be seen standing on the top deck.

A Busy Scene by Derry's Clock

The earlier photograph again shows the area near to Derry's Clock and the number 2 tram is on its way to Prince Rock. All the passengers on board are sat upstairs probably to take in the view of the town. Many more wait to get on as the conductor collects their fares. Much of George Street was destroyed in the Blitz and the only structure that survives in the older photograph is Derry's Clock.

The London and South Western Railway Offices
A tram belonging to the Plymouth Corporation Tramways leaves on its way to Beaumont Road. An advert for the London Furnishing Company is featured on its side. In the background is the Domestic Bazaar Company which offered any article for 6d. The later photograph shows a bus passing by the same area today.

Jack 'Legs' Diamond's Killer Car

Jack 'Legs' Diamond was a gangster and bootlegger in America who was shot and killed in 1931 at the age of 34. In the earlier photograph, elephants carry advertising boards announcing that Jack Diamond's armoured car will be on display at Derry's Clock. Many American gangsters drove in similar armoured cars including the more infamous, Al Capone.

Mutley Plain.   Plymouth.   E 18607

A Tram at Mutley

The number 26 tram travels along Mutley Plain towards Peverell. Many of the buildings on the left of the picture still stand although much has changed. A horse and cart approaches from the other direction. The Wesleyan Chapel with its tall spire, seen in the background, stood at the junction to Belgrave Road. It was demolished in the 1980s.

The Tram Depot at Milehouse

Several trams can be seen in the earlier photograph parked up at the depot at Milehouse. They include adverts for Arnold's Seeds of 7 Drake Street, Jacob's Cream Crackers and Harding's Furniture. The trams are probably in for repair and the front end of a newer motor bus stands nearby.

A Football Special Passing the Britannia Inn

The empty tram shown in the older photograph was a football special, laid on to take passengers to the match at Plymouth Argyle's ground at nearby Home Park. It has just travelled past the Britannia Inn and is heading along Milehouse Road. The later photograph shows the scene today and many of the old buildings still stand.

A Busy Scene by the Technical College in Tavistock Road
A large crowd has gathered near to the old Technical College in Tavistock Road in the earlier photograph. A coal cart passes nearby. The Plymouth Science, Art and Technical Schools in Tavistock Road were built in 1892 on a site opposite to where the current main library stands. Today, Plymouth University stands in their place.

A Tram in Old Town Street

Nothing survives from the older photograph which shows a horse-drawn tram in Old Town Street. Much was destroyed during the Blitz of 1941. The tram carries an advert for Spooner & Co. who, at the time, operated from premises that stretched from Bedford Street to Old Town Street. Old Town Street today leads towards the recently built Mall at Drake Circus.

The Number 6 Tram at Stonehouse on its Way to the Theatre
The tram shown is on its way towards Derry's Clock via Union Street. Many trams showed their destination as 'Theatre' long after the Theatre Royal had been demolished. Even later buses displayed the same destination. The more recent photograph shows the far end of Union Street where the tram would have originally passed.

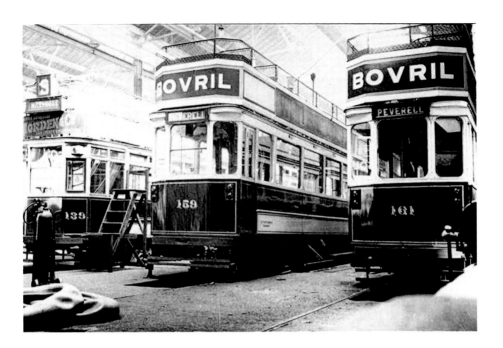

Trams at Milehouse Depot

Gleaming trams with their destinations shown as Milehouse and Peverell stand at the main depot, probably having repair work undertaken. Two have adverts for Bovril. The depot at Milehouse is still very busy today with many buses travelling all over the city. The later photograph shows a bright yellow school bus and a coach parked at the depot.

Much Transport in Old Town Street

Two trams and a motor car can be seen in the older photograph taken in Old Town Street in the early 1900s. Several horses and carts can also be seen. The building on the left belongs to Messrs. Spooners & Co. who were drapers, milliners and haberdashers. The company's name is carved into the building and flags fly outside. Swiss's toyshop stands next door.

A Tram at Union Street

A tram travels down a very neat and tidy Union Street in the earlier photograph. The building on the right advertises Orgel's Furnishing Mart and further up the street, on the left, is the New Palace Theatre. The later photograph shows the far end of Union Street. Some buildings still stand although many have been demolished over the years.

Much Activity in Union Street

Another photograph showing a busy Union Street includes two trams passing close to Halford's Cycle Shop. Many adverts for the businesses of the day can be seen including ones for the Posada Wine Store, A. Levy & Co., Oliver's and Wright's hairdressers. Apart from the trams, there are also many cyclists using the road.

A Tram Passes by Sherwell Church in Tavistock Road

The number 24 tram heads from Compton towards the heart of Plymouth in the earlier photograph. The cobbled road can be seen following the lines of the tramway. On the right of the photograph, someone is being transported in a horse and buggy. Many of the buildings in the earlier photograph still exist. The later photograph shows the scene from further back, close to the library and museum.

A Charabanc Leaving from St Budeaux

A charabanc trip packed with people leaves from a garage in St Budeaux in the earlier photograph. Charabanc trips were very popular in the 1920s and would take people on day trips to the country or seaside. It's amazing just how many people could fit into one of these large cars. The recent photograph shows St Budeaux as it is today with the Co-op and Victoria Road in the background.

The Hoe Slopes, Plymouth.

Children on the Hoe Slopes

A tram follows the road close to the pier in the earlier photograph while many children watch from the Hoe Slopes. The scene is still much the same today although the trams, the pier and bandstand have now long-gone. The Queen Victoria Jubilee fountain is to the left of the tram in front of the Belvedere but it also disappeared many years ago.

A Steam Train at Mutley

A steam train pulls into Mutley station in the earlier photograph. The station was opened in 1871 and was eventually closed in 1939. In the background is the Royal Eye Infirmary which was opened in October 1901 by Lady Mary Parker. The later photograph shows the eye infirmary as it is today.

The Number 3 Tram at Milehouse Depot

Known as a 'Squareface' model, the tram would have been painted yellow. It is pictured at the back of the Milehouse sheds. Trams suffered a lot of wear and tear and had to be maintained regularly. They also had to be updated to comply with the strict safety regulations of the day.

St John's Ambulance Members at Union Place

Members of the St John Ambulance Association are shown complete with their bicycles in Union Place in Stonehouse. All are dressed in uniforms and one member is proudly displaying his medals. A young boy, also in uniform, salutes to the camera. Union Place runs parallel behind Union Street and is situated where the flats are seen on the left of the later photograph.

A Tram at Mutley

The tram in the older photograph advertises 'Oatbread Ale and Stout', a business long forgotten. A car slows down nearby to let passengers cross the road. The long-since demolished Wesleyan Chapel is on the right of the photograph. The later photograph shows that many of the older buildings still survive in Mutley and most escaped the Blitz of 1941.

A Busy Scene at George Street

There are many passengers queueing close to the Theatre Royal, waiting to board trams in the earlier photograph. The closest tram is heading towards Morice Square in Devonport. Derry's Clock, in the background, is festooned with decorations as is the building behind. The area is a lot quieter today and a car park stands where all this activity once took place.

An Ice Cream Seller at King Street

The earlier view shows many motor vehicles travelling along King Street. On the right of the photograph is a man with a handcart selling ice creams. King Street has changed greatly over the years and many of the buildings shown have now long gone. The later photograph shows the far end of King Street where the old railway arch once stood.

Plymouth's First Car

Dr Francis Pearse, who was a dental surgeon, was the first person to own a car in Plymouth. The car was a German Benz and dated from around 1896. The car ended up at the Brooklands racing circuit and the older photograph shows the doctor driving it to Friary Station so that it could be transported there by train. The later photograph shows how traffic has greatly increased in the years in between.

Vehicles Pass on Stonehouse Bridge

Motor vehicles cross the old Stonehouse Bridge in the earlier photograph. The bridge once featured many billboards which included adverts for local businesses and attractions. One shown here advertises the Theatre Royal which, at the time, was putting on a performance of *The Beggar's Opera*. The lorry in the photograph belongs to Alford Stores Ltd. of Plymouth and Devonport. The later photograph shows the bridge as it is today.

A Tram Travelling down Peverell Park Road

The number 158 tram travels down Peverell Park Road towards the terminus at Peverell Corner. The conductor and a couple of passengers can be seen on the top deck. An advert for Bovril appears on the front and its destination is again given as 'Theatre'. The later photograph shows the far end of Peverell Park Road where it joins Outland Road.

The Back of the Old Market
An early vehicle is shown at
the back of the market which
once stood alongside East Street.
The photograph shows a shop
belonging to Marshall's Farms
of Roborough which specialised
in vegetables and rabbits. They
proudly display their model T
Ford. The later photograph shows
today's indoor market as seen
from Frankfort Gate.

Camels at Pennycomequick

A huge crowd has gathered in the earlier photograph to watch a parade, which includes many camels, heading towards Pennycomequick. The circus was probably in town and, with few people having television sets, was much more of an event than it would be today. The event was probably being held on land at Central Park. The later photograph shows Pennycomequick as it is today.

St Andrew's Church and Guildhall

The older photograph shows traffic close to St Andrew's Church. To the left of Bateman's Opticians is Basket Street and the road on the far right of the picture is Bedford Street. Double-decker buses are now being used in this pre-blitz scene although the tramlines can be seen embedded in the road. The later photograph shows St Andrew's Church from the top of Finewell Street.

A Motorbike in Fore Street, Devonport

A man travels down Fore Street in Devonport on a motorbike in the earlier photograph. In the background, close to the Electric Cinema, is a tram packed with passengers. Lipton's can be seen, at number 94 on the left, close to the junction at Lambert Street. Heavy bombing in the Second World War obliterated the area and, today, it is much different.

King George VI at Plymouth Railway Station

The older photograph shows King George VI in full Naval attire arriving at Plymouth. He was met at the main station by local dignitaries and high ranking naval personnel. The Royal train can be seen on the left. The later photograph shows the railway bridge crossing the road towards the main station and Pennycomequick can be seen in the background.

A Tram and Bus at Milehouse Depot

Trams and buses ran side-by-side with each other in Plymouth until the last tram completed its journey in 1945. From the 1930s, plans were put in place to replace all trams in the city with more modern transport and only the route between Drake Circus and Peverell Corner remained. By the end of the war, the decision was made to halt the tram service altogether.

A Busy Scene at Frankfort Street

The earlier photograph showing Frankfort Street is busy with both people and traffic and there are many lorries, cars and wagons. On the left is the Costers building and, beside it, the offices of the *Western Morning News*. Nearly all was destroyed in the bombing of 1941, although the *Western Morning News* building survived and today houses Waterstone's.

The Pier

Two cars and many boats can be seen near to the ornate pier at Plymouth Hoe. The signs on the pier advertise concerts, cafés, entertainment and 'public bathing for ladies and gents'. The pier was destroyed in the Blitz and the remnants of it were removed in the early 1950s. The later photograph shows where the entrance once stood.

A Bombed Frankfort Street

The earlier photograph shows the devastation caused to Frankfort Street due to enemy bombing. Again, the *Western Morning News* building can be seen standing on the left of the photograph. The road is impassable due to rubble and fallen debris and several vehicles block the way while a building in the background is hosed down.

The Scene from St Andrew's Church

In the older photograph, many buildings have been destroyed by enemy bombing. Many buildings still stand but these would later be cleared away for future development. Several double-decker buses pass nearby. The cross of St Andrew's Church can be seen in the foreground surrounded by scaffold. It was later removed as it was deemed to be unsafe.

A Destroyed Locomotive at Keyham

During April 1941, the locomotive *Bowden Hall* was destroyed when a bomb hit the nearby station at Keyham. Services in and out of Cornwall were halted by the blast. The Great Western Railway locomotive, number 4911, was later taken to Swindon and scrapped. The station still exists but is little used.

US Troops Clearing Away Debris

In the earlier photograph, American troops, who were stationed in the city in the 1940s prior to DDay, help with the removal of damaged buildings and tons of fallen debris. The area would later be re-developed during the rebuilding of the city after the war. The more recent photograph shows land being cleared at Derry's Cross in preparation of new building work.

A Classic Car Event on the Hoe

Although the cars shown are much older, the earlier photograph shows a classic car event on the Hoe during the late 1950s. Much of the area remains the same today although the popular café in the background, which resembled an aircraft hangar, is long gone. Classic car events still take place yearly on the Hoe. The later photograph shows another attraction, the very popular Plymouth Wheel.

The Hoe Promenade

The pre-war shot of the Hoe shows two old cars of the day and a motorcycle parked near to the promenade. The area remains much the same although the bandstand was removed to help the war effort. The view has been taken from the Grand Hotel which has had many celebrity visitors over the years including Laurel and Hardy.

A Coach by Smeaton's Tower

In the earlier photograph a coach belonging to the Co-op Travel Service can be seen on the road close to Smeaton's Tower. The coaches took people on trips all over Devon and Cornwall during the 1950s and also made extended trips all over the country. This part of the Hoe has changed little over the years although the lighthouse has now been repainted in its original colours.

The Oil Refinery at Cattedown

The older photograph shows the staff of the Shell depot at Cattedown with their many transport vehicles in the background. The depot at Cattedown is situated on the site where the oldest human remains in Britain were discovered dating back approximately 140,000 years. Also found were the bones of Ice Age woolly mammoth, woolly rhinoceroses, hyena and reindeer.

The Millbay Laundry

The Millbay Laundry was located at Millbay Road although they had premises all over Plymouth. The company's original works were destroyed during bombing in 1941 but their Eddystone Works at Millbay Road survived. The older photograph shows one of their vans and the later photograph shows Millbay Road as it is today leading towards the Duke of Cornwall Hotel.

The Elburton Hotel

Several cars can be seen in the earlier photograph which shows the Elburton Hotel. A group of women, who appear to be nurses, are gathered at the door. The road has been widened greatly over the years and now carries much more traffic. The public house, now just 'The Elburton', still stands and remains open for business.

A Double-Decker Bus at the Top of Royal Parade

On the right of the older photograph are the bombed remains of St Andrew's Church which would later be restored to its original glory. The reconstruction of Plymouth has begun and Royal Parade is in place and open to traffic. The double-decker bus in the foreground is the number 13 and has an advert for 'Devon Brown Ale' on its side.

A Double-Decker Bus at Saltash Passage

The number 95 bus, bound for Hooe, is shown by the Royal Albert Bridge in the earlier photograph. Parked behind it is a vintage car of the day. The area was also, years before, a stopping off point for the many trams that once visited Saltash Passage. The same area today is used to store boats and other water craft.

The *Western Morning News* Delivery Men
The *Western Morning News* van was once
a popular sight in Plymouth delivering
newspapers to various shops around the
city. Their deliveries continued in darkness
during the blackouts of the Second World
War. Featured in the earlier photograph on the
far left is Percy Colton. His brother, Sid, also
appears in this picture standing beside him.
The later photograph shows the old *Western
Morning News* building as it is today.

Buses Passing by North Road Station
Buses and cars pass by the railway station as the office block known as 'Intercity House' is
being built. It was later officially opened by Dr Richard Beeching on 26 March 1962. The
later photograph shows the completed building together with the railway line leading from
the main station towards Mutley.

A Diesel Train at North Road Station

A diesel train, the *D802*, arrives at Plymouth's main railway station sometime in the 1960s. Known as *Formidable*, the train, as with others, were named after well-known warships. It was first used in 1958 but was withdrawn from service ten years later and taken to Swindon and dismantled.

A Busy New George Street

Plymouth's city centre was once packed with pedestrians and the older photograph from the 1960s shows hundreds of shoppers jostling for space on the pavements. Many vehicles are parked in the busy street including a lorry belonging to Frank H. Mann, a fruit and vegetable dealer. Today, the whole area is pedestrianised and very few vehicles pass this way.

Shoppers in Armada Way

A 1960s photograph shows cars parked in Armada Way together with many pedestrians. On the right is the British Home Stores building. The buildings look much the same today although, again, the area has now been pedestrianised. The later view shows Armada Way as seen from the other side of Royal Parade. In the middle of the photograph is the Piazza, an open public area, together with its large television screen.

Ivor Dewdney's, Cornwall Street

Many cars can be seen in the 1960s shot of Cornwall Street. On the right is Ivor Dewdney's pasty shop. Dewdney's first shop was opened in King Street in the 1930s. After the war, Dewdney's took over the newly built premises in Cornwall Street and have been there ever since. The later photograph shows the view looking down Cornwall Street from the junction at Armada Way.

ARMADA WAY, PLYMOUTH

A Busy Armada Way

Many cars appear in the 1960s photograph of Armada Way. Much of the area seen is now also pedestrianised. The buildings remain much the same today and the tower of the Guildhall can be seen in the background. The later photograph shows the same area looking down towards the heart of the town.

81

The Lifeboys at St Budeaux Station

The earlier photograph shows the 12th Plymouth Lifeboys on Church Parade beside St Budeaux Railway Station sometime after the war. The adverts in the background make interesting reading. One is for Goodbody's and says, 'The sign of good bread'. The billboard beside it advertises a box of cakes called, 'Week End'.

The Royal Albert and Tamar Bridges

The Royal Albert Bridge opened up the rail route into Cornwall in 1859 and just over 100 years later, the road bridge opened. It was much in demand as vast amounts of traffic needed to travel to and from Plymouth. Previously, the main route to and from Cornwall had been by the small ferries at Devonport and Saltash Passage and these had very quickly become congested.

The Impressive Royal Parade

The older view, taken in the 1950s, shows Royal Parade looking much the same as it does today. For many years, an underpass took pedestrians under the busy road but today this has been filled in and a pedestrian crossing once again crosses the main road. Of course, traffic has increased greatly in the last sixty years or so and the crossing has seen several accidents in recent years.

Armada Way Looking Towards the Civic Centre

Cars once parked all along Armada Way making it handy for anyone who just wanted to pop in and out of shops quickly. There were many car parks around the city at the time and the main parking areas were on places previously cleared of buildings such as the sites where Sainsbury's and Toys R Us now stand.

Looking Towards Cornwall Street from Armada Way

An aerial shot of Armada Way shows the many cars that once parked along its streets. In the distance, the buildings at the top of Armada Way, which would later become banks, are yet to be built. The photograph appears to be taken from the Guildhall Tower and the Dingles building can be seen on the right.

Greenbank Hospital

An ambulance pulls into Greenbank hospital in the earlier photograph, taken in the 1960s. Many now-classic cars can be seen in the car park. The hospital was built in 1840 and was demolished in the 1990s and new homes were built on the site. The main hospital at Derriford took the place of all of the smaller hospitals around the city.

Western Approach from the New Continental Hotel
A Morris Traveller heads down towards Union Street on the road leading down from the Crescent. Today, the Pavilions stand on the site on the left where Millbay Station once stood and in the middle distance, again on the left, is where Toys R Us stands. The later view shows the scene from the top of the road looking down Millbay Road past the New Continental Hotel.

A Busy Royal Parade

Royal Parade is packed with lovely old double-decker buses and cars in the earlier photograph which was taken in the 1960s. All of the buildings shown in the photograph remain much the same today. The yellow van in the foreground belongs to Stephens. The later photograph is taken halfway down Royal Parade and shows the busy scene today.

The Palace Theatre in Union Street

Union Street is marked as the A38 in the earlier photograph but wouldn't be referred to as that nowadays. There are many cars and vans parked along the road in this 1960s scene. It's amazing to see just how much of Union Street still existed back then. Unfortunately, many of the old buildings have been cleared and replaced with buildings such as Aldi and Lidl. The Palace Theatre can be seen on the left of the picture.

Southside Street, the Barbican

Some of the buildings have changed or disappeared over the years and parts of Southside Street have been rebuilt. The very old building with the sloped roof, on the right in the earlier photograph, has long since disappeared. In the far distance is the Navy Inn and the Maritime Inn is advertised on the left. The later photograph shows the view from the other direction.

The Lockyer Tavern in Lockyer Street

Many old cars, including a Morris Minor, line the street leading towards Derry's Clock in the earlier photograph. On the right is the Lockyer Tavern which was demolished many years ago. The land where it once stood now forms part of the beer garden area at the rear of the Bank public house.

Armada Way and the Civic Centre
A Ford Cortina and a Mini can be seen in
the foreground of the earlier photograph
from the 1970s which shows the Civic
Centre in the background. The Civic Centre
was opened in 1962 and, today, has Grade 2
listed status. The area shown in the older
photograph now forms part of the Piazza.

The Palace Theatre

The earlier 1970s photograph shows the Palace Theatre in Union Street when it incorporated the Star Social Club. The van on the left belongs to Westcountry Furnishers Ltd and a Singer Gazelle and a Ford Corsair wait to pull out onto Union Street. The later photograph shows the Palace Theatre today, closed and worse for wear.

King Street Arch

An old SWEB van and the number 5 bus can be seen from the old railway arch at King Street which was removed in the 1970s. Jack Cohen's very popular joke shop, which was in business for many years, is in the background in between Warne News and Reynolds. Today, much has changed and a car park, adjoining Toys R Us, is situated on the right of the later photograph.

The Drake Cinema

A photograph taken in the 1980s shows a car passing by the Drake Cinema. *Ghostbusters* is the main feature which would make the year 1984. Today, in the distance, the road layout has changed and some buildings have been demolished. The Drake Cinema has now gone and a casino stands in its place. The later photograph shows the view from beside the cinema looking towards the bottom end of Royal Parade.